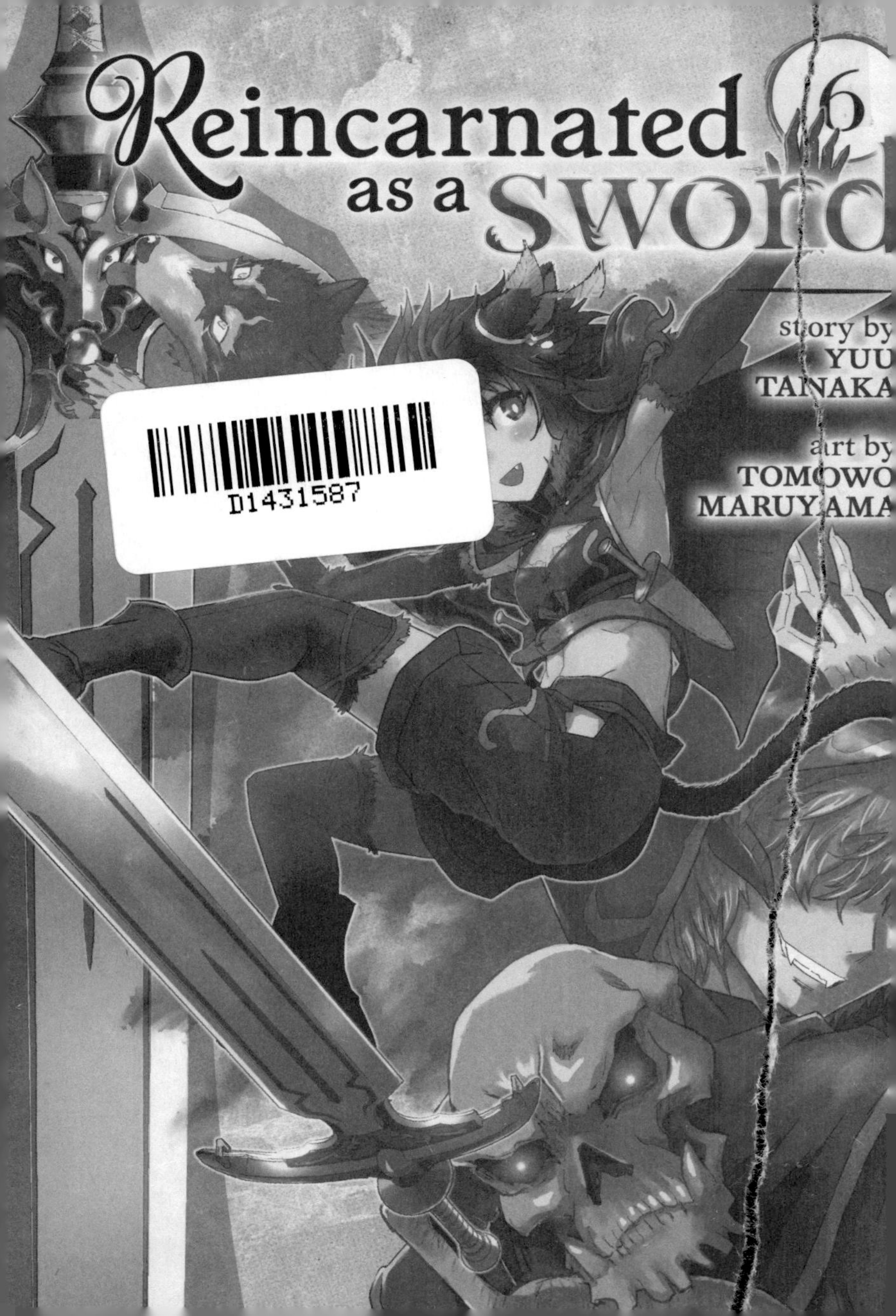
Reincarnated as a Sword
6
story by
YUU TANAKA
art by
TOMOWO MARUYAMA

ATLAS

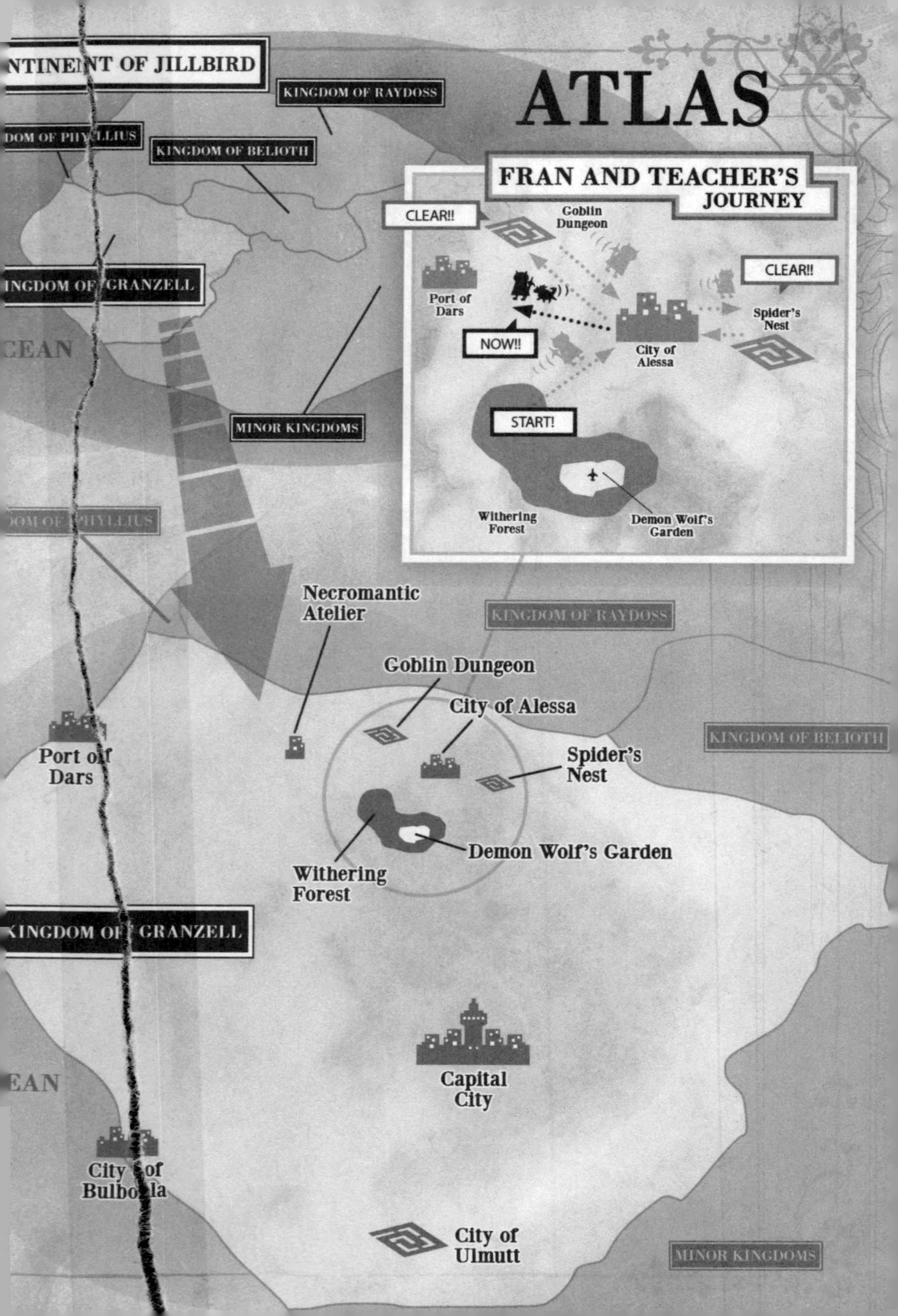

NTINENT OF JILLBIRD
KINGDOM OF RAYDOSS
DOM OF PHYLLIUS
KINGDOM OF BELIOTH
INGDOM OF GRANZELL
CEAN
MINOR KINGDOMS
FRAN AND TEACHER'S JOURNEY
CLEAR!!
Goblin Dungeon
Port of Dars
CLEAR!!
Spider's Nest
NOW!!
City of Alessa
START!
Withering Forest
Demon Wolf's Garden
DOM OF PHYLLIUS
Necromantic Atelier
KINGDOM OF RAYDOSS
Goblin Dungeon
City of Alessa
KINGDOM OF BELIOTH
Port of Dars
Spider's Nest
Demon Wolf's Garden
Withering Forest
KINGDOM OF GRANZELL
Capital City
EAN
City of Bulbola
City of Ulmutt
MINOR KINGDOMS

SUMMARY

Fran, a Black Cat slave girl, escaped being mauled by a Twinhead Bear thanks to a sword she found stuck in the ground. That sword was Teacher, an Intelligent Weapon capable of using Spells and Skills. Teacher in hand, Fran traveled to Alessa and became a member of the Adventurers' Guild.

Soon after, she ventured into the Goblin Dungeon and defeated a Greater Demon, then vanquished the Spider's Nest, becoming a Blademage. Now, together with their new direwolf named Jet, Fran and Teacher make their way to the port of Dars.

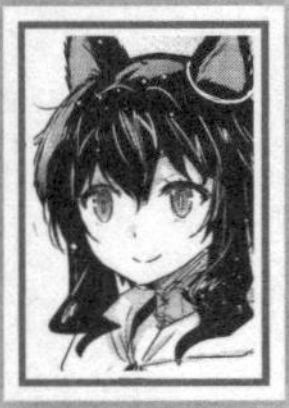

Fran

Black Cat slave girl, formerly nameless. Became an adventurer after meeting Teacher during a close brush with death. Willing to take on dangerous quests for the sake of evolving. Favorite food is Teacher's curry. Currently a D-Rank adventurer.

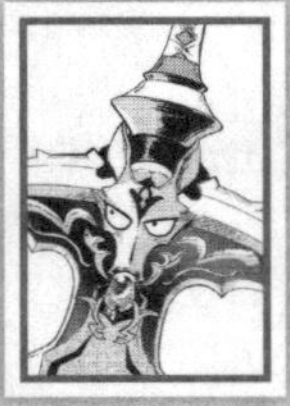

Teacher

Reincarnated as a sword after getting hit by a car. Now on a quest to become the strongest sword in the world while watching over his beloved pupil, Fran. An excellent cook.

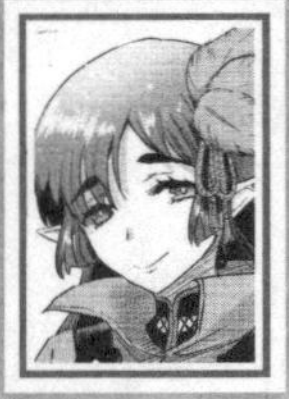

Amanda

Half-Elf A-Rank adventurer of Alessa. Called "the Hariti" because of her love for children. Watches over Fran's adventures like a loving mother.

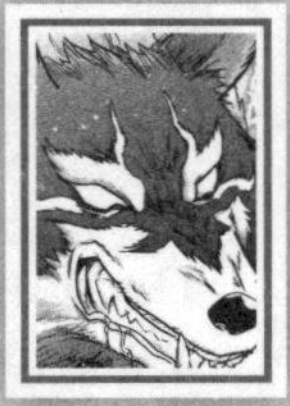

Jet

A direwolf familiar summoned by Teacher in the Spider's Nest. Actually very friendly to Fran and Teacher.

Reincarnated as a Sword

6

Chapter 28: Aerial Conquest

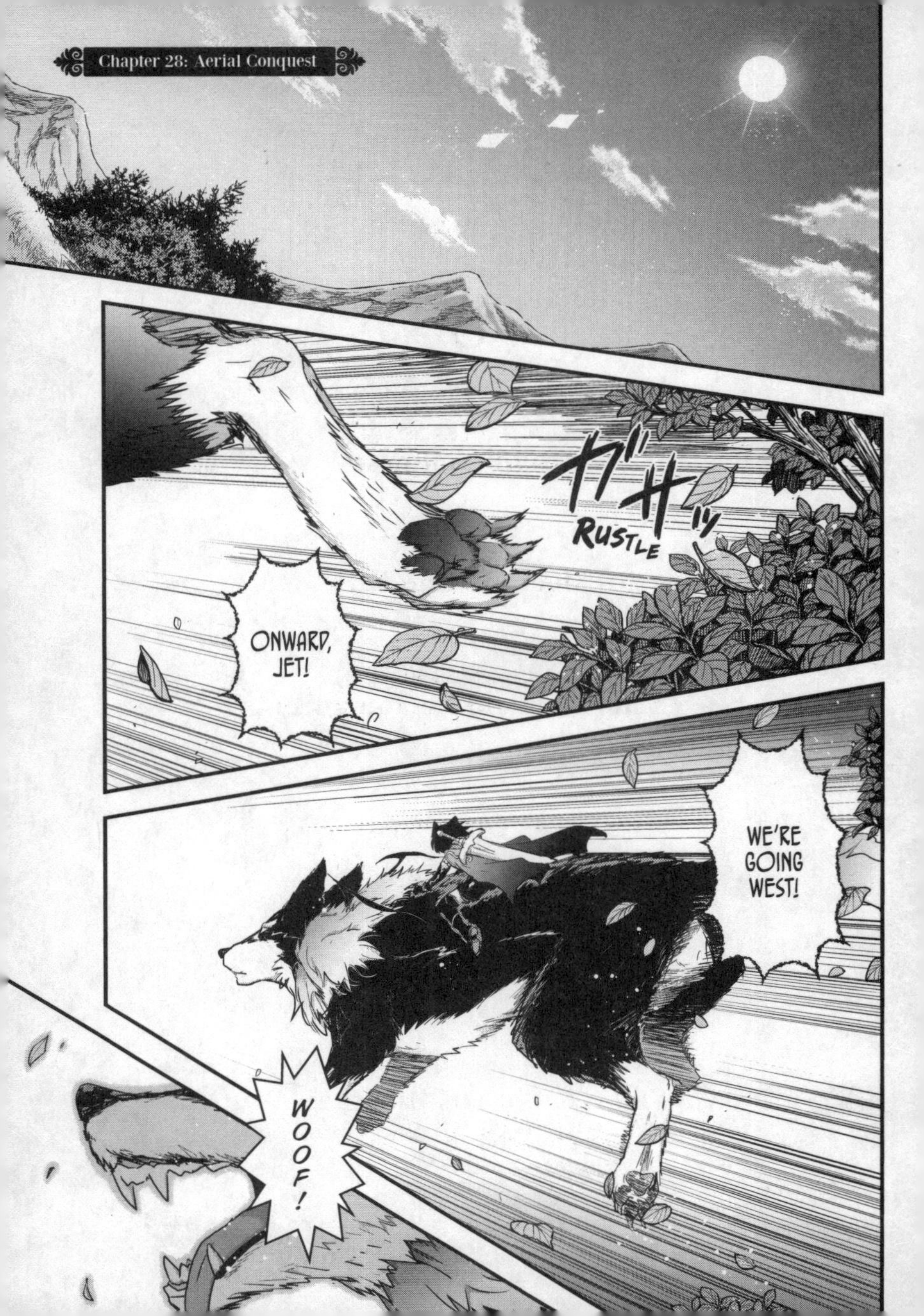
ガサッ
RUSTLE
ONWARD, JET!
WE'RE GOING WEST!
WOOF!

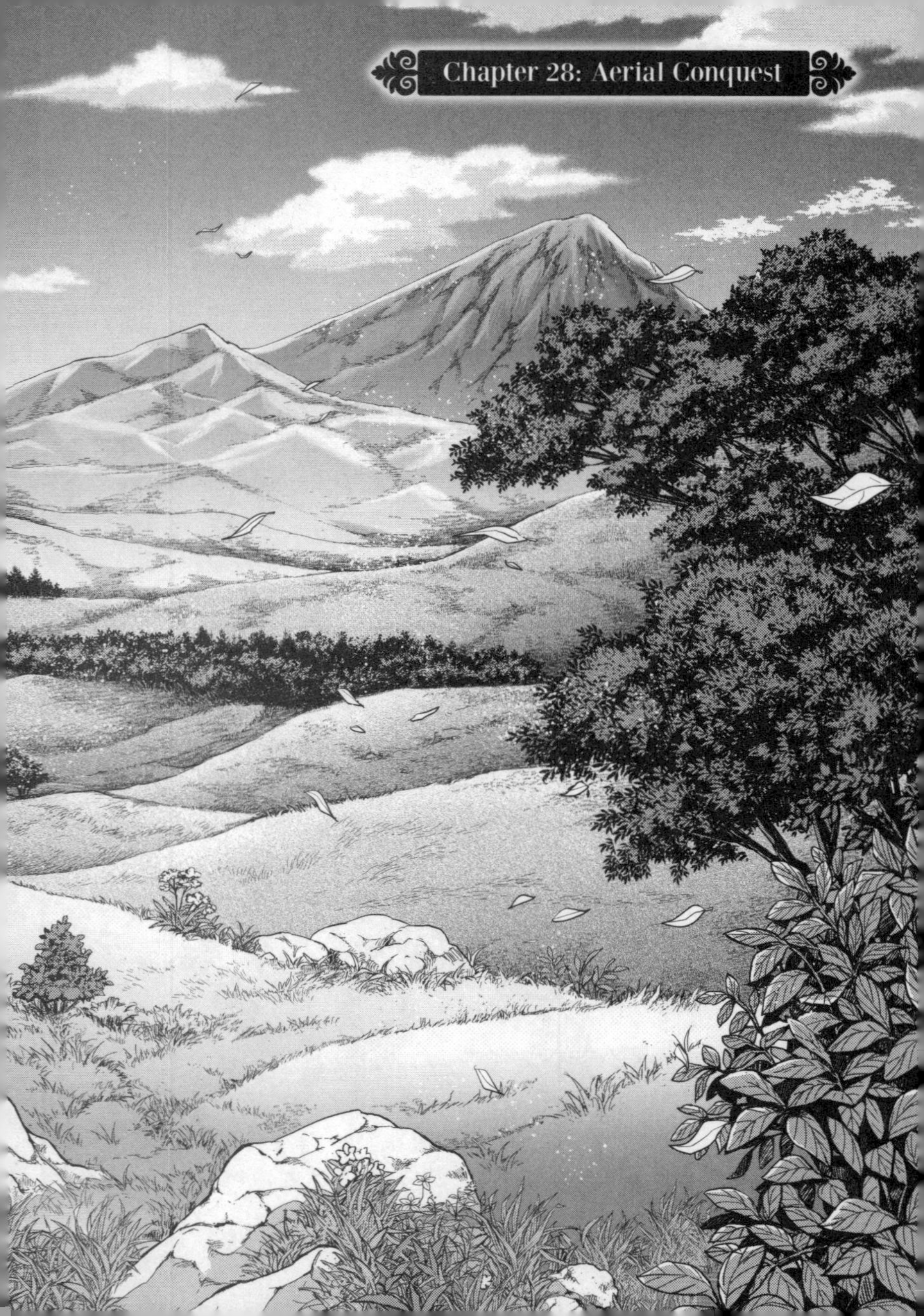
Chapter 28: Aerial Conquest

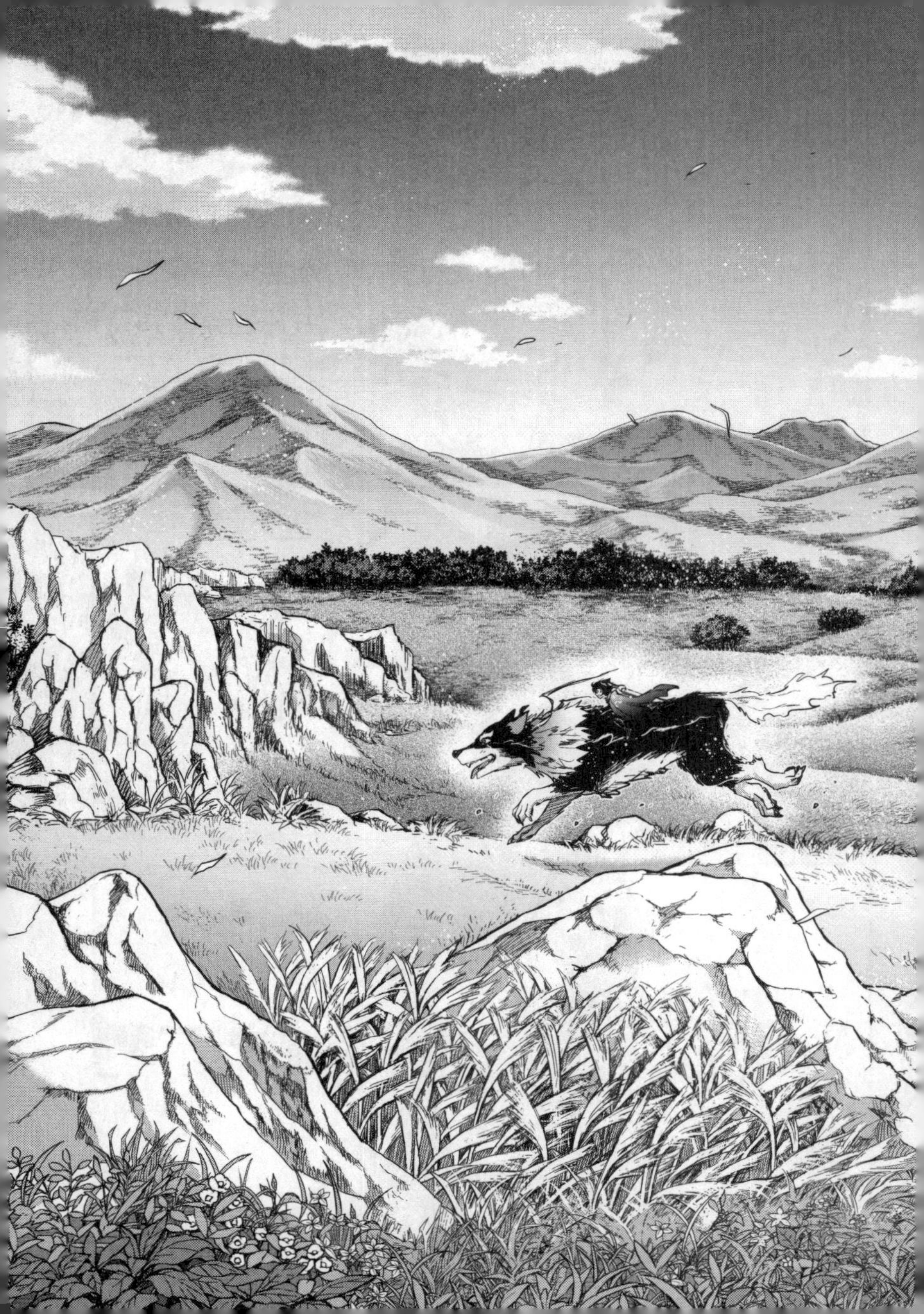

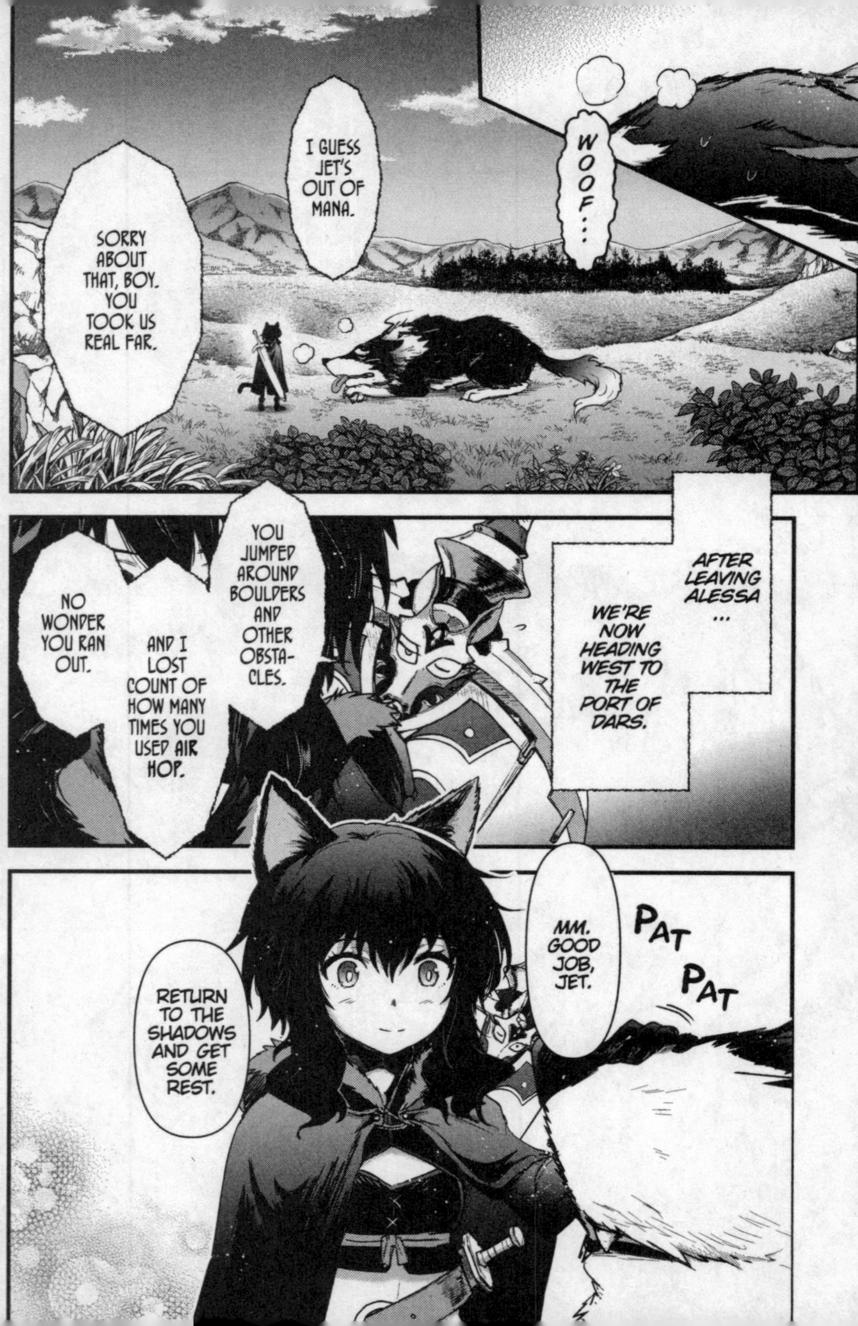
WOOF...
I GUESS JET'S OUT OF MANA.
SORRY ABOUT THAT, BOY. YOU TOOK US REAL FAR.
AFTER LEAVING ALESSA...
WE'RE NOW HEADING WEST TO THE PORT OF DARS.
YOU JUMPED AROUND BOULDERS AND OTHER OBSTACLES.
AND I LOST COUNT OF HOW MANY TIMES YOU USED AIR HOP.
NO WONDER YOU RAN OUT.
PAT PAT
MM. GOOD JOB, JET.
RETURN TO THE SHADOWS AND GET SOME REST.

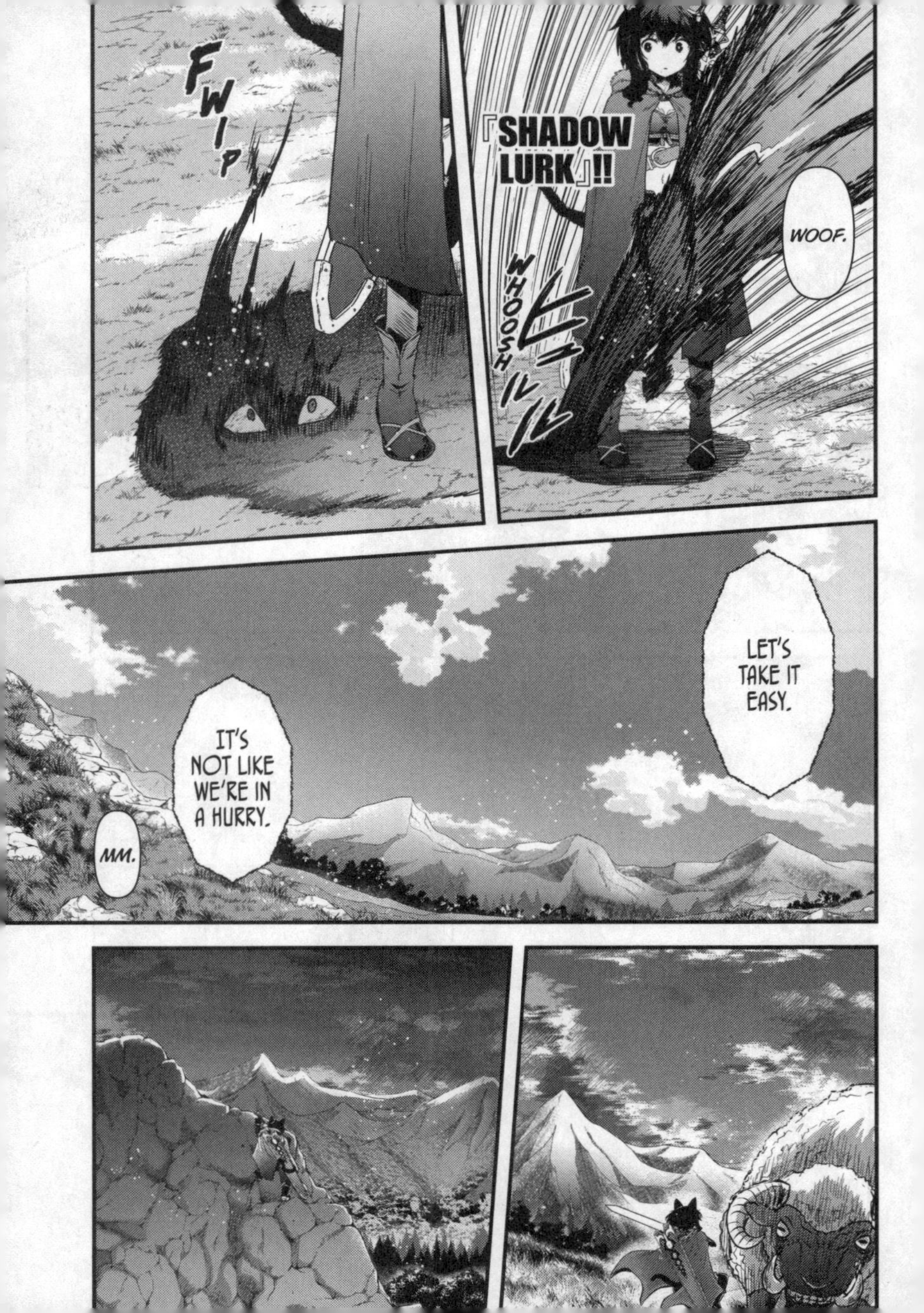
『SHADOW LURK』!!
WOOF.
WHOOSH
FWIP
LET'S TAKE IT EASY.
IT'S NOT LIKE WE'RE IN A HURRY.
MM.

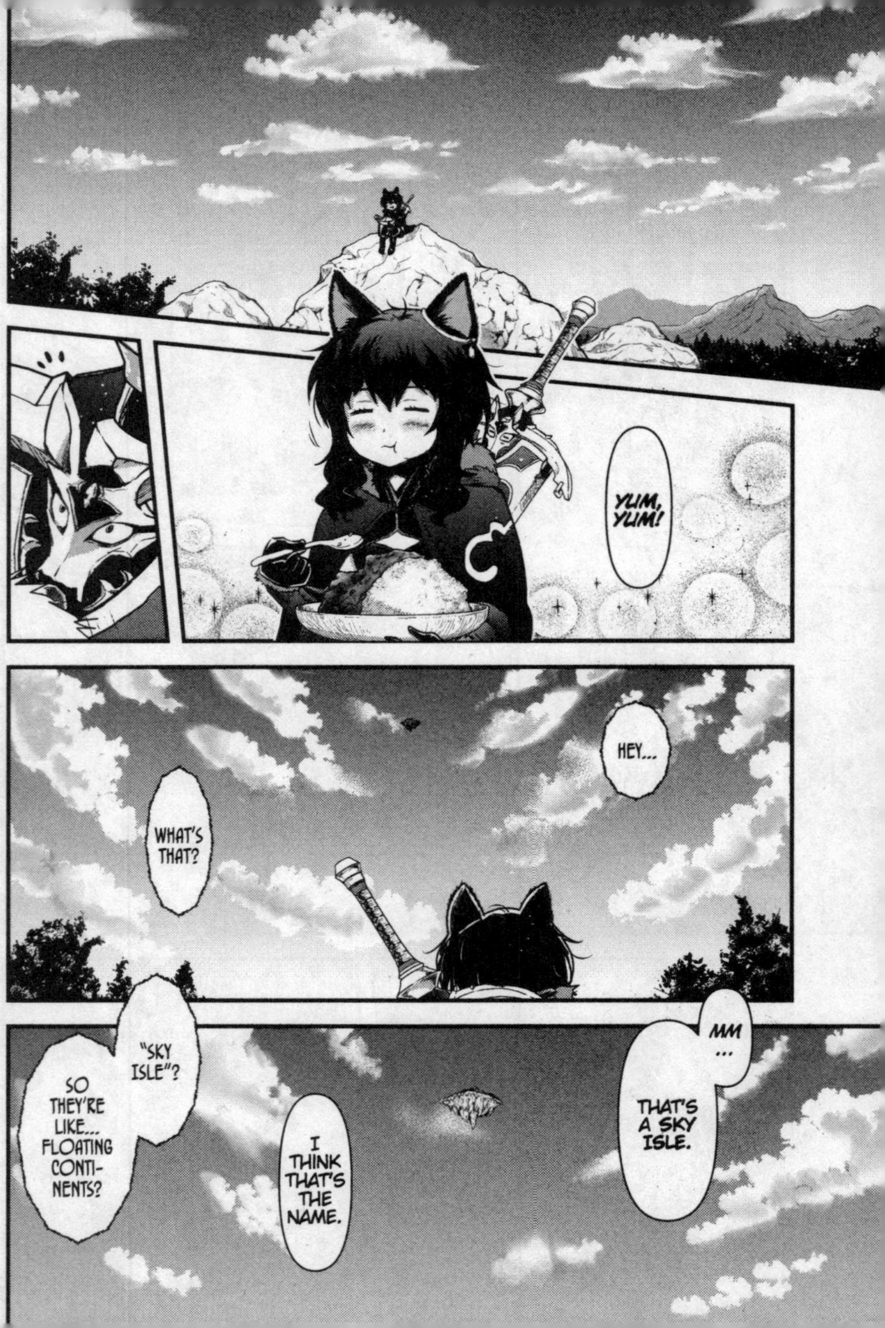
YUM, YUM!
HEY...
WHAT'S THAT?
MM...
THAT'S A SKY ISLE.
I THINK THAT'S THE NAME.
"SKY ISLE"?
SO THEY'RE LIKE... FLOATING CONTI-NENTS?

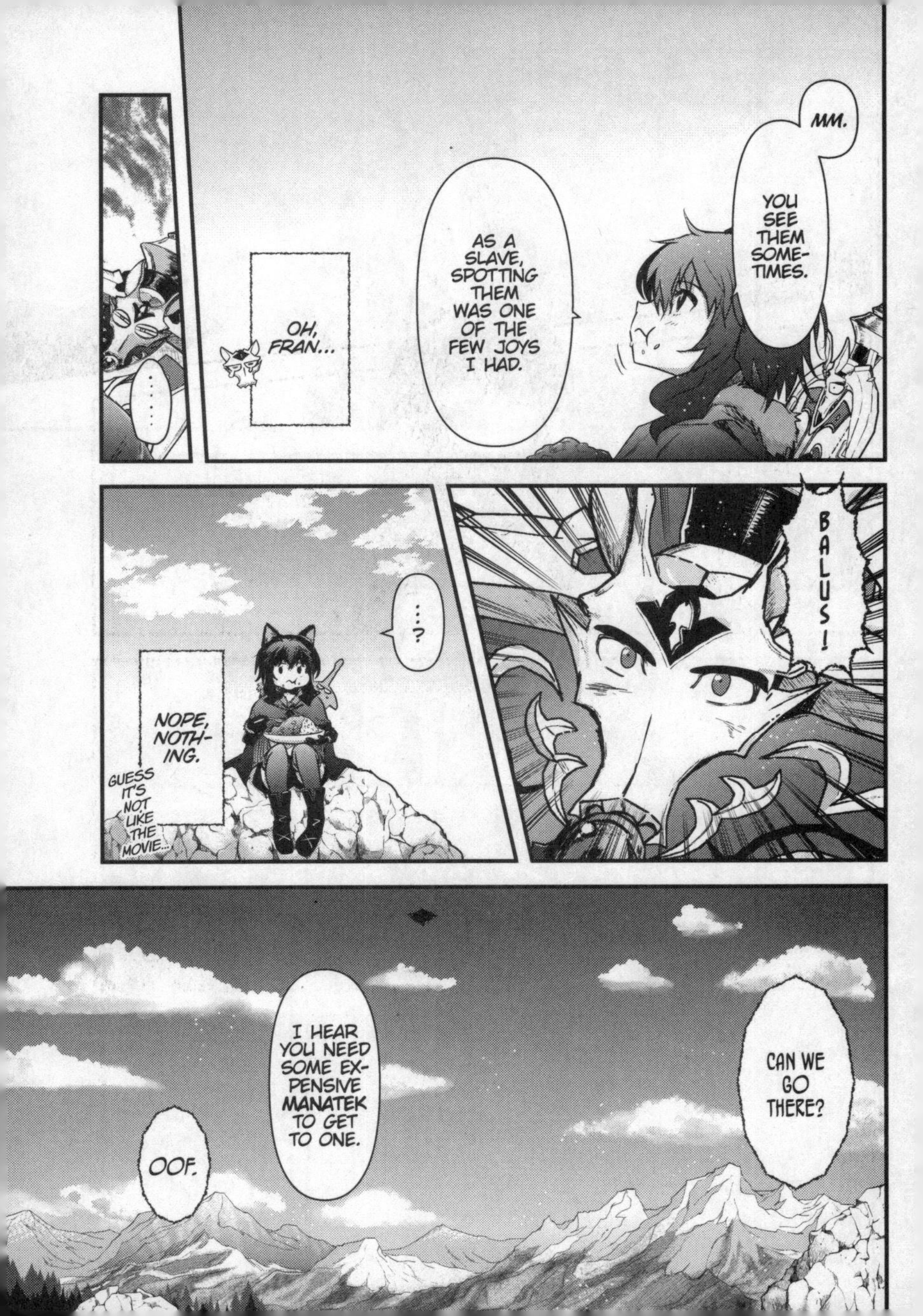
MM.
YOU SEE THEM SOME-TIMES.
AS A SLAVE, SPOTTING THEM WAS ONE OF THE FEW JOYS I HAD.
OH, FRAN...
......
BALUS!
...?
NOPE, NOTH-ING.
GUESS IT'S NOT LIKE THE MOVIE...
CAN WE GO THERE?
I HEAR YOU NEED SOME EX-PENSIVE MANATEK TO GET TO ONE.
OOF.

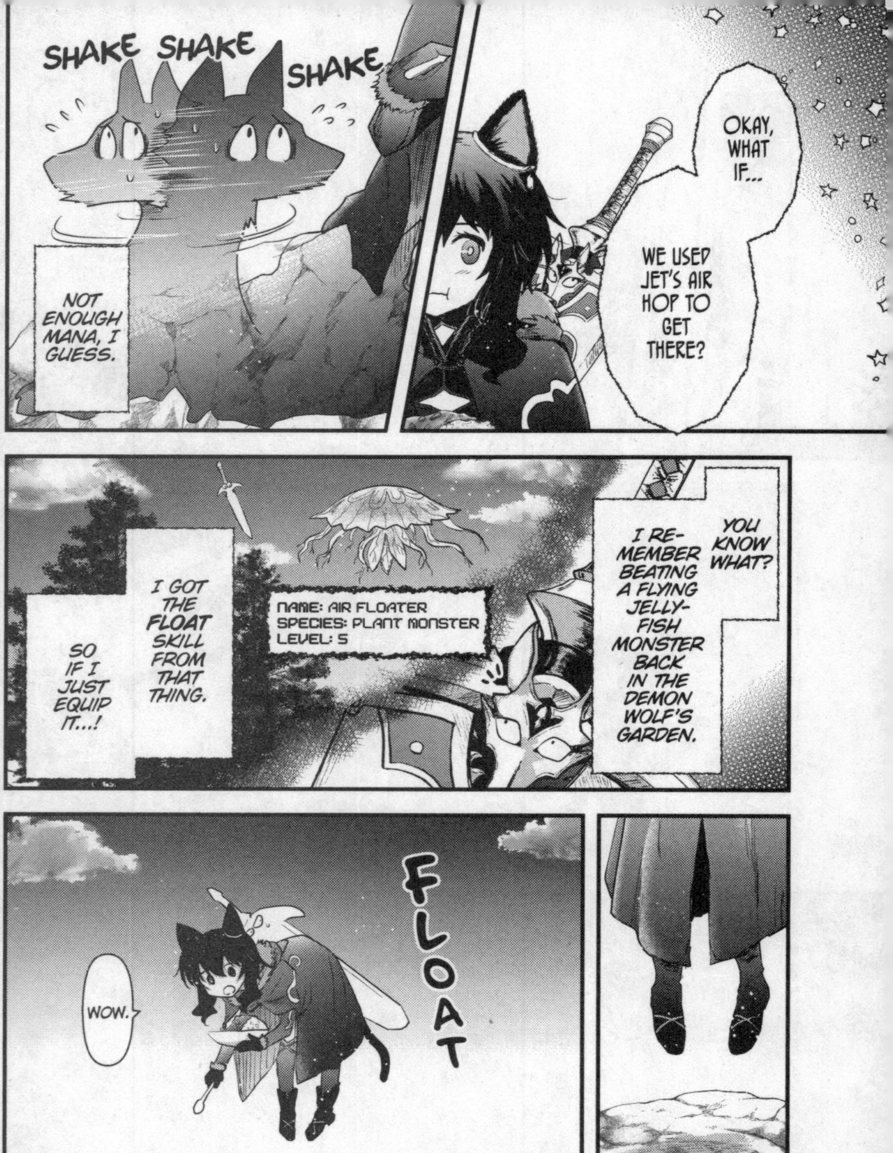
OKAY, WHAT IF...
WE USED JET'S AIR HOP TO GET THERE?
SHAKE SHAKE
SHAKE
NOT ENOUGH MANA, I GUESS.
YOU KNOW WHAT?
I RE-MEMBER BEATING A FLYING JELLY-FISH MONSTER BACK IN THE DEMON WOLF'S GARDEN.
NAME: AIR FLOATER
SPECIES: PLANT MONSTER
LEVEL: 5
I GOT THE FLOAT SKILL FROM THAT THING.
SO IF I JUST EQUIP IT...!
FLOAT
FLOAT
WOW.

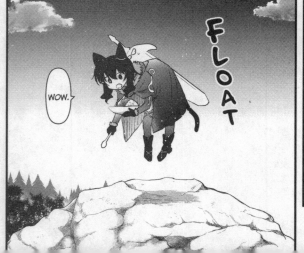

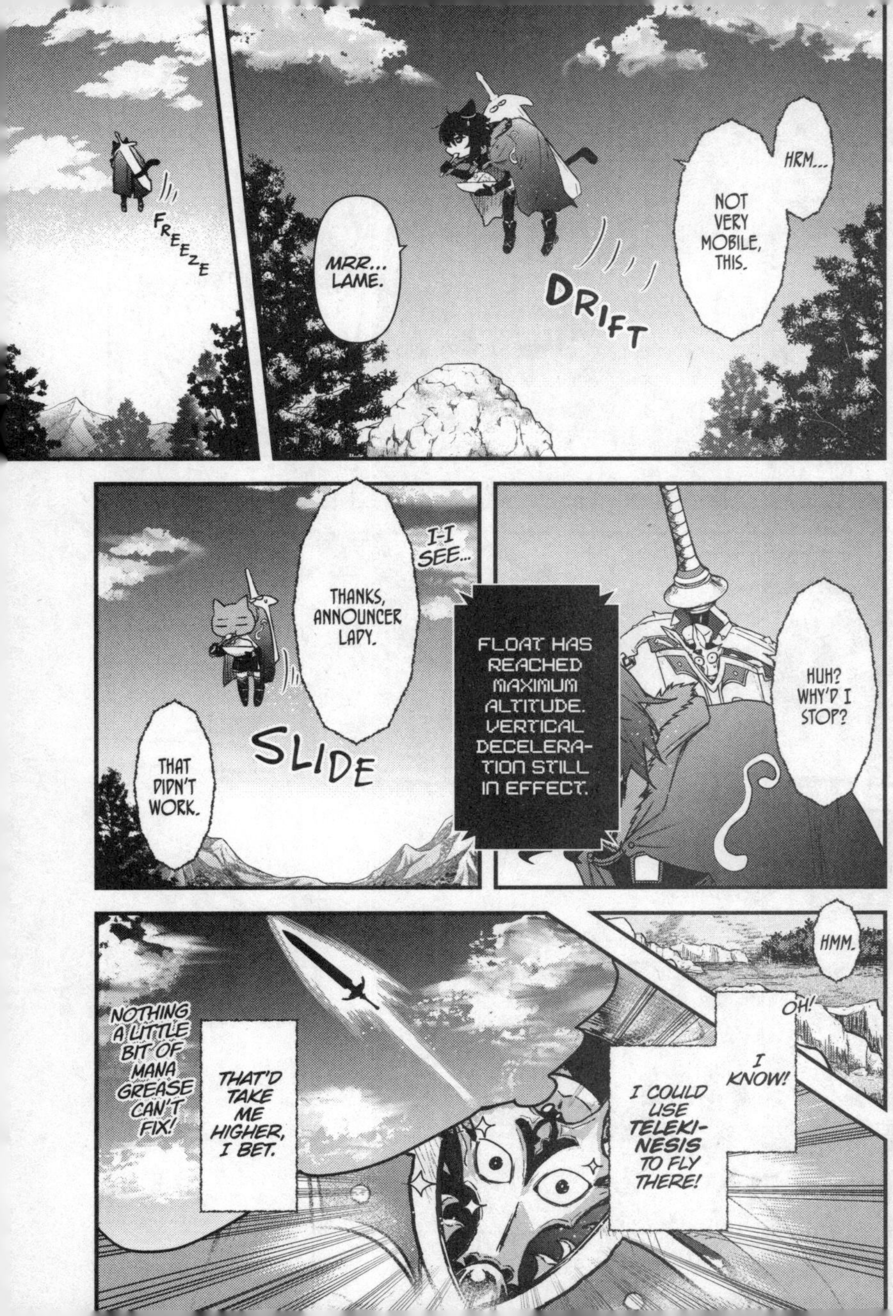
HRM...
NOT VERY MOBILE, THIS.
DRIFT
MRR... LAME.
FREEZE
HUH? WHY'D I STOP?
FLOAT HAS REACHED MAXIMUM ALTITUDE. VERTICAL DECELERA-TION STILL IN EFFECT.
I-I SEE...
THANKS, ANNOUNCER LADY.
SLIDE
THAT DIDN'T WORK.
HMM.
OH!
I KNOW!
I COULD USE TELEKI-NESIS TO FLY THERE!
THAT'D TAKE ME HIGHER, I BET.
NOTHING A LITTLE BIT OF MANA GREASE CAN'T FIX!

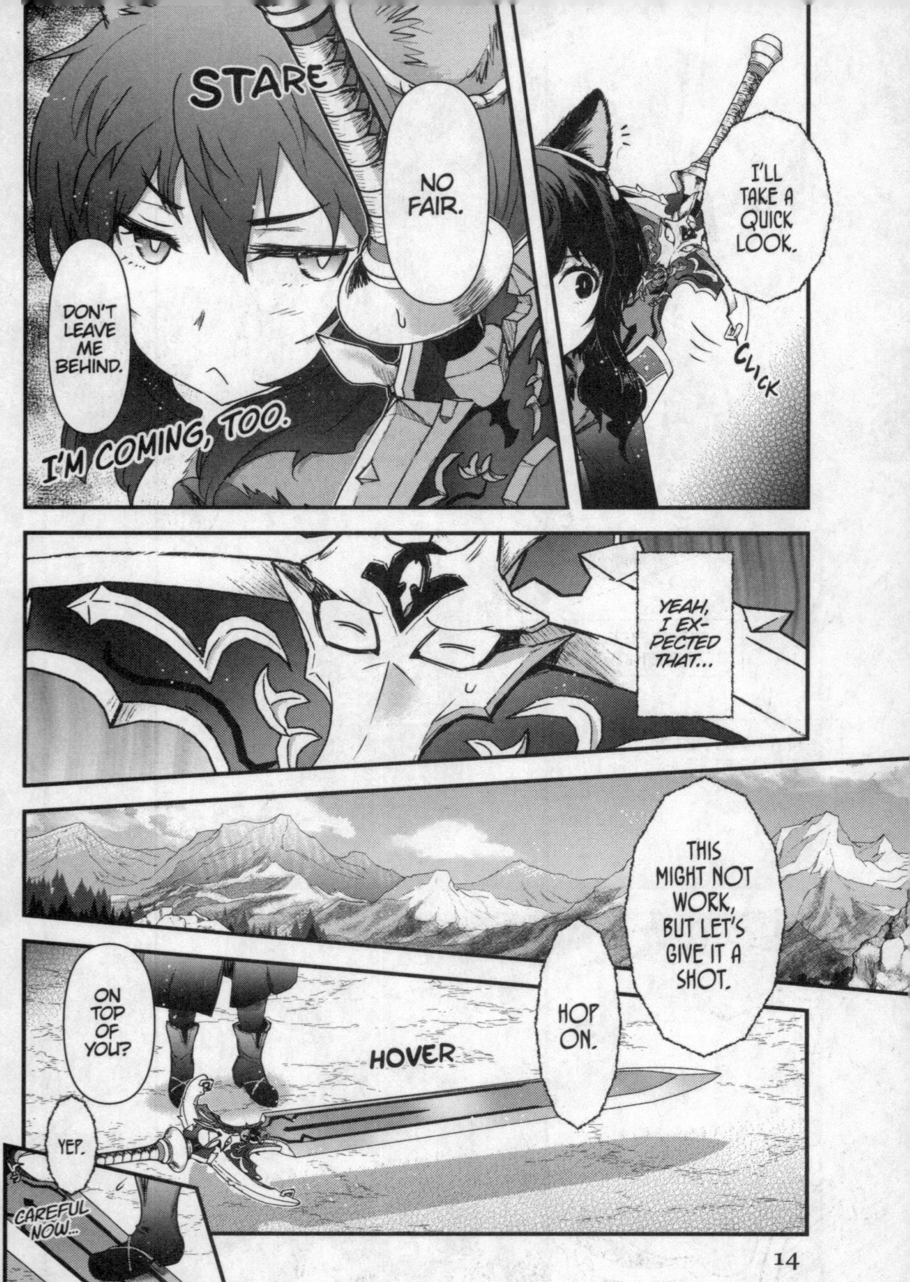
I'LL TAKE A QUICK LOOK.
CLICK
NO FAIR.
STARE
DON'T LEAVE ME BEHIND.
I'M COMING, TOO.
YEAH, I EXPECTED THAT...
THIS MIGHT NOT WORK, BUT LET'S GIVE IT A SHOT.
HOP ON.
ON TOP OF YOU?
HOVER
YEP.
CAREFUL NOW...

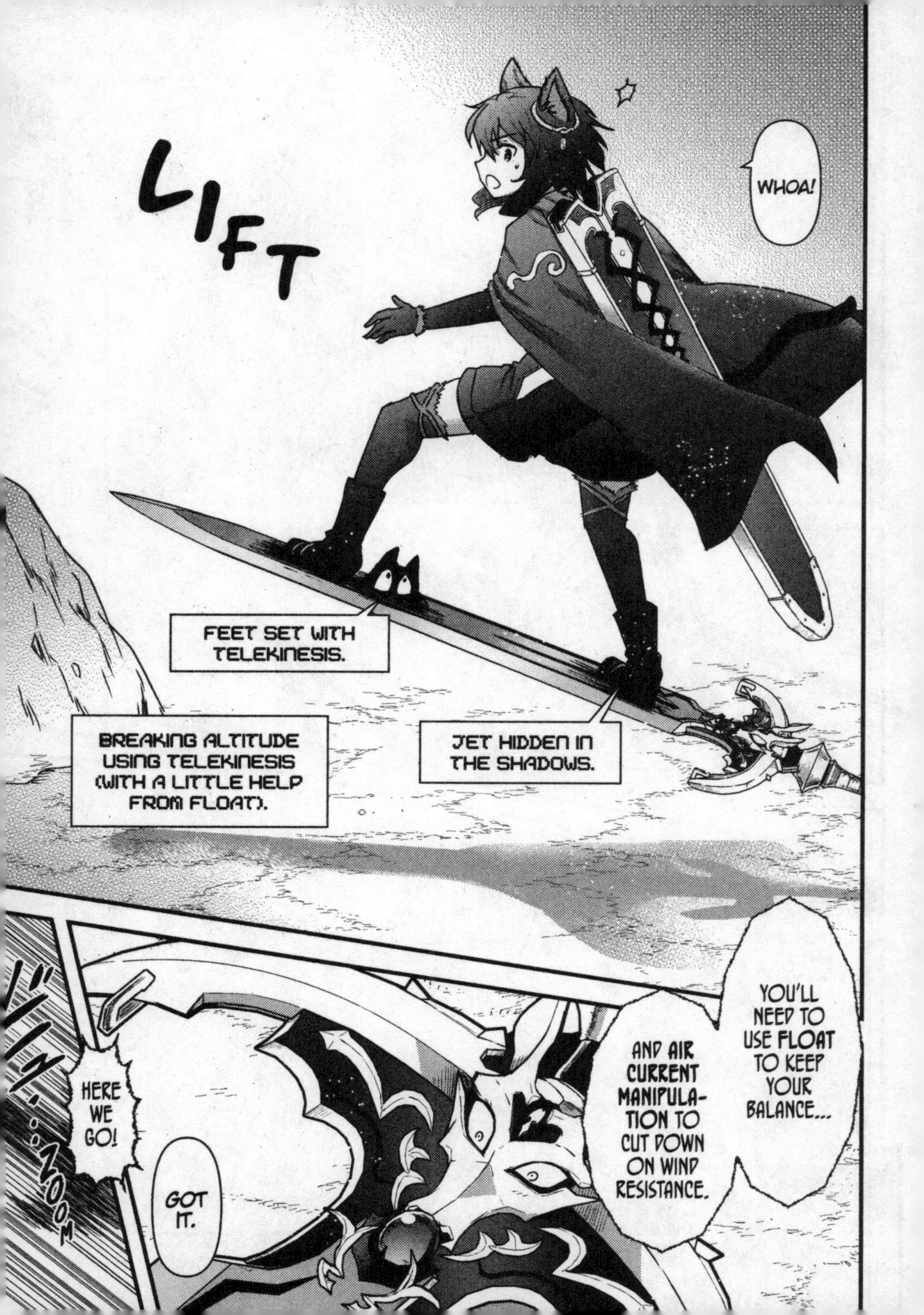
WHOA!
LIFT
FEET SET WITH TELEKINESIS.
JET HIDDEN IN THE SHADOWS.
BREAKING ALTITUDE USING TELEKINESIS (WITH A LITTLE HELP FROM FLOAT).
YOU'LL NEED TO USE FLOAT TO KEEP YOUR BALANCE...
AND AIR CURRENT MANIPULATION TO CUT DOWN ON WIND RESISTANCE.
HERE WE GO!
GOT IT.
...ZOOM

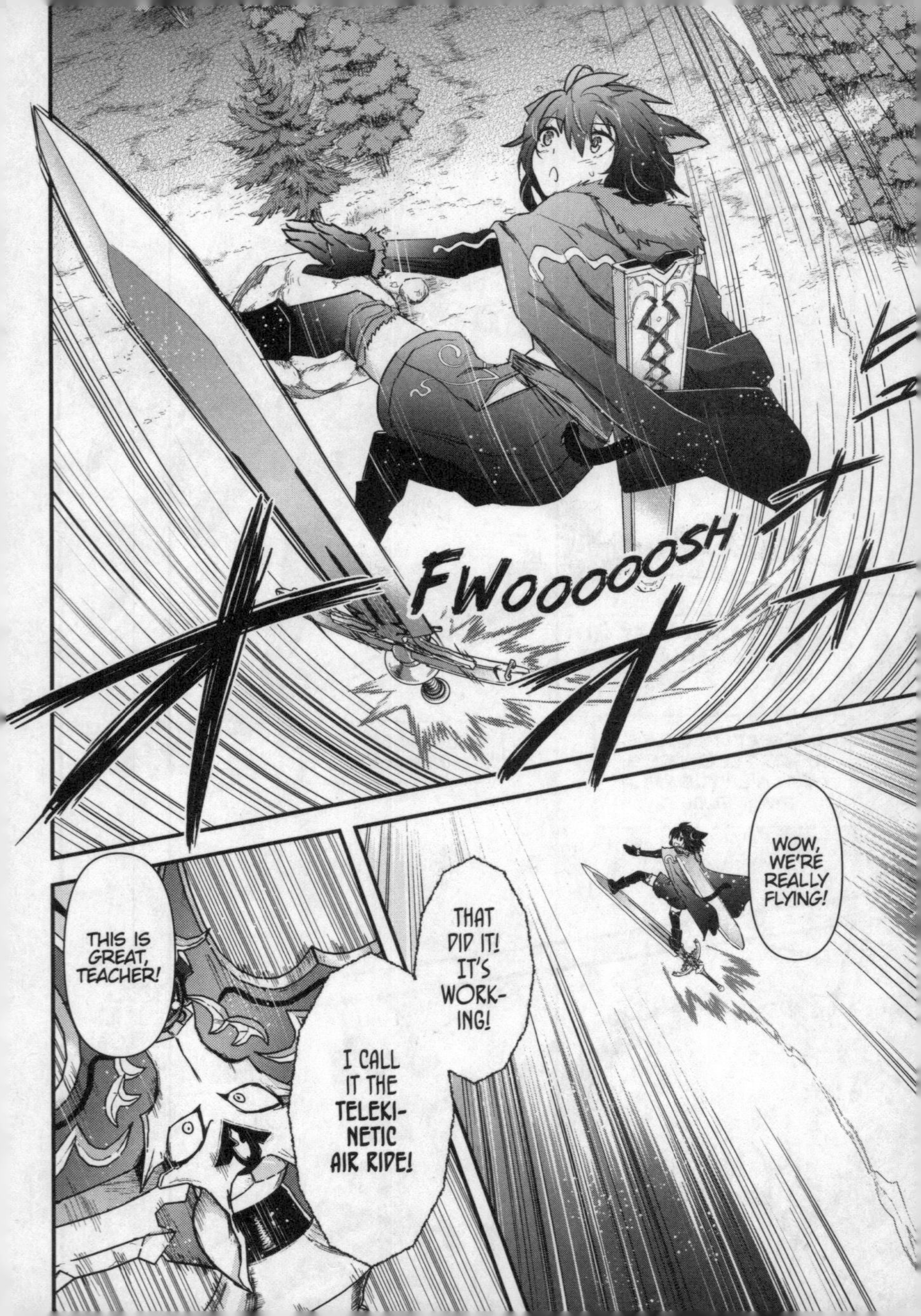
FWOOOOOOSH
WOW, WE'RE REALLY FLYING!
THAT DID IT! IT'S WORK-ING!
I CALL IT THE TELEKI-NETIC AIR RIDE!
THIS IS GREAT, TEACHER!

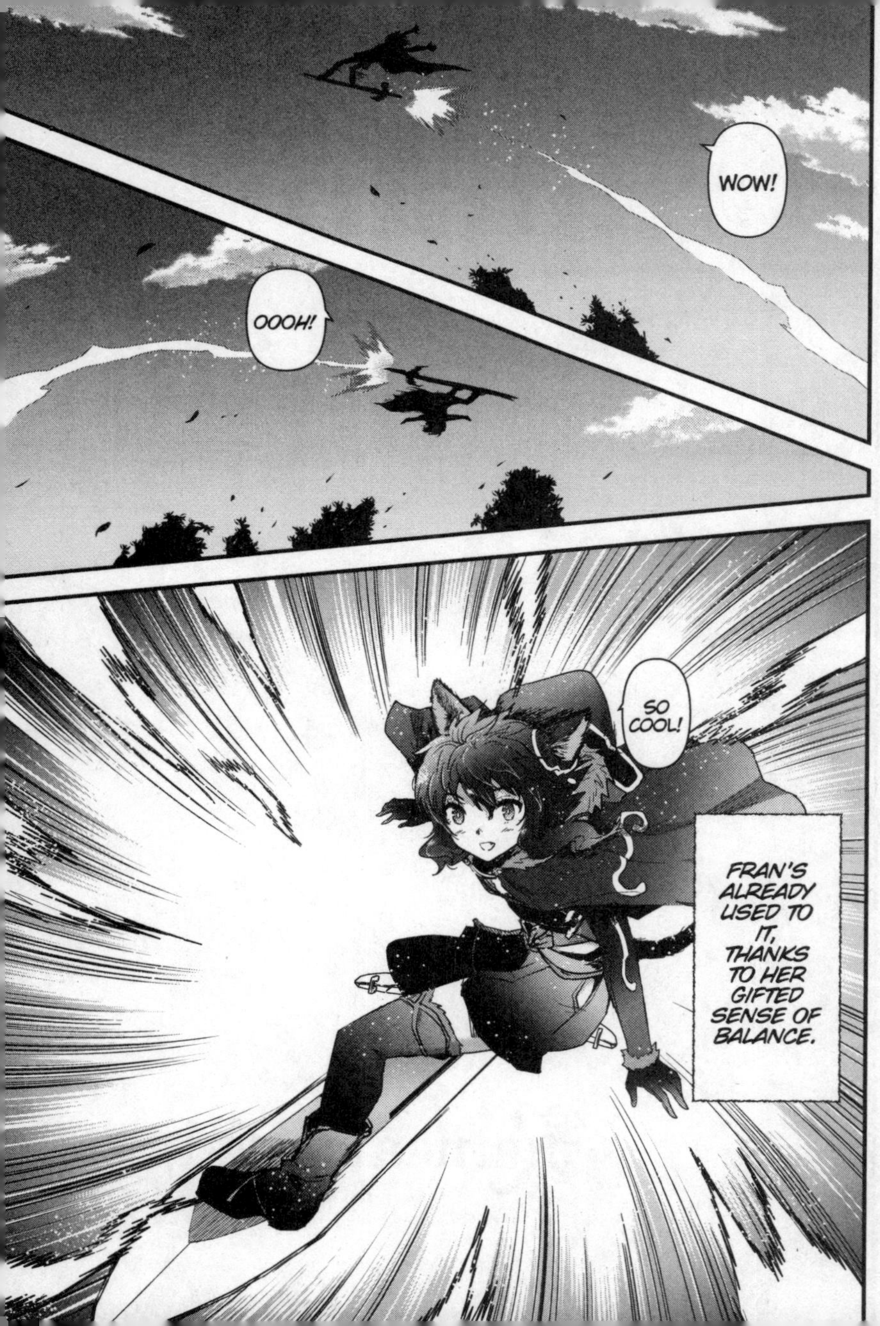
WOW!
OOOH!
SO COOL!
FRAN'S ALREADY USED TO IT, THANKS TO HER GIFTED SENSE OF BALANCE.

Reincarnated
as a sword

Chapter 29: Meet the Undead

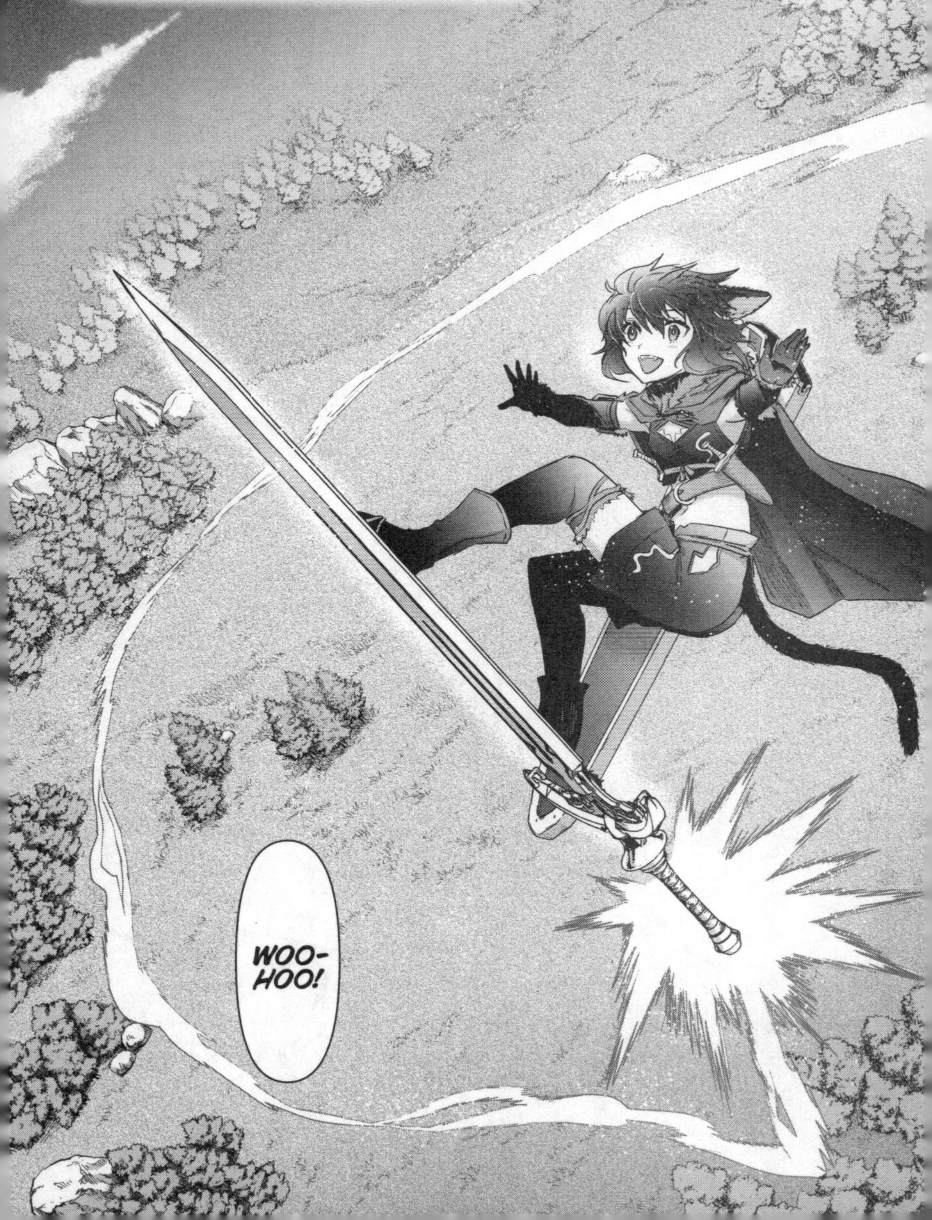
WOO-HOO!

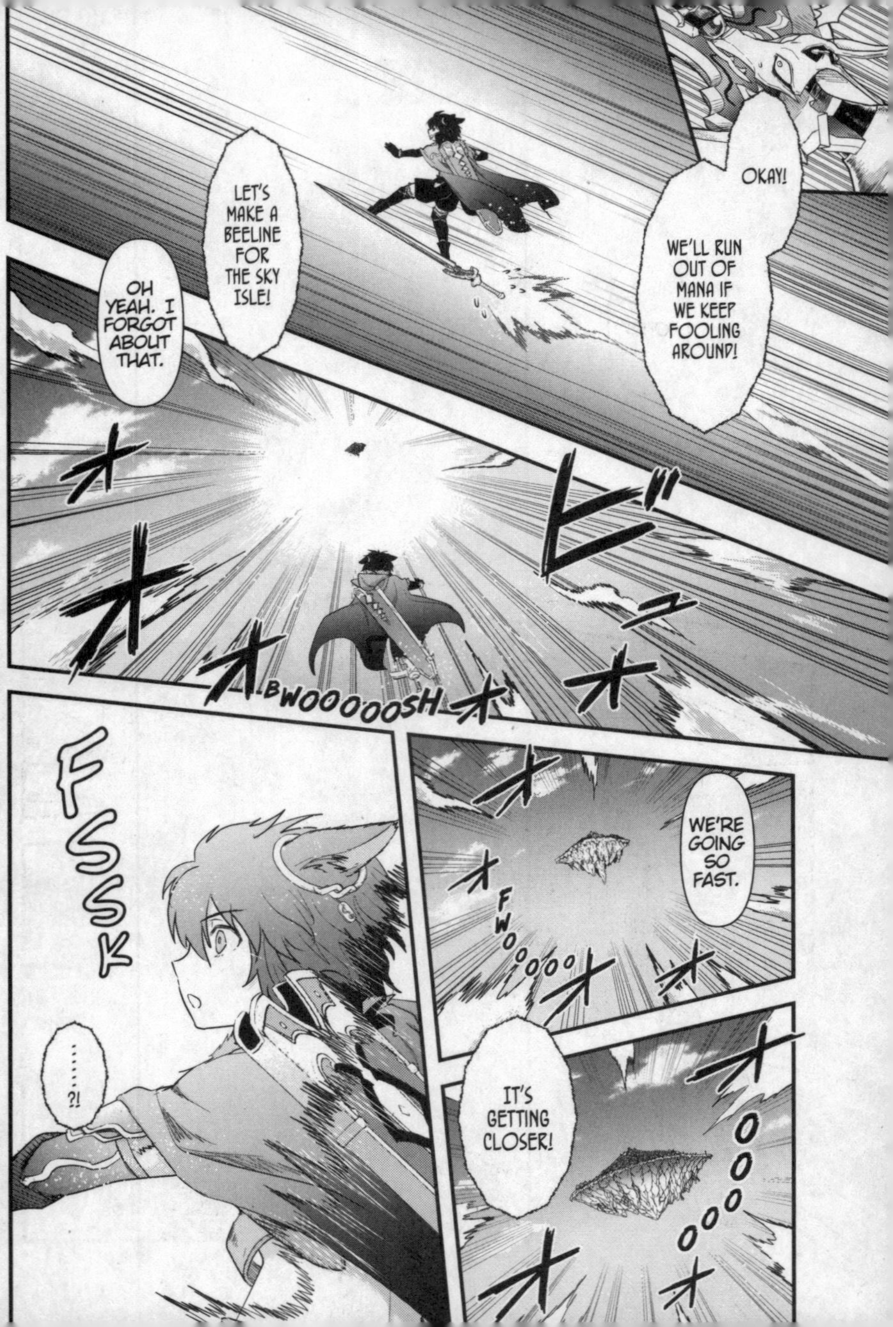
OKAY!
WE'LL RUN OUT OF MANA IF WE KEEP FOOLING AROUND!
LET'S MAKE A BEELINE FOR THE SKY ISLE!
OH YEAH. I FORGOT ABOUT THAT.
BWOOOOOOSH
WE'RE GOING SO FAST.
FWOOOOO
IT'S GETTING CLOSER!
FSSK
......?!

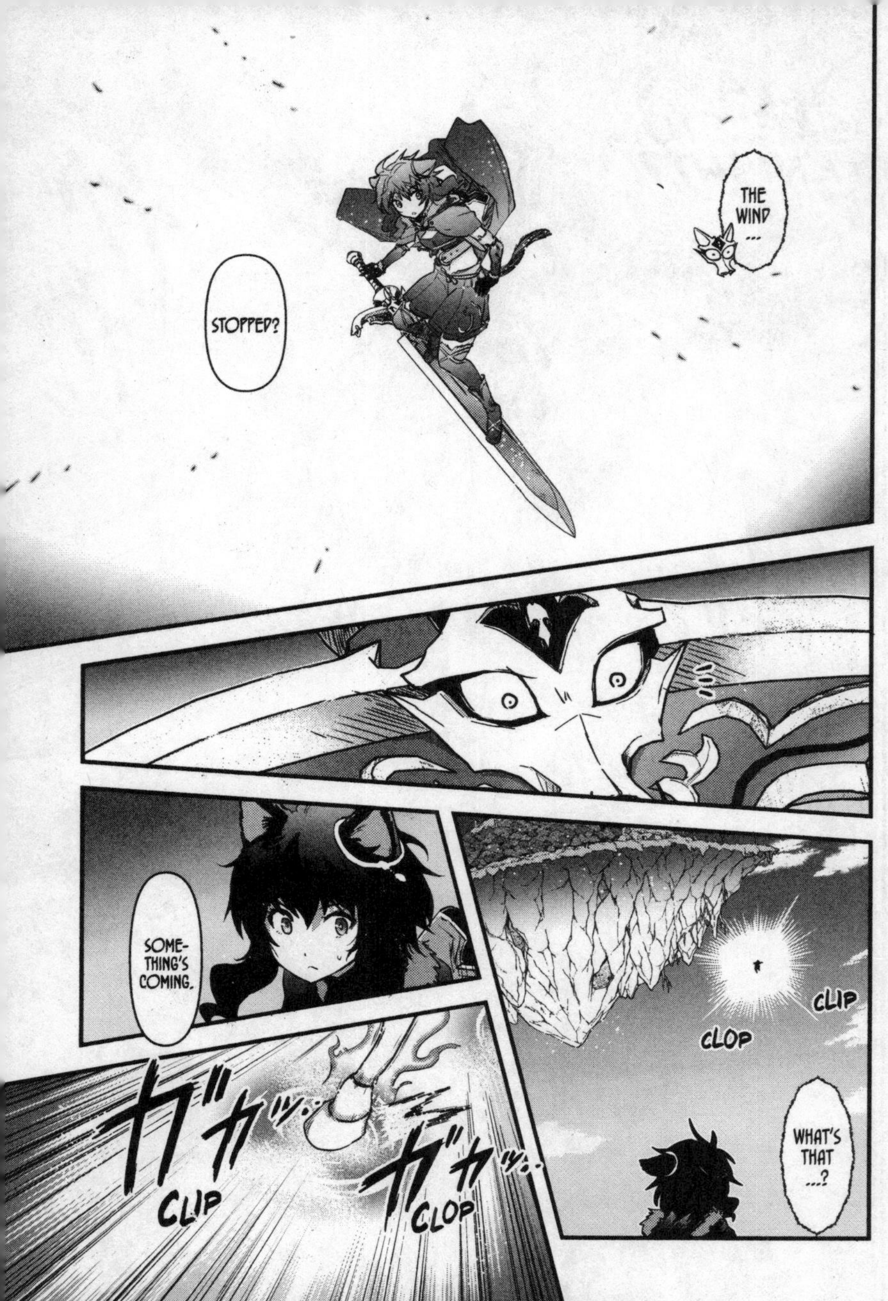
THE WIND ...
STOPPED?
CLIP
CLOP
WHAT'S THAT ...?
SOME-THING'S COMING.
ガカッ..
CLOP
ガカッ..
CLIP

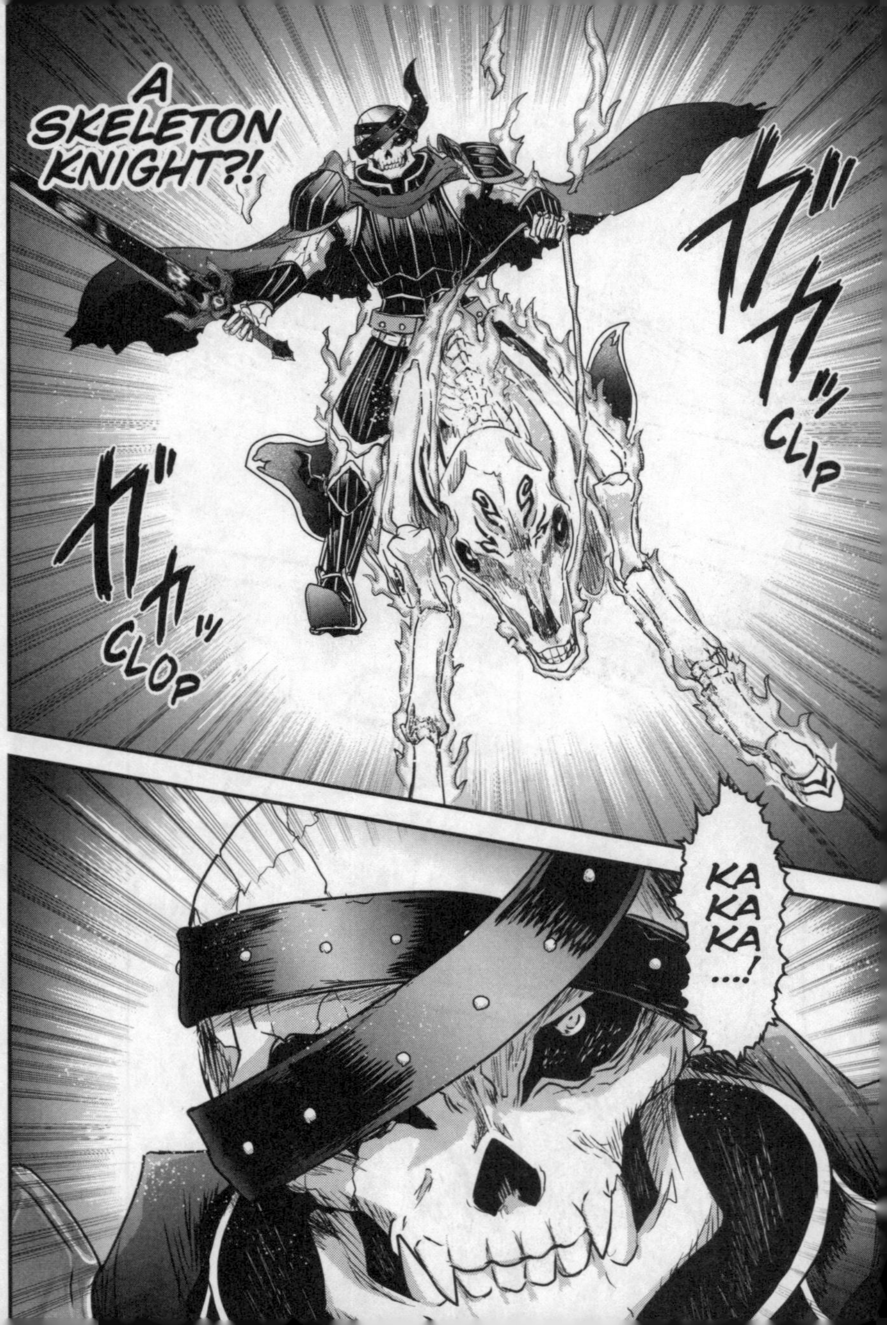
A SKELETON KNIGHT?!
ガガッ
CLIP
ガガッ
CLOP
KA KA KA...!

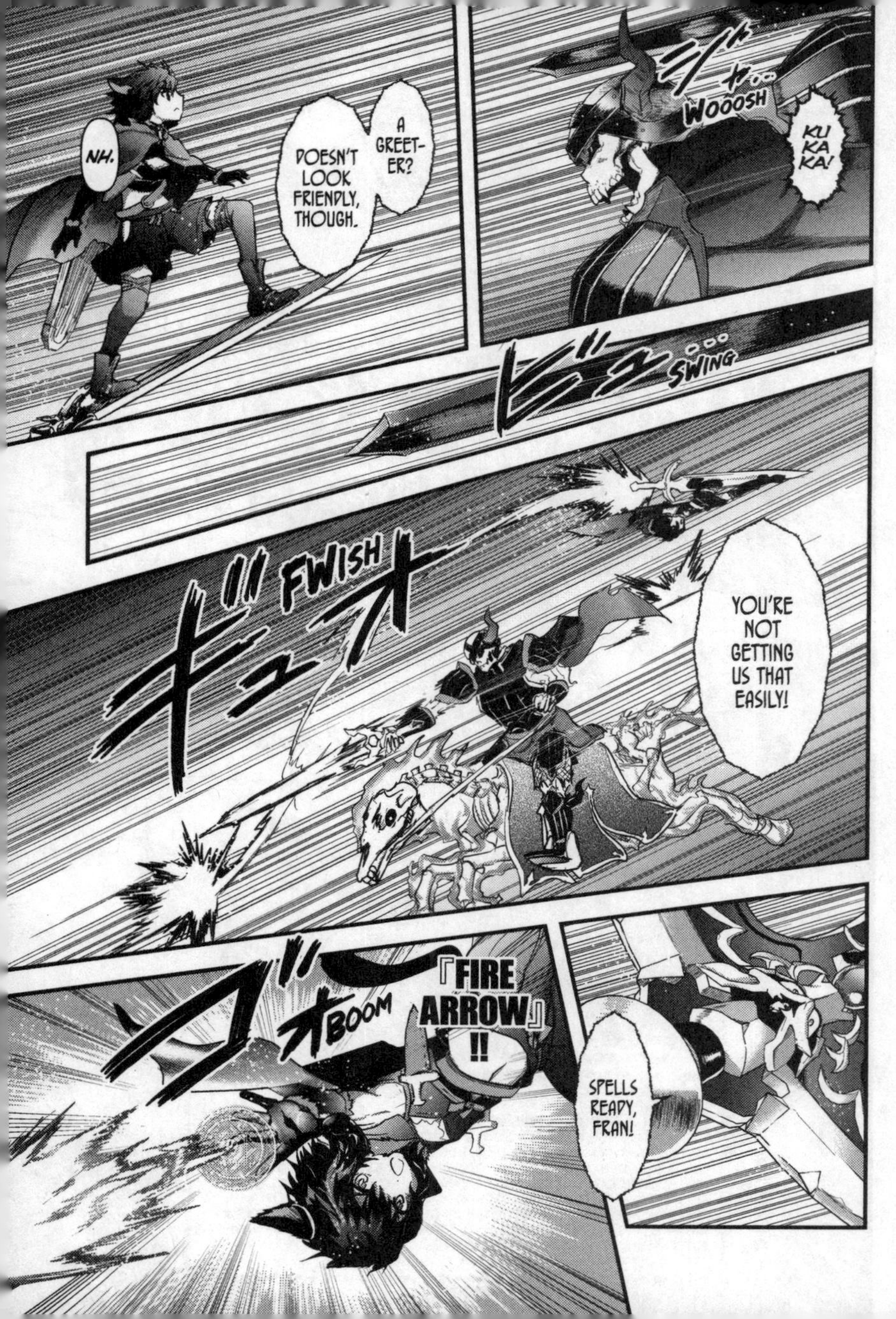
WOOOSH
KU KA KA!
A GREET-ER?
DOESN'T LOOK FRIENDLY, THOUGH.
NH.
SWING
YOU'RE NOT GETTING US THAT EASILY!
FWISH
SPELLS READY, FRAN!
『FIRE ARROW』!!
BOOM

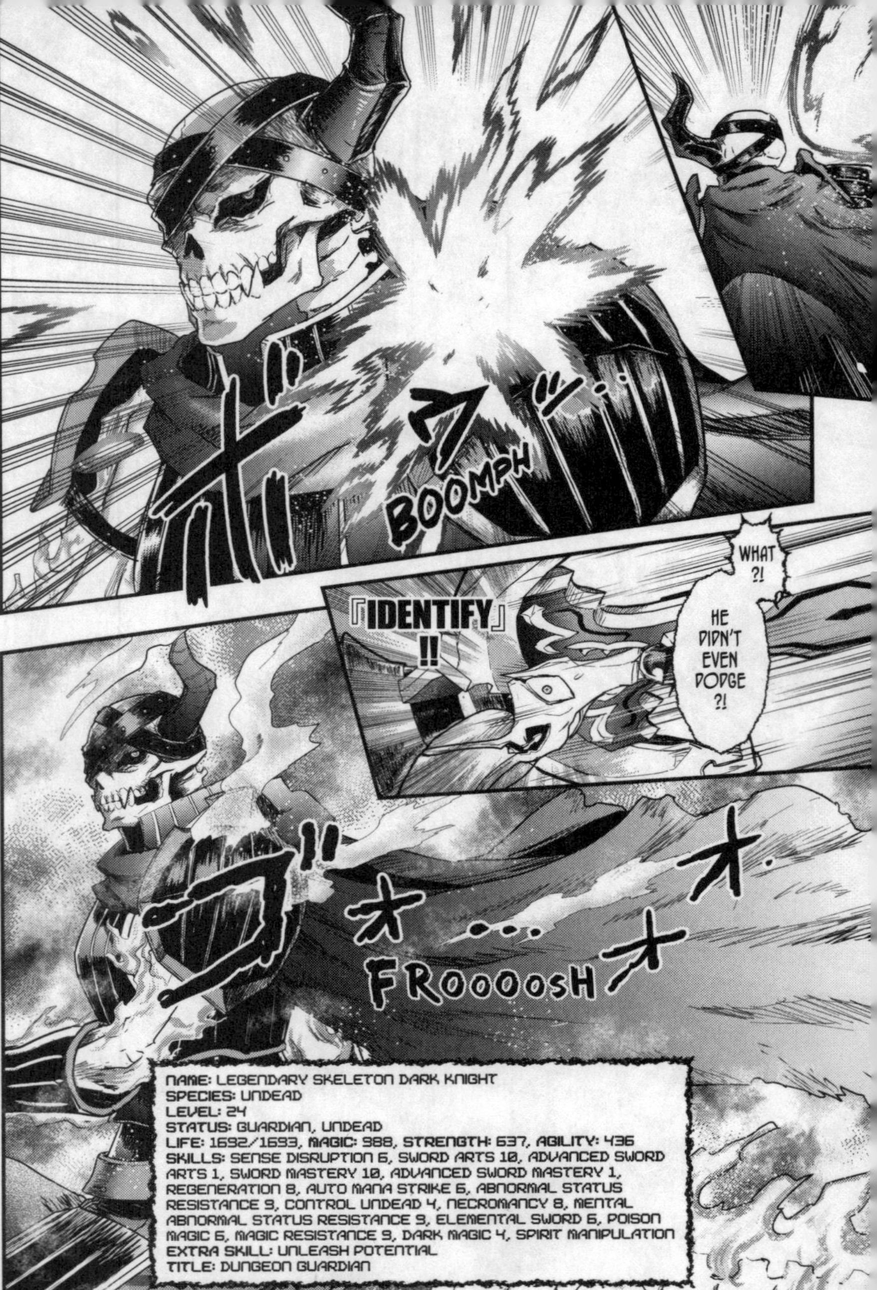

BOOMPH
WHAT ?!
HE DIDN'T EVEN DODGE ?!
『IDENTIFY』 !!
FROOOOSH
NAME: LEGENDARY SKELETON DARK KNIGHT
SPECIES: UNDEAD
LEVEL: 24
STATUS: GUARDIAN, UNDEAD
LIFE: 1692/1693, MAGIC: 988, STRENGTH: 637, ABILITY: 436
SKILLS: SENSE DISRUPTION 6, SWORD ARTS 10, ADVANCED SWORD ARTS 1, SWORD MASTERY 10, ADVANCED SWORD MASTERY 1, REGENERATION 8, AUTO MANA STRIKE 6, ABNORMAL STATUS RESISTANCE 9, CONTROL UNDEAD 4, NECROMANCY 8, MENTAL ABNORMAL STATUS RESISTANCE 9, ELEMENTAL SWORD 6, POISON MAGIC 6, MAGIC RESISTANCE 9, DARK MAGIC 4, SPIRIT MANIPULATION
EXTRA SKILL: UNLEASH POTENTIAL
TITLE: DUNGEON GUARDIAN

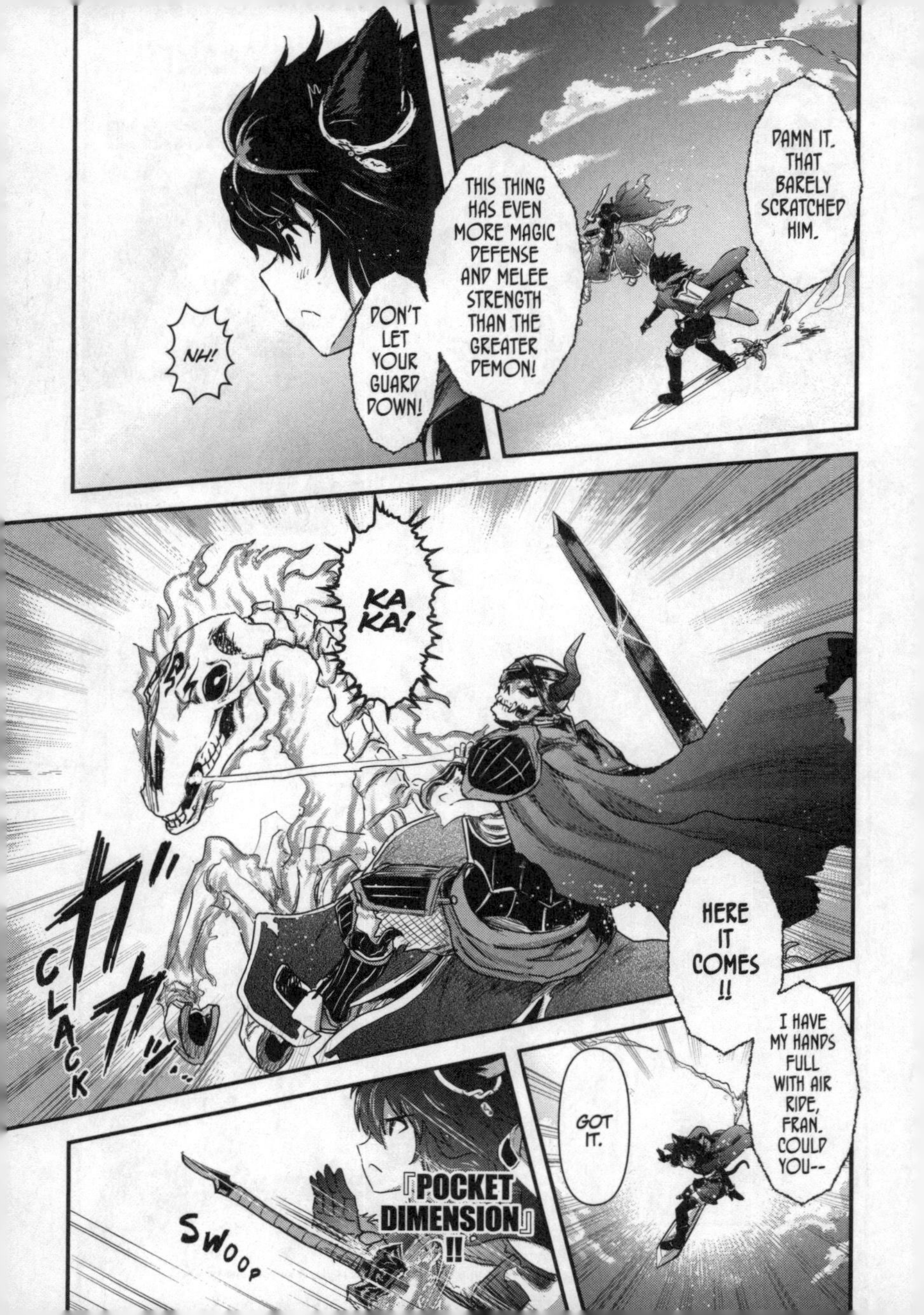
DAMN IT. THAT BARELY SCRATCHED HIM.
THIS THING HAS EVEN MORE MAGIC DEFENSE AND MELEE STRENGTH THAN THE GREATER DEMON!
DON'T LET YOUR GUARD DOWN!
NH!
KA KA!
HERE IT COMES!!
CLACK
I HAVE MY HANDS FULL WITH AIR RIDE, FRAN. COULD YOU--
GOT IT.
『POCKET DIMENSION』!!
SWOOP

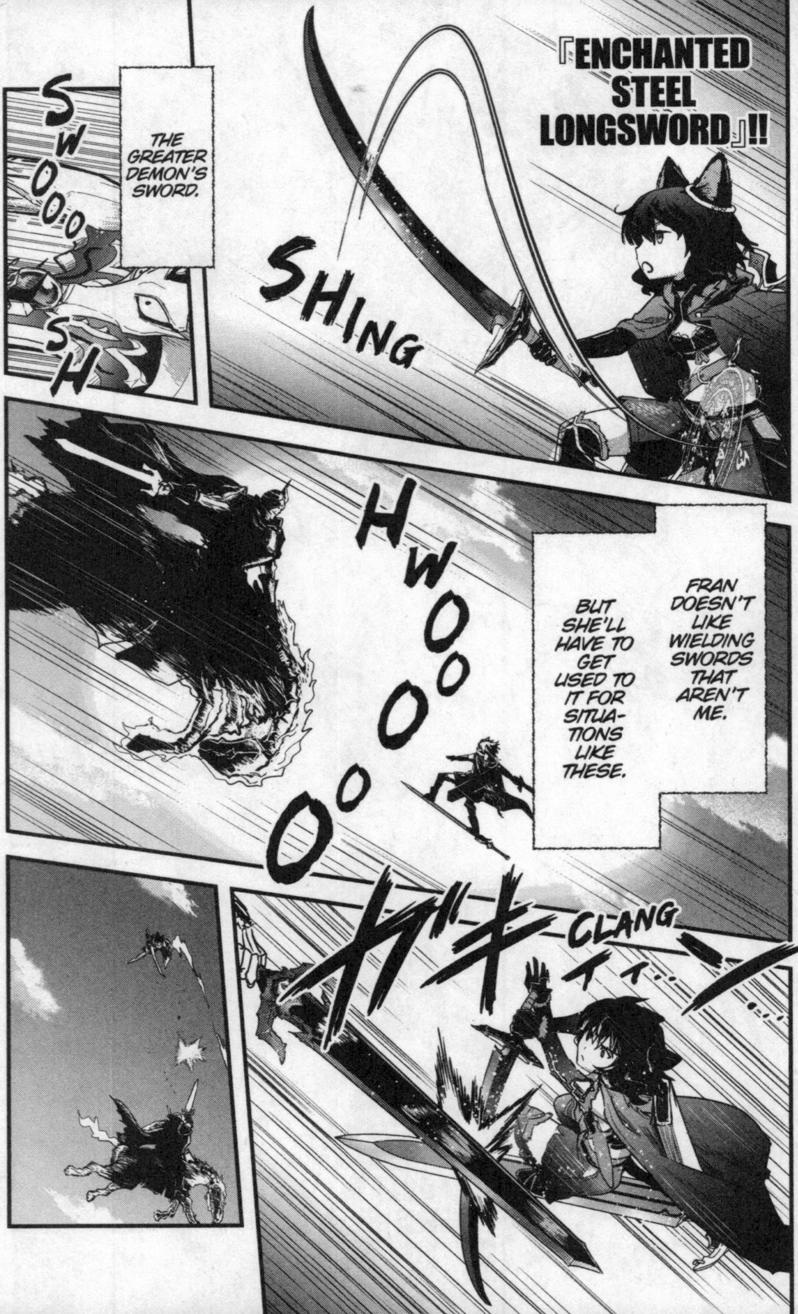
『ENCHANTED STEEL LONGSWORD』!!
SHING
THE GREATER DEMON'S SWORD.
SWOOOOSH
HWOOOOO
FRAN DOESN'T LIKE WIELDING SWORDS THAT AREN'T ME.
BUT SHE'LL HAVE TO GET USED TO IT FOR SITUATIONS LIKE THESE.
ガキ
CLANG

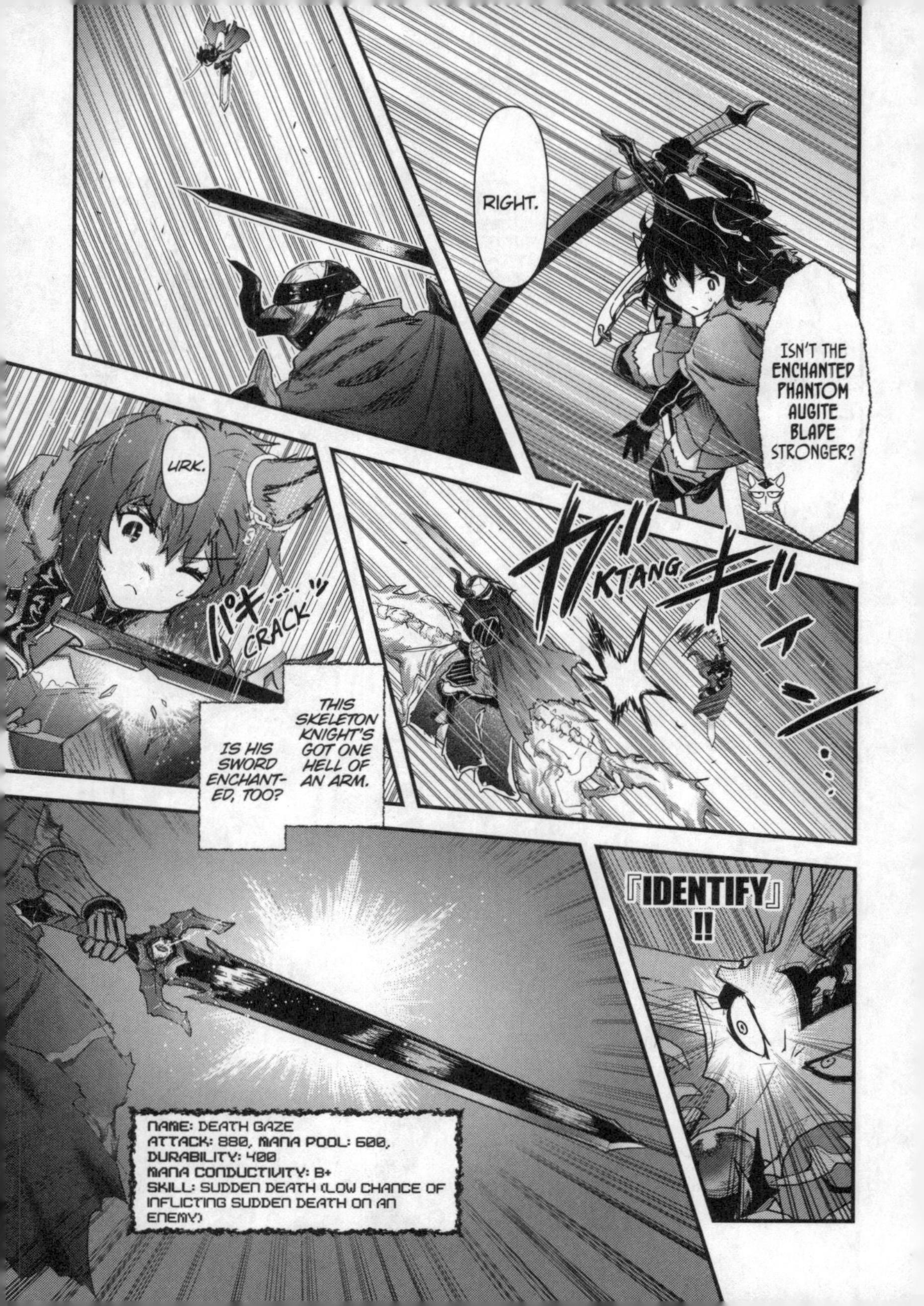
RIGHT.
ISN'T THE ENCHANTED PHANTOM AUGITE BLADE STRONGER?
KTANG
URK.
CRACK
THIS SKELETON KNIGHT'S GOT ONE HELL OF AN ARM.
IS HIS SWORD ENCHANTED, TOO?
『IDENTIFY』!!
NAME: DEATH GAZE
ATTACK: 880, MANA POOL: 600,
DURABILITY: 400
MANA CONDUCTIVITY: B+
SKILL: SUDDEN DEATH (LOW CHANCE OF INFLICTING SUDDEN DEATH ON AN ENEMY)

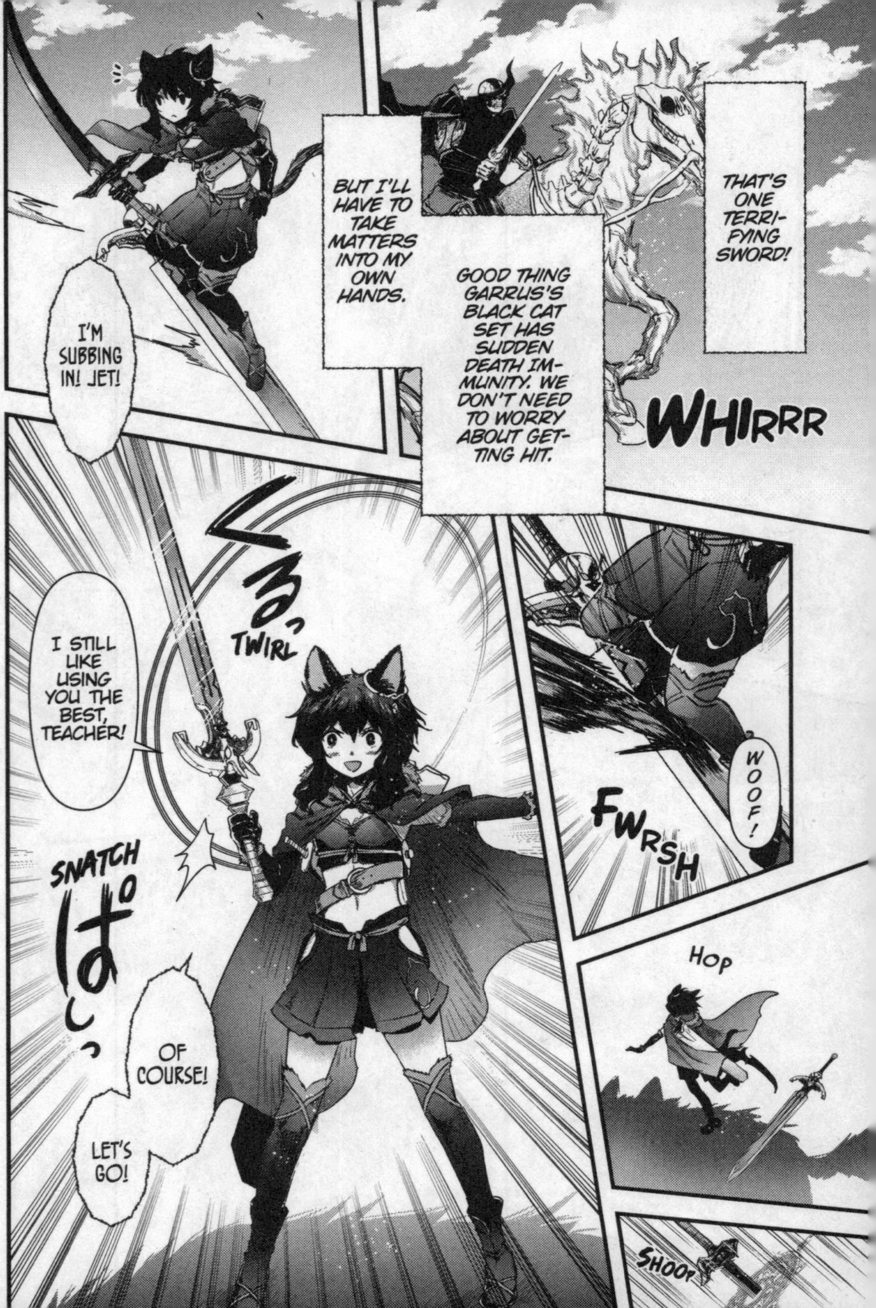
THAT'S ONE TERRIFYING SWORD!
WHIRRR
GOOD THING GARRUS'S BLACK CAT SET HAS SUDDEN DEATH IMMUNITY. WE DON'T NEED TO WORRY ABOUT GETTING HIT.
BUT I'LL HAVE TO TAKE MATTERS INTO MY OWN HANDS.
I'M SUBBING IN! JET!
WOOF!
FWRSH
HOP
SHOOP
くるっ
TWIRL
I STILL LIKE USING YOU THE BEST, TEACHER!
SNATCH
ぱしっ
OF COURSE!
LET'S GO!

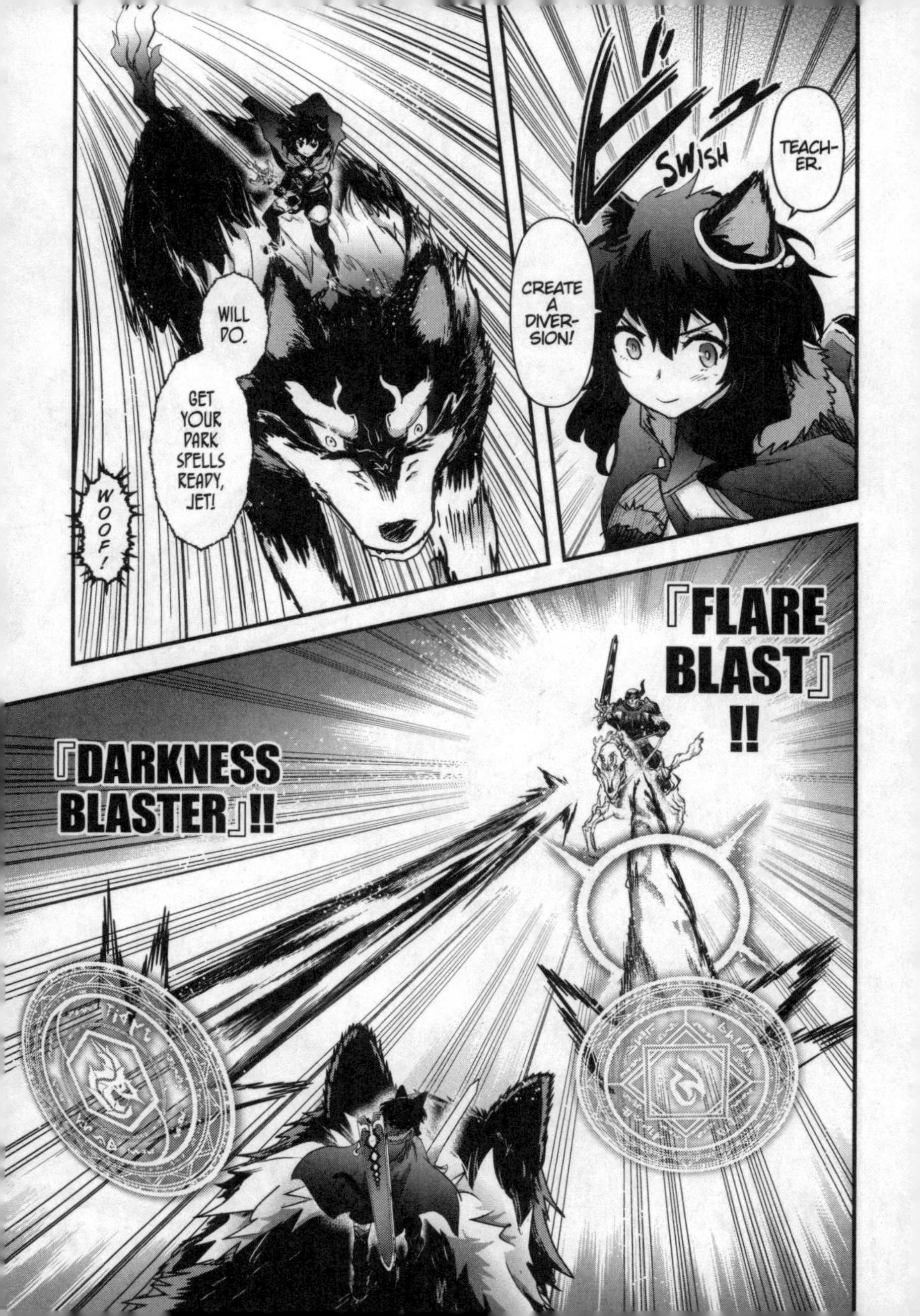
SWISH
TEACHER.
CREATE A DIVERSION!
WILL DO.
GET YOUR DARK SPELLS READY, JET!
WOOF!
『FLARE BLAST』!!
『DARKNESS BLASTER』!!

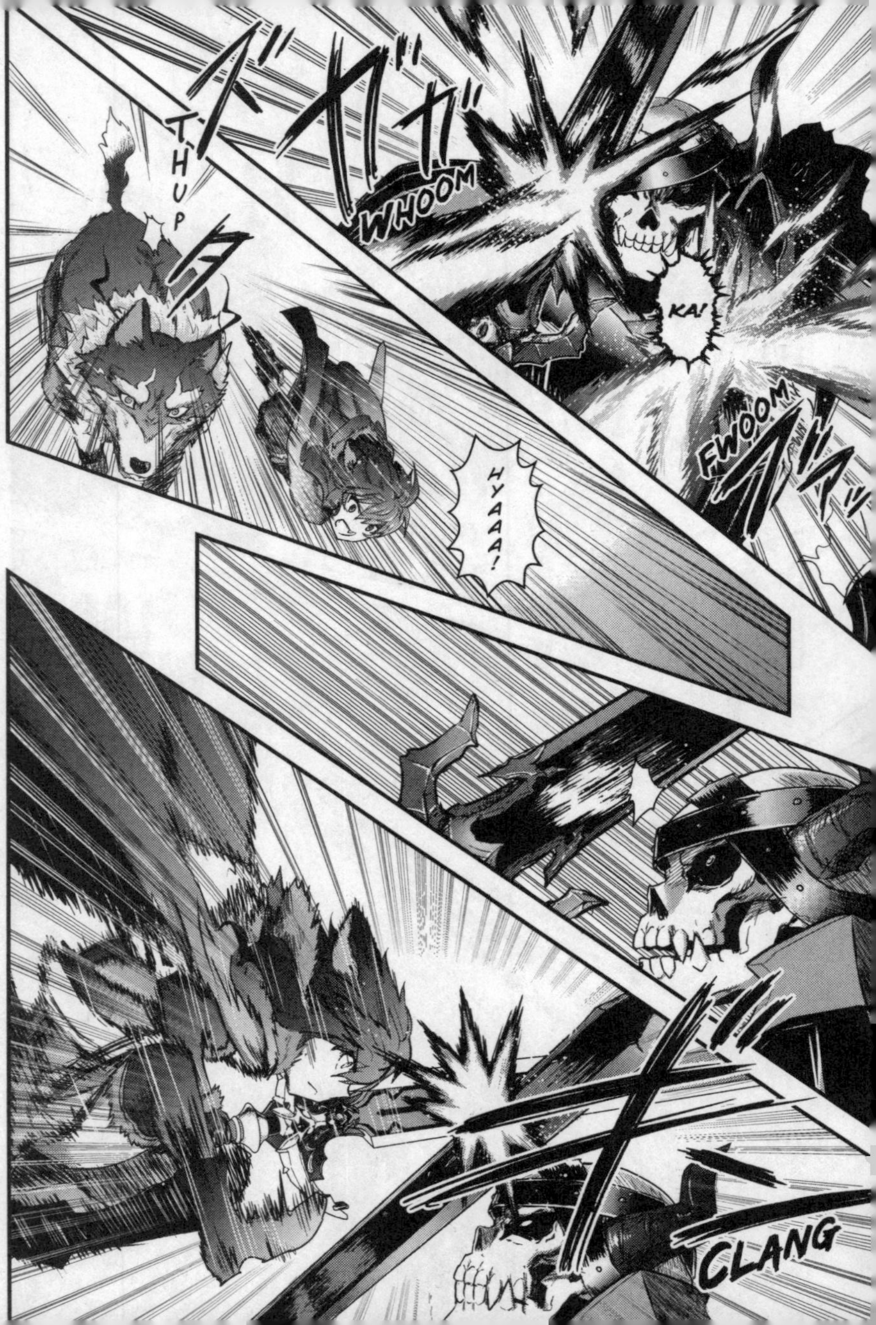
WHOOM
KA!
FWOOM
THUP
HYAAAA!
CLANG

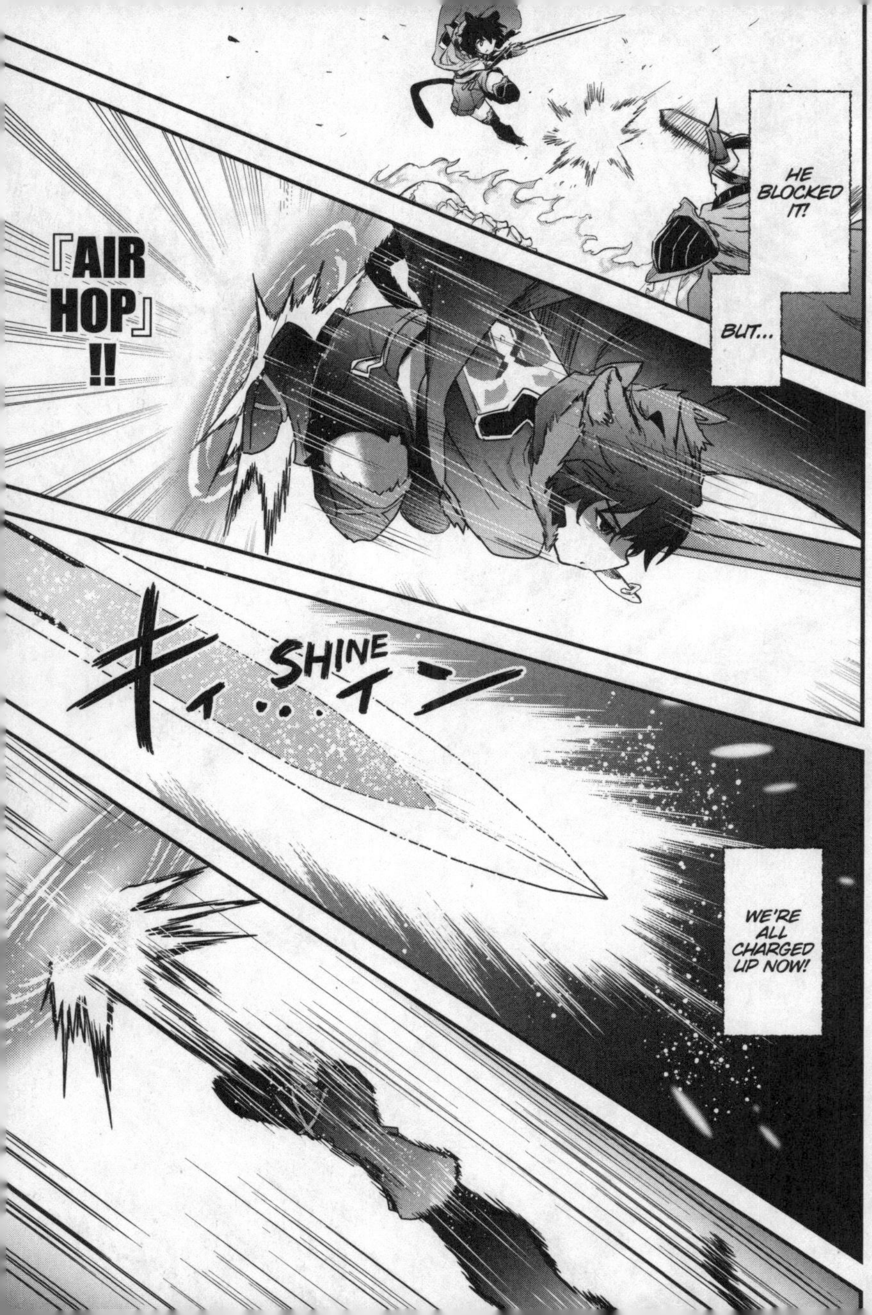
HE BLOCKED IT!
BUT...
『AIR HOP』!!
SHINE
WE'RE ALL CHARGED UP NOW!

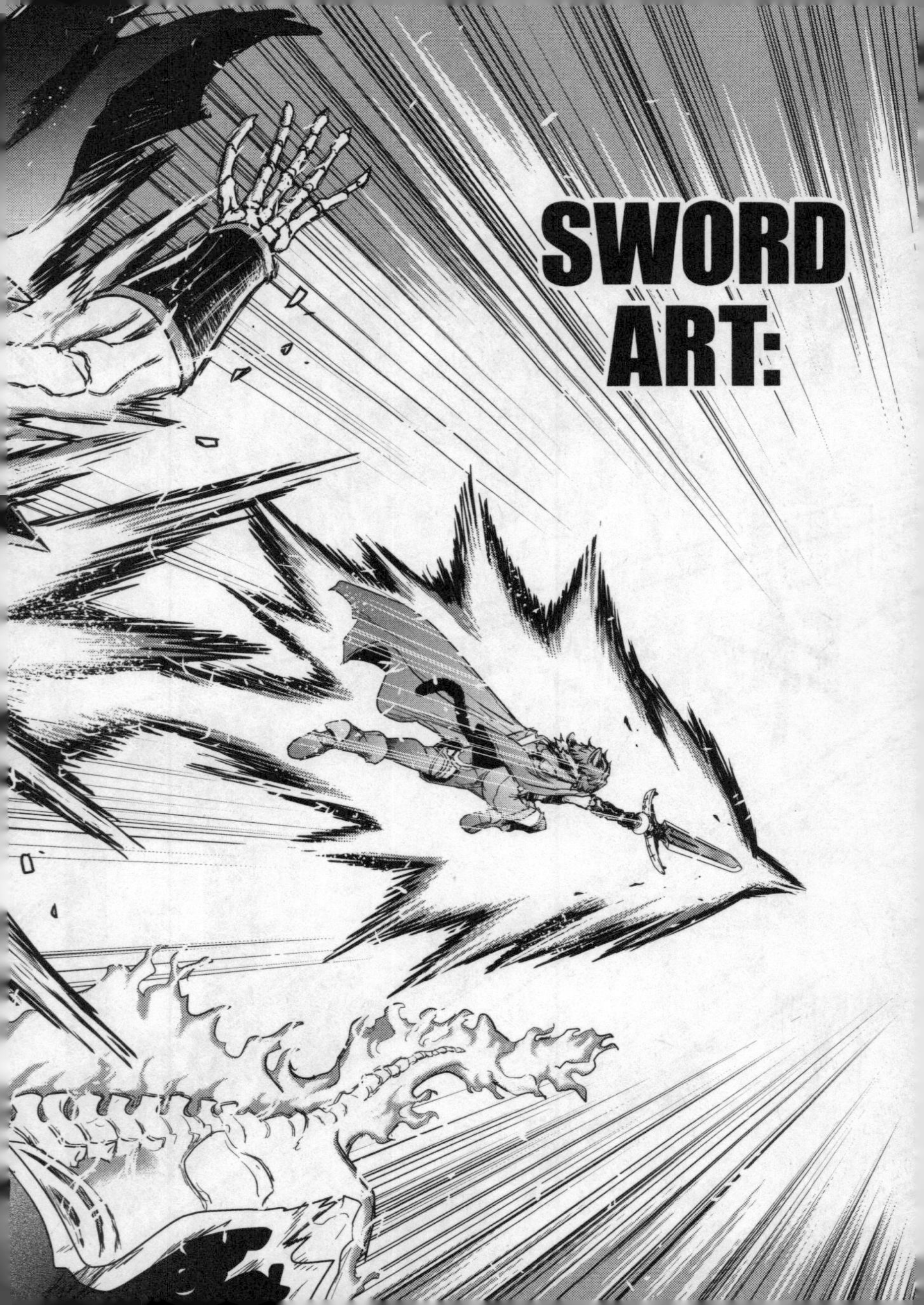
SWORD ART:

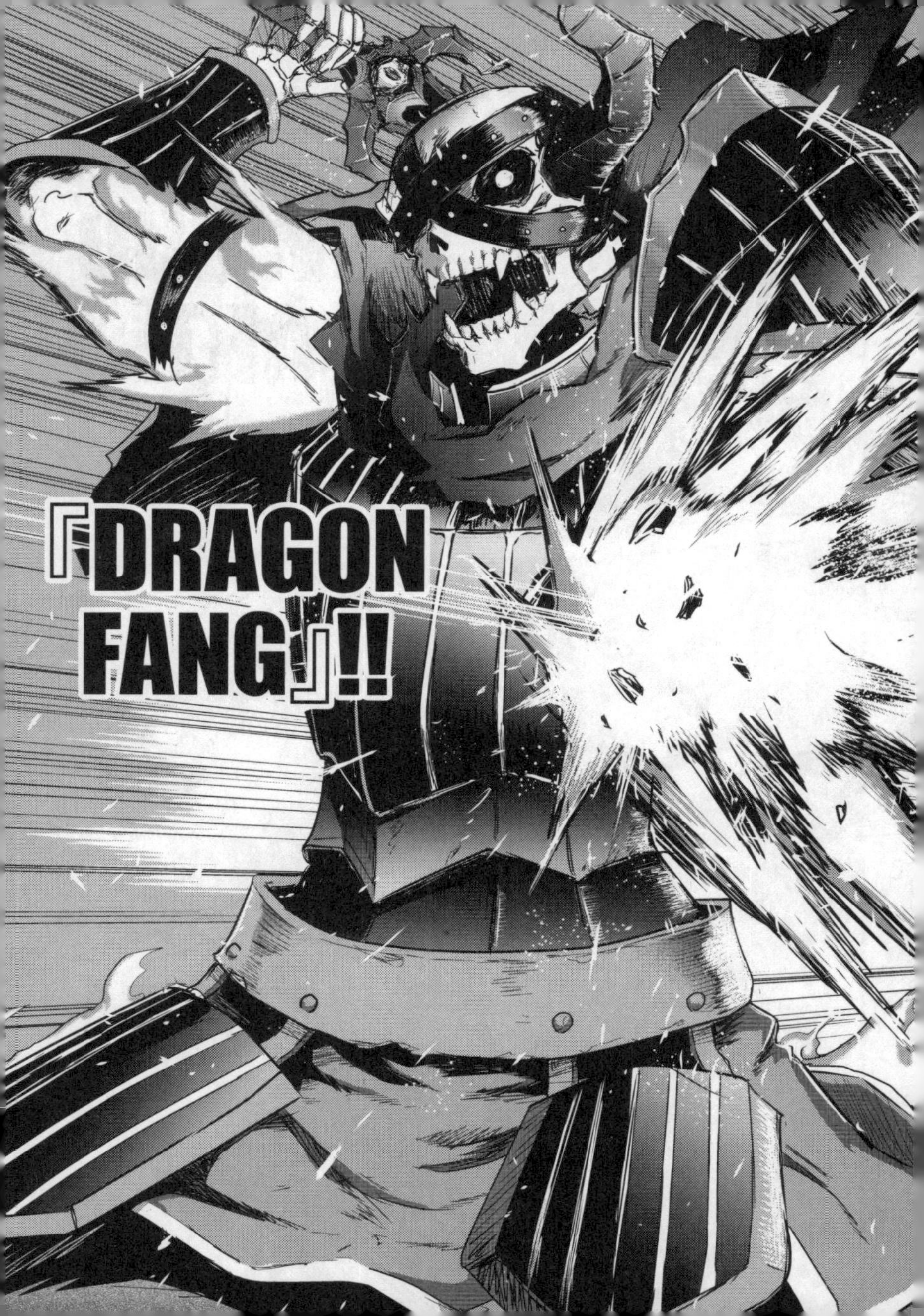
「DRAGON FANG」!!

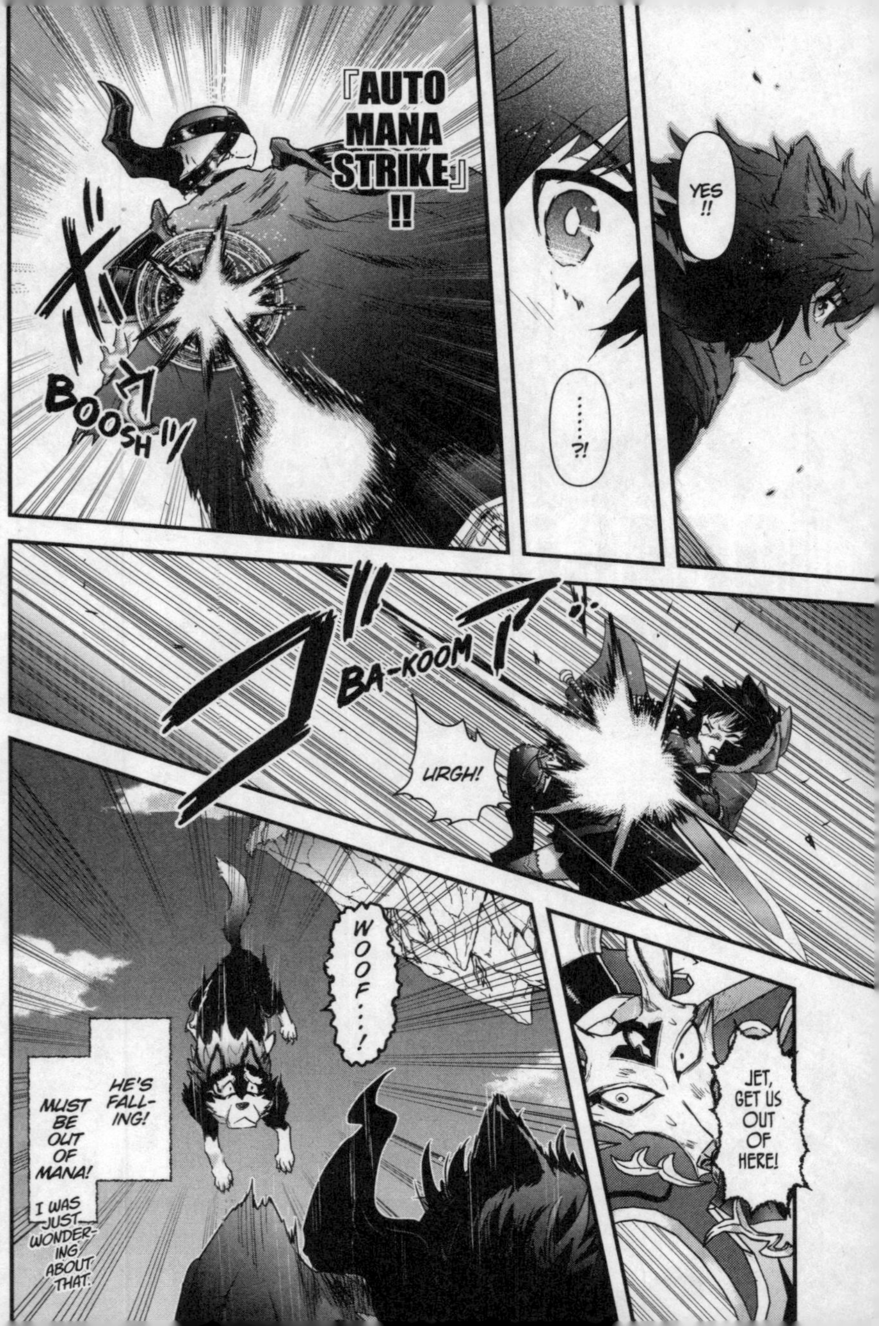

YES !!
......?!
『AUTO MANA STRIKE』!!
BOOSH
BA-KOOM
URGH!
JET, GET US OUT OF HERE!
WOOF...!
HE'S FALLING!
MUST BE OUT OF MANA!
I WAS JUST WONDERING ABOUT THAT.

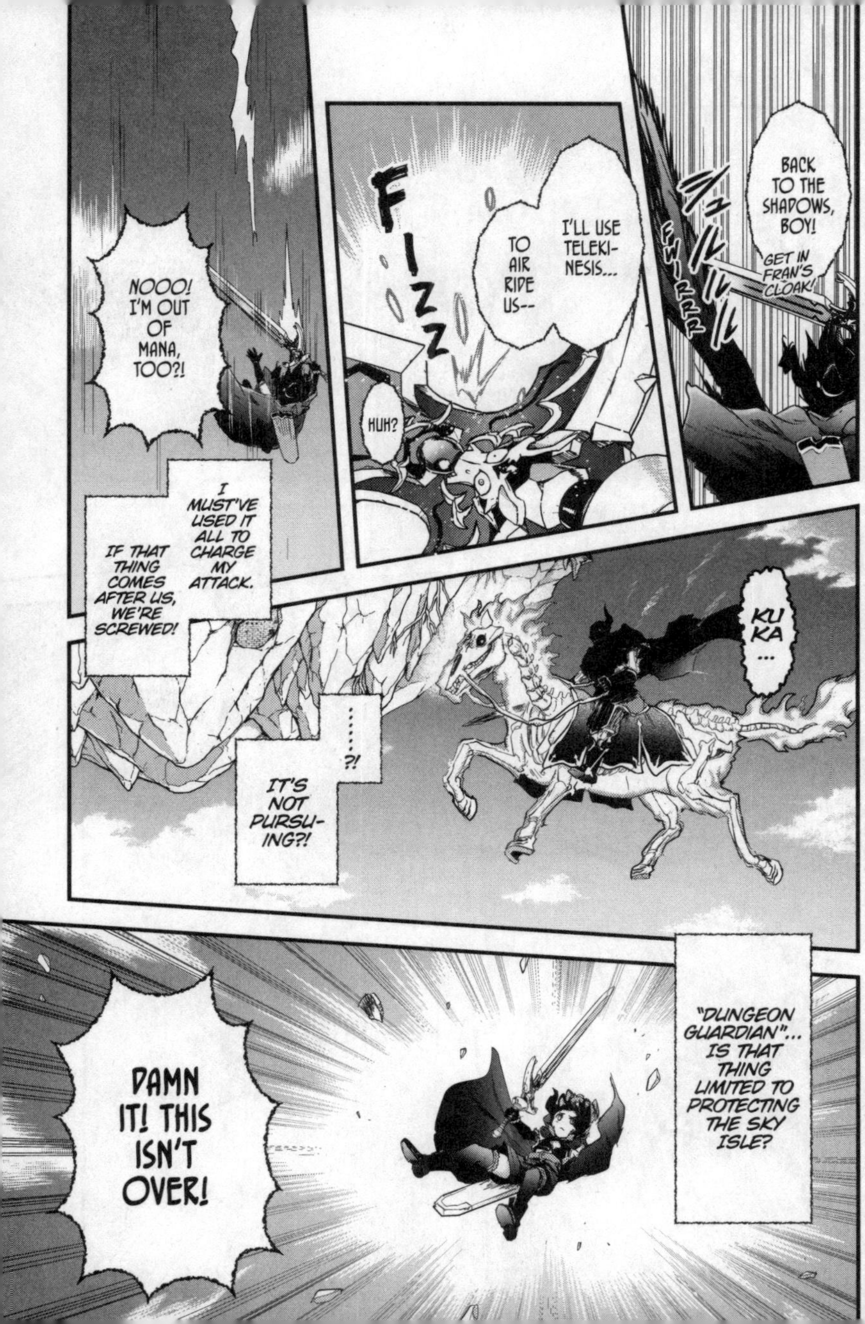
BACK TO THE SHADOWS, BOY!
GET IN FRAN'S CLOAK!
FWIRRR
I'LL USE TELEKINESIS...
TO AIR RIDE US--
FIZZ
HUH?
NOOO! I'M OUT OF MANA, TOO?!
I MUST'VE USED IT ALL TO CHARGE MY ATTACK.
IF THAT THING COMES AFTER US, WE'RE SCREWED!
KUKA...
......?!
IT'S NOT PURSUING?!
"DUNGEON GUARDIAN"... IS THAT THING LIMITED TO PROTECTING THE SKY ISLE?
DAMN IT! THIS ISN'T OVER!

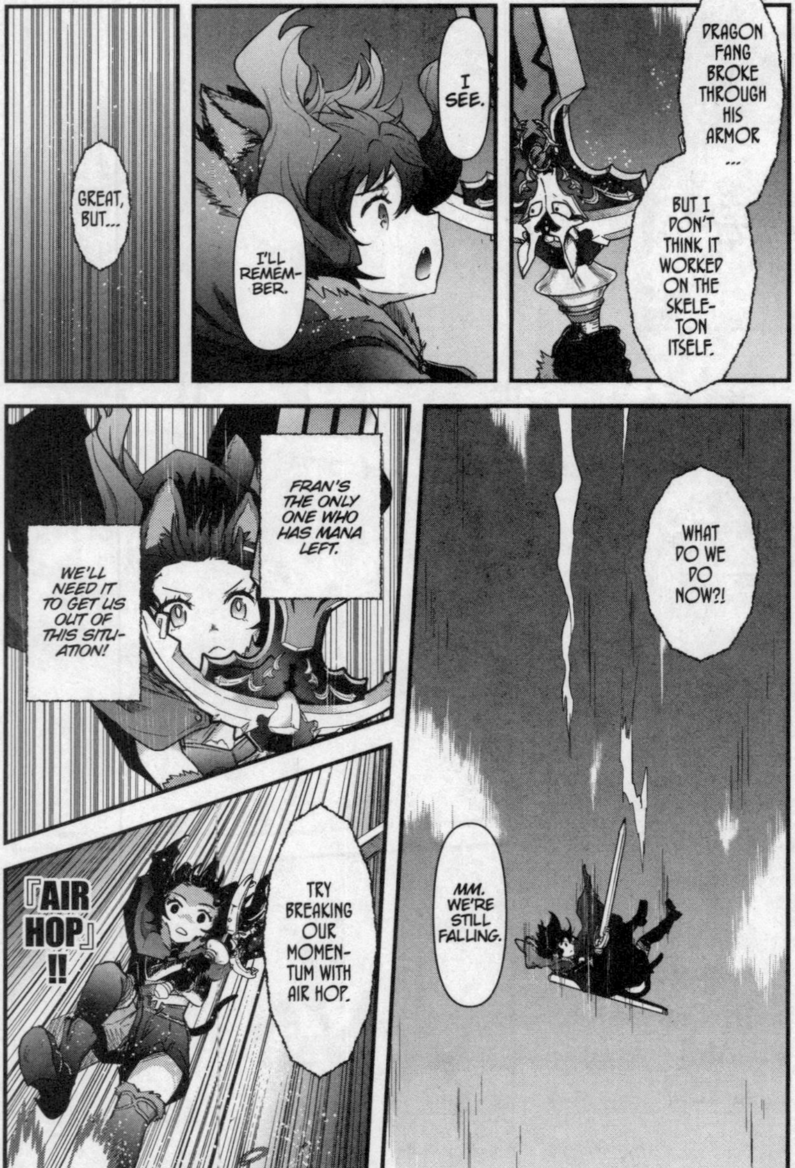
DRAGON FANG BROKE THROUGH HIS ARMOR...
BUT I DON'T THINK IT WORKED ON THE SKELETON ITSELF.
I SEE.
I'LL REMEMBER.
GREAT, BUT...
WHAT DO WE DO NOW?!
MM. WE'RE STILL FALLING.
FRAN'S THE ONLY ONE WHO HAS MANA LEFT.
WE'LL NEED IT TO GET US OUT OF THIS SITUATION!
TRY BREAKING OUR MOMENTUM WITH AIR HOP.
『AIR HOP』!!

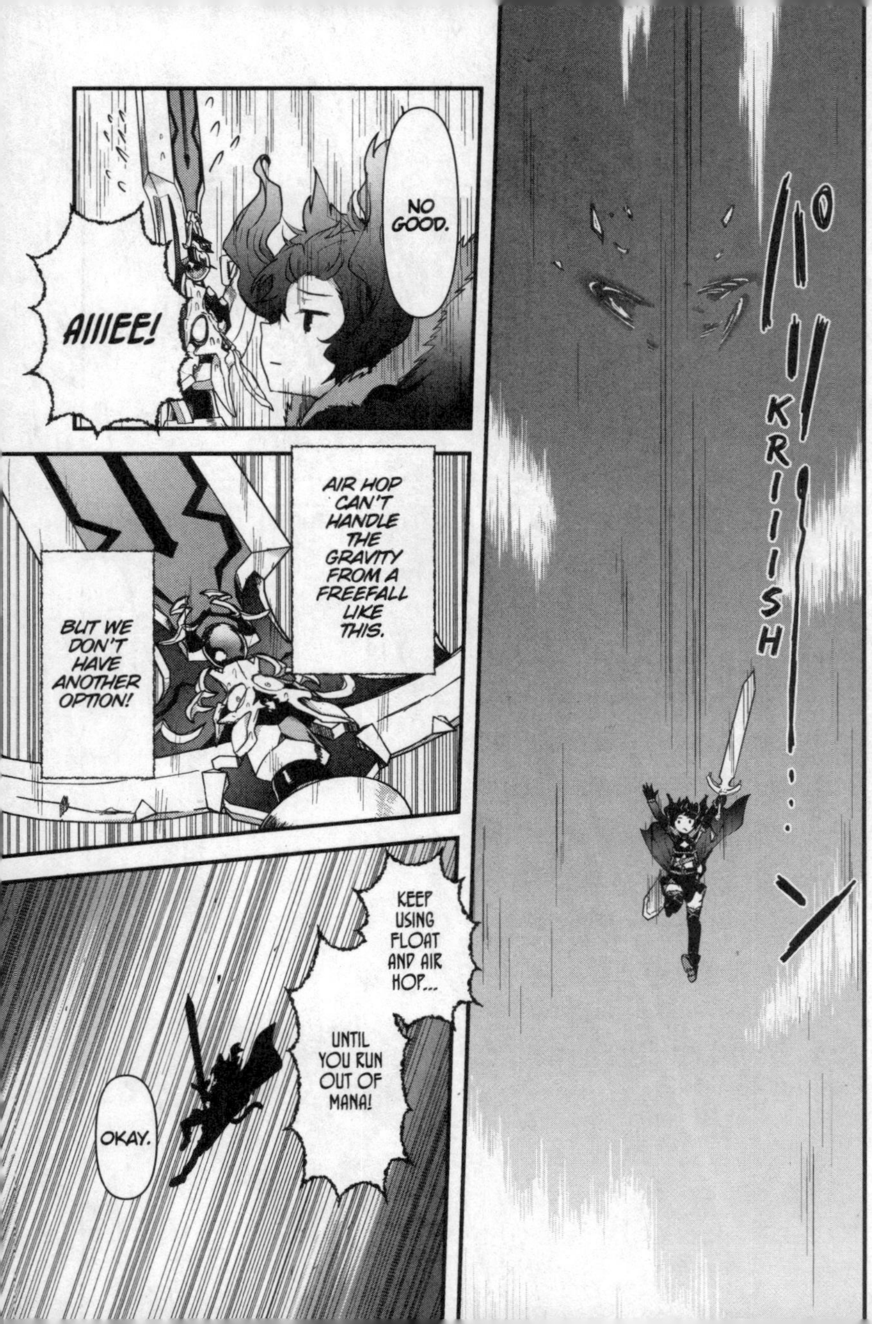

パリーン…
KRIIISH
NO GOOD.
AIIIEE!
AIR HOP CAN'T HANDLE THE GRAVITY FROM A FREEFALL LIKE THIS.
BUT WE DON'T HAVE ANOTHER OPTION!
KEEP USING FLOAT AND AIR HOP...
UNTIL YOU RUN OUT OF MANA!
OKAY.

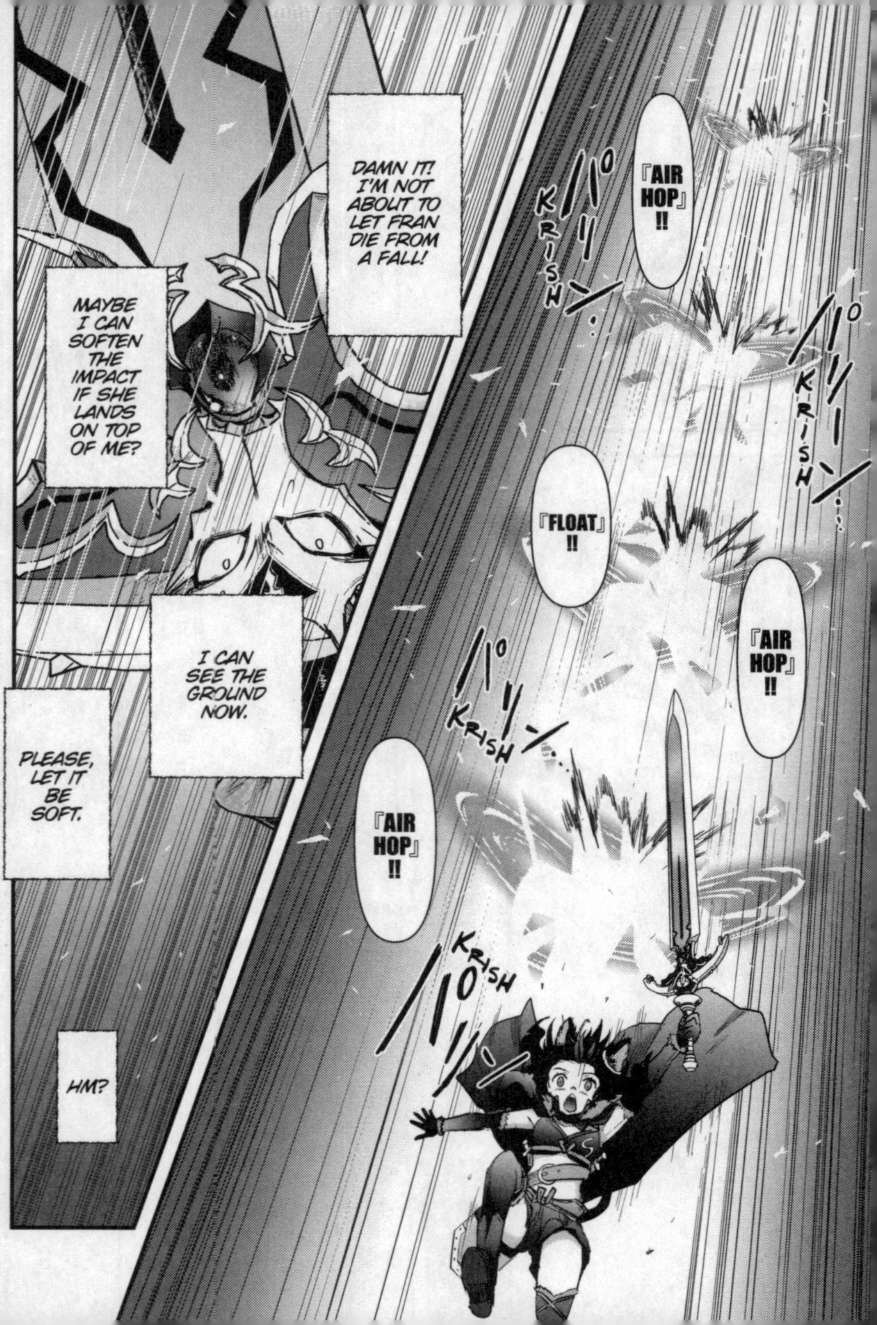

KRISH
『AIR HOP』!!
KRISH
『FLOAT』!!
『AIR HOP』!!
KRISH
『AIR HOP』!!
KRISH
DAMN IT! I'M NOT ABOUT TO LET FRAN DIE FROM A FALL!
MAYBE I CAN SOFTEN THE IMPACT IF SHE LANDS ON TOP OF ME?
I CAN SEE THE GROUND NOW.
PLEASE, LET IT BE SOFT.
HM?

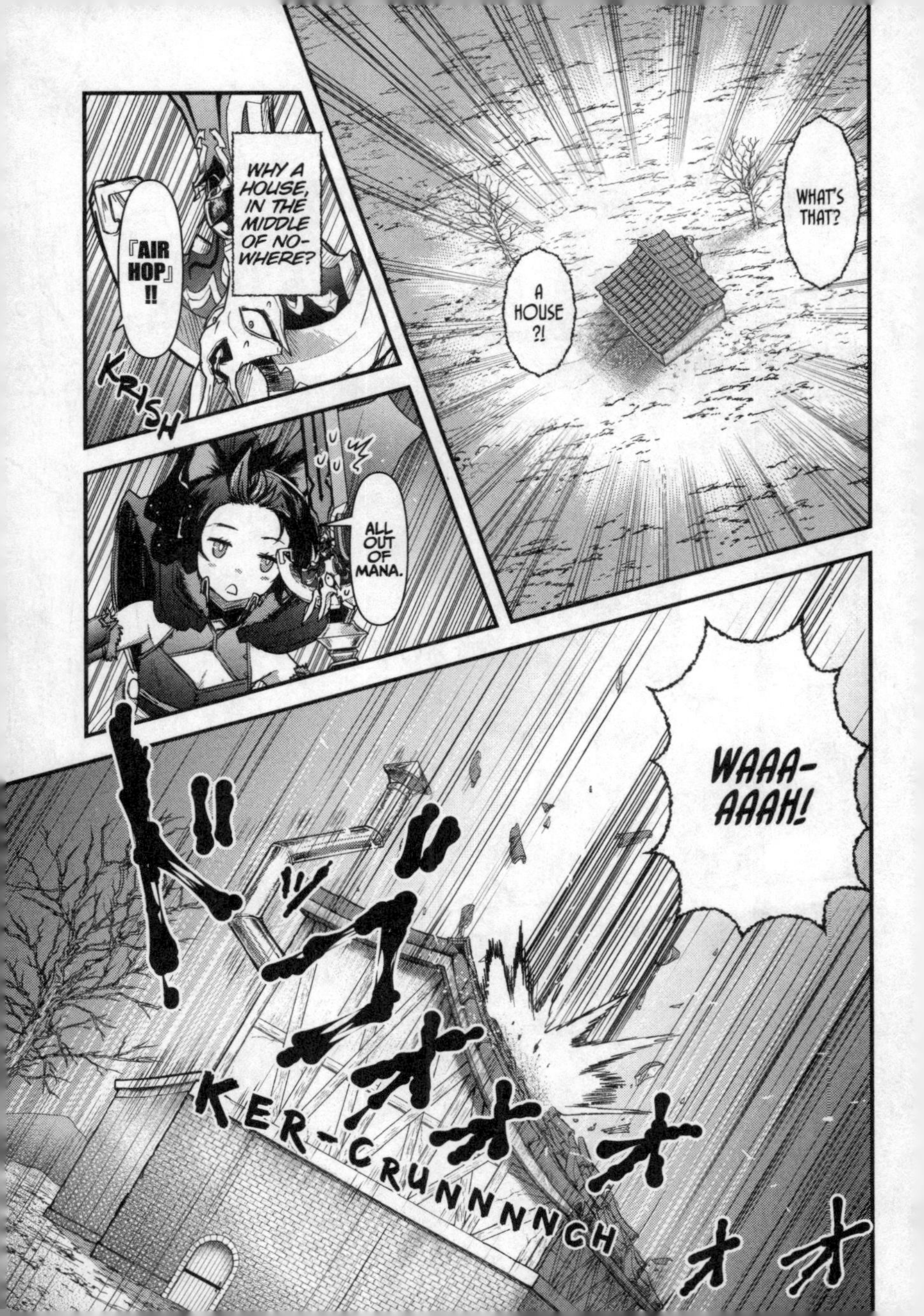
WHAT'S THAT?
A HOUSE ?!
WHY A HOUSE, IN THE MIDDLE OF NO-WHERE?
『AIR HOP』!!
KRISH
ALL OUT OF MANA.
WAAA-AAAH!
KER-CRUNNNNNCH

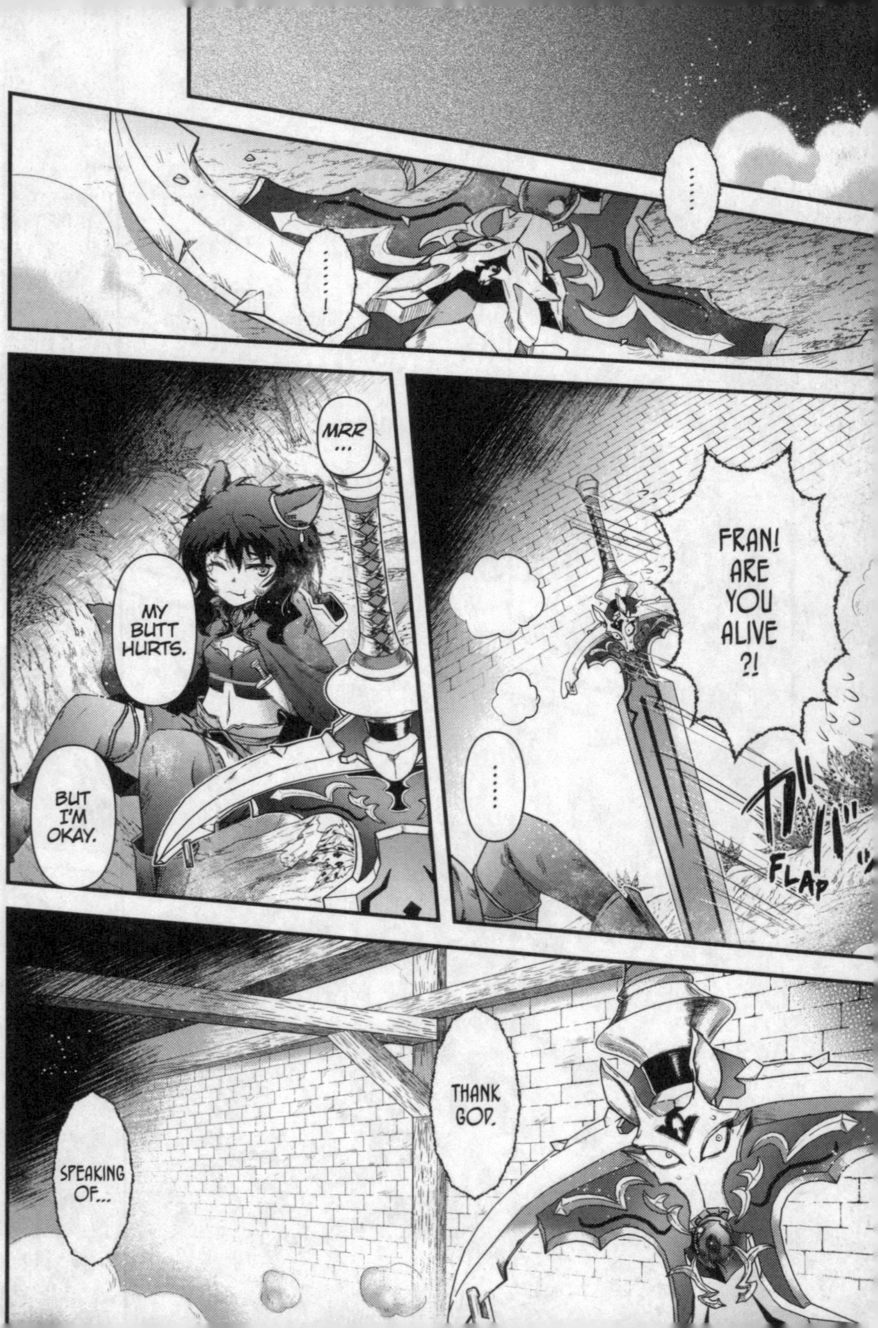
......
......!
FRAN! ARE YOU ALIVE?!
......
ガバッ
FLAP
MRR ...
MY BUTT HURTS.
BUT I'M OKAY.
THANK GOD.
SPEAKING OF...

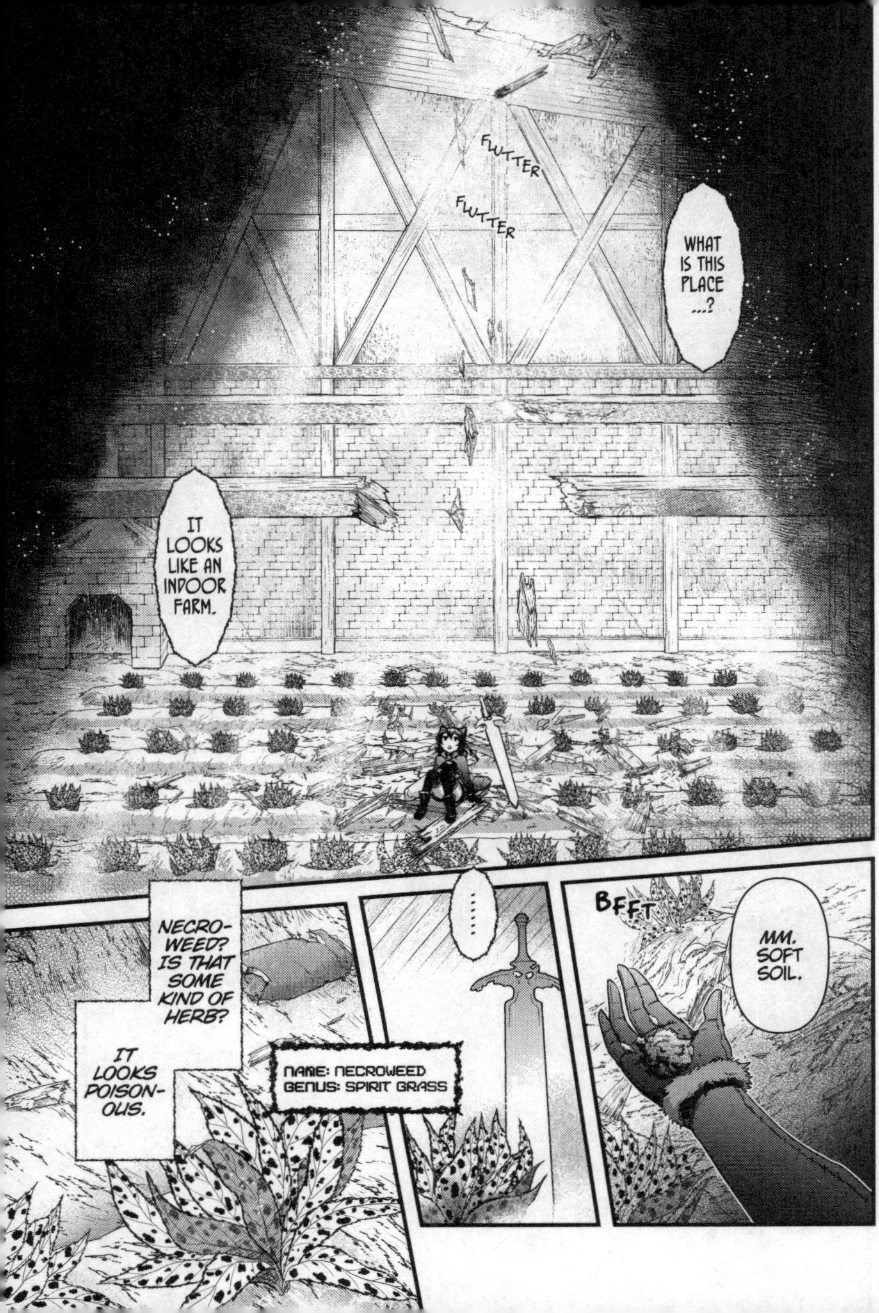
FLUTTER
FLUTTER
WHAT IS THIS PLACE ...?
IT LOOKS LIKE AN INDOOR FARM.
BFFT
MM. SOFT SOIL.
......
NAME: NECROWEED
GENUS: SPIRIT GRASS
NECRO-WEED? IS THAT SOME KIND OF HERB?
IT LOOKS POISON-OUS.

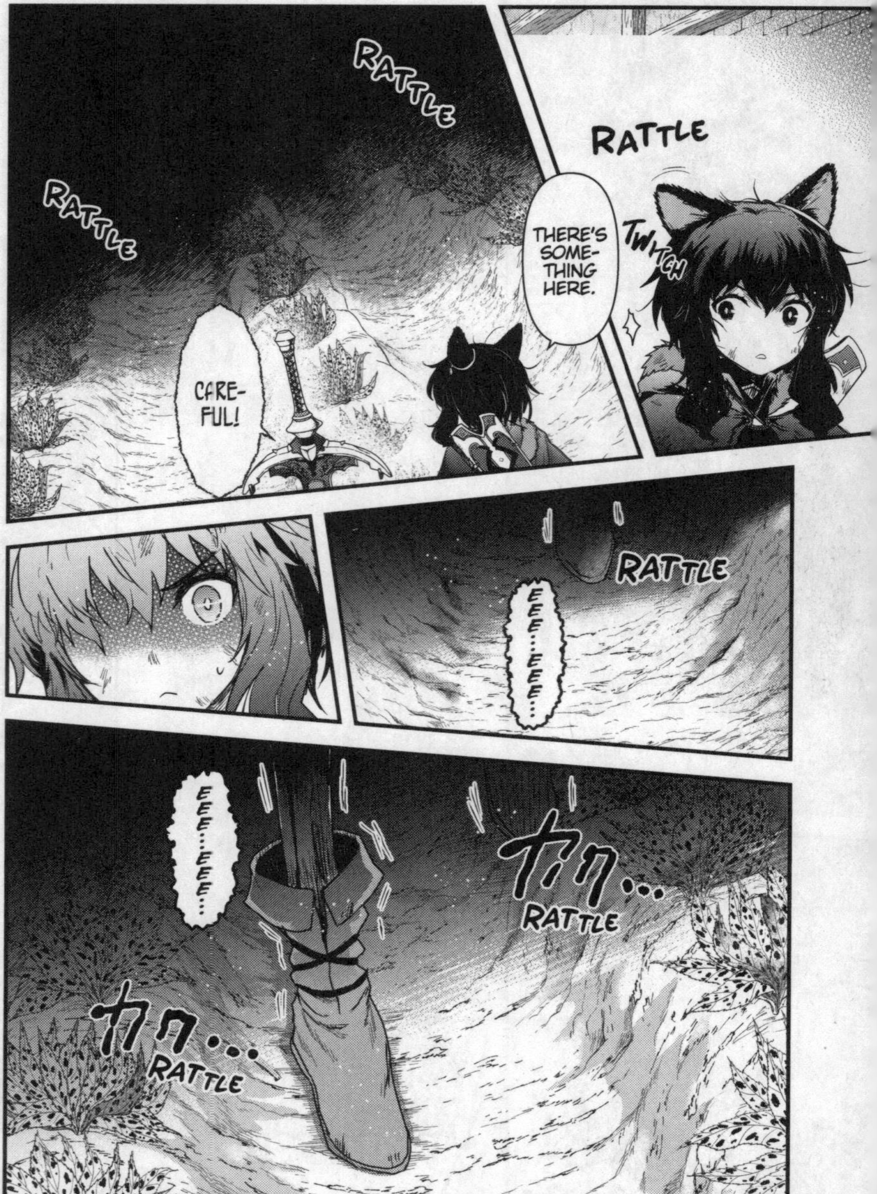
RATTLE
THERE'S SOME-THING HERE.
TWITCH
RATTLE
RATTLE
CARE-FUL!
RATTLE
EEE...EEE...
EEE...EEE...
カク...
RATTLE
カク...
RATTLE

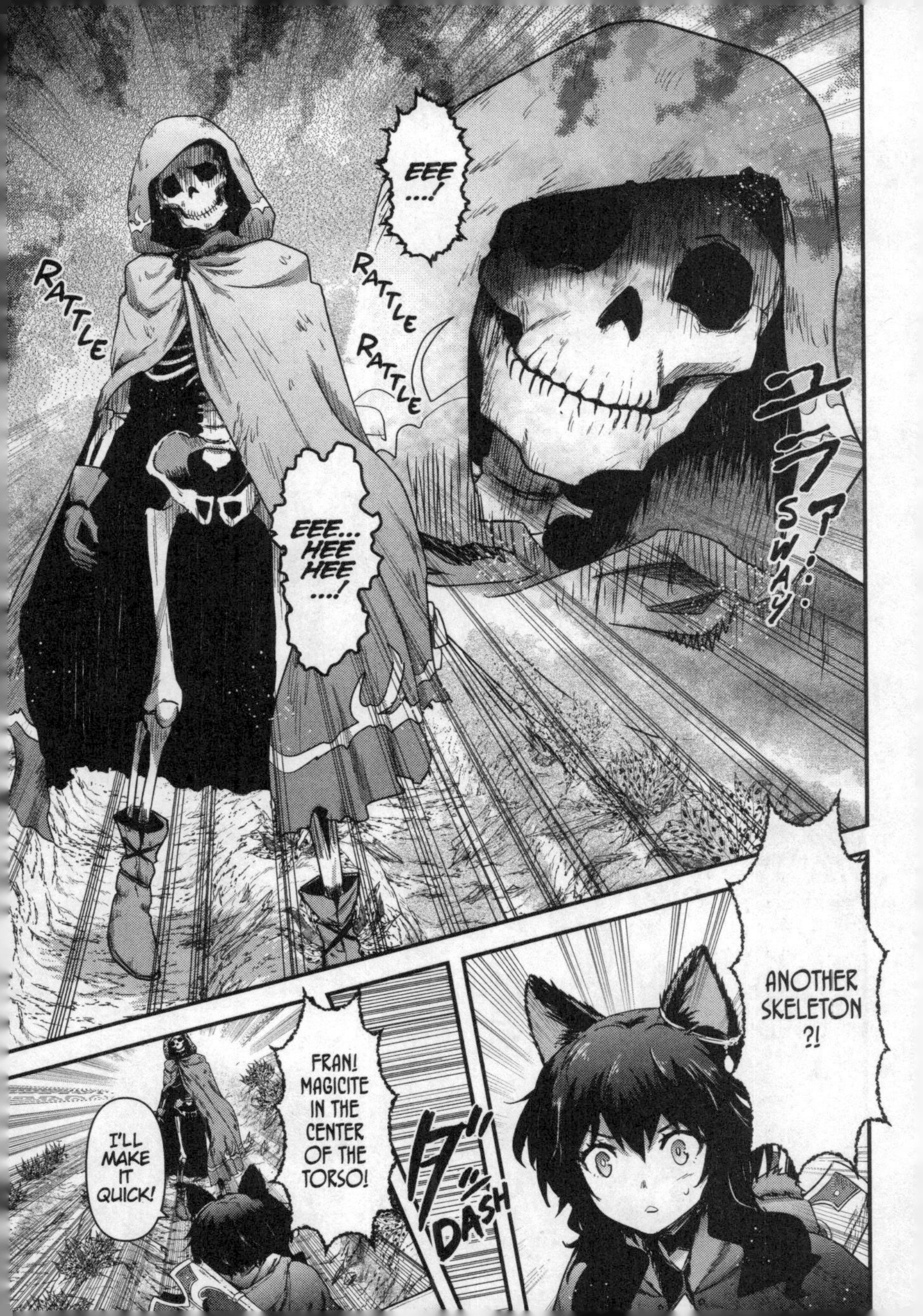
EEE....!
ユラァ…
SWAY
RATTLE
RATTLE
EEE... HEE HEE....!
RATTLE
ANOTHER SKELETON?!
ドッ
DASH
FRAN! MAGICITE IN THE CENTER OF THE TORSO!
I'LL MAKE IT QUICK!

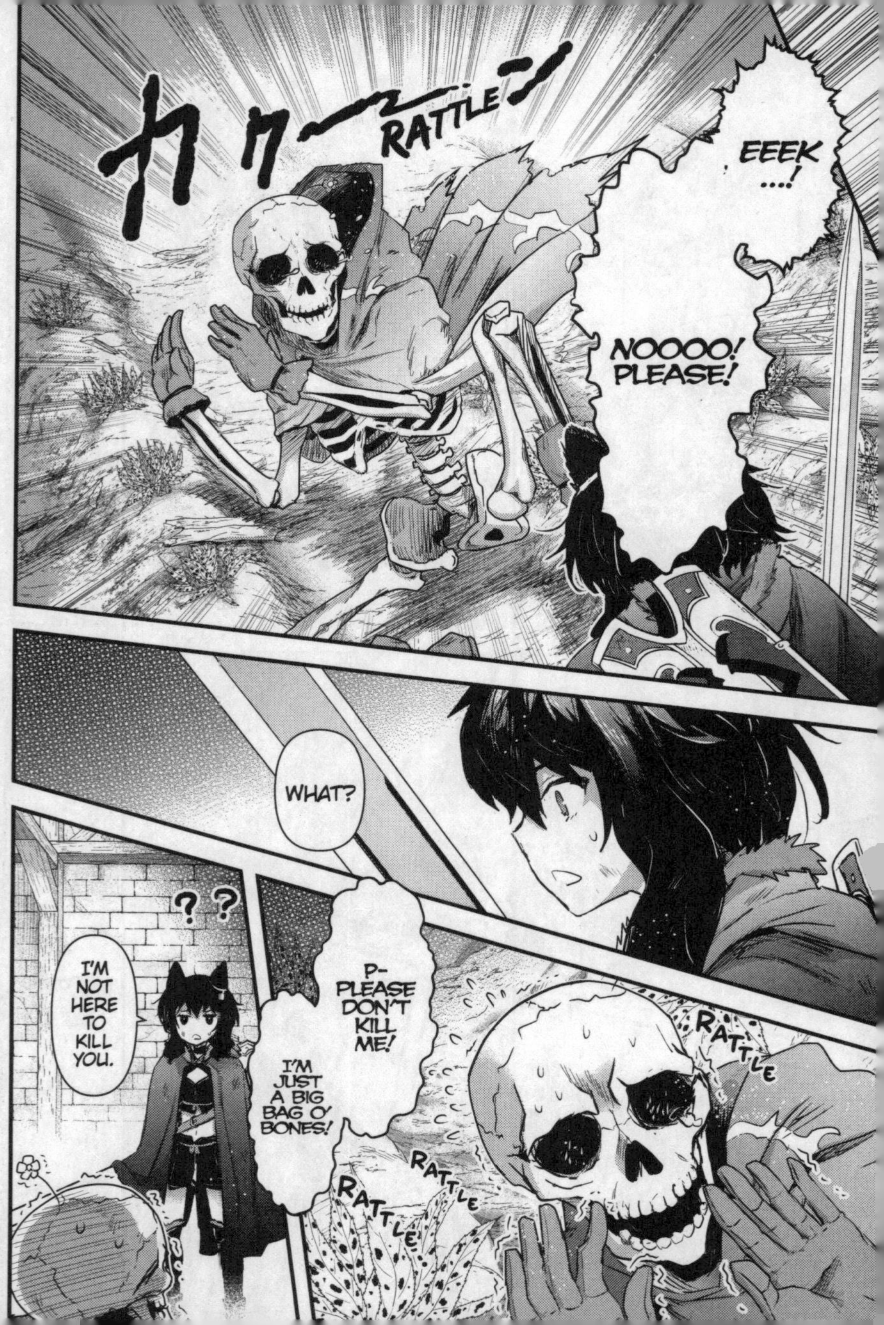
EEEK ...!
NOOOO! PLEASE!
カクーン
RATTLE
WHAT?
RATTLE
P-PLEASE DON'T KILL ME!
I'M JUST A BIG BAG O' BONES!
RATTLE
RATTLE
RATTLE
? ?
I'M NOT HERE TO KILL YOU.

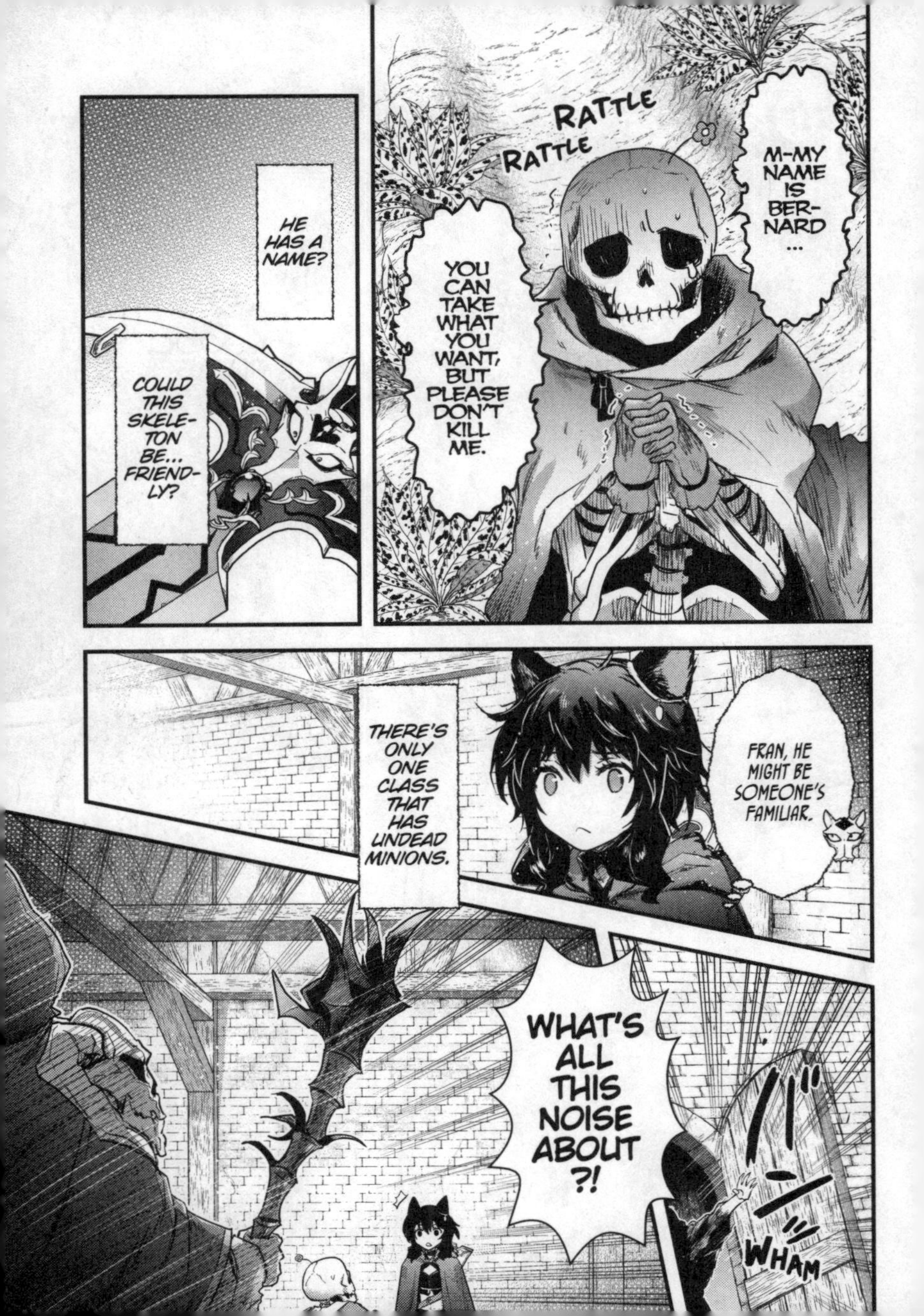
RATTLE
RATTLE
M-MY NAME IS BER-NARD...
YOU CAN TAKE WHAT YOU WANT, BUT PLEASE DON'T KILL ME.
HE HAS A NAME?
COULD THIS SKELE-TON BE... FRIEND-LY?
FRAN, HE MIGHT BE SOMEONE'S FAMILIAR.
THERE'S ONLY ONE CLASS THAT HAS UNDEAD MINIONS.
WHAM
WHAT'S ALL THIS NOISE ABOUT?!

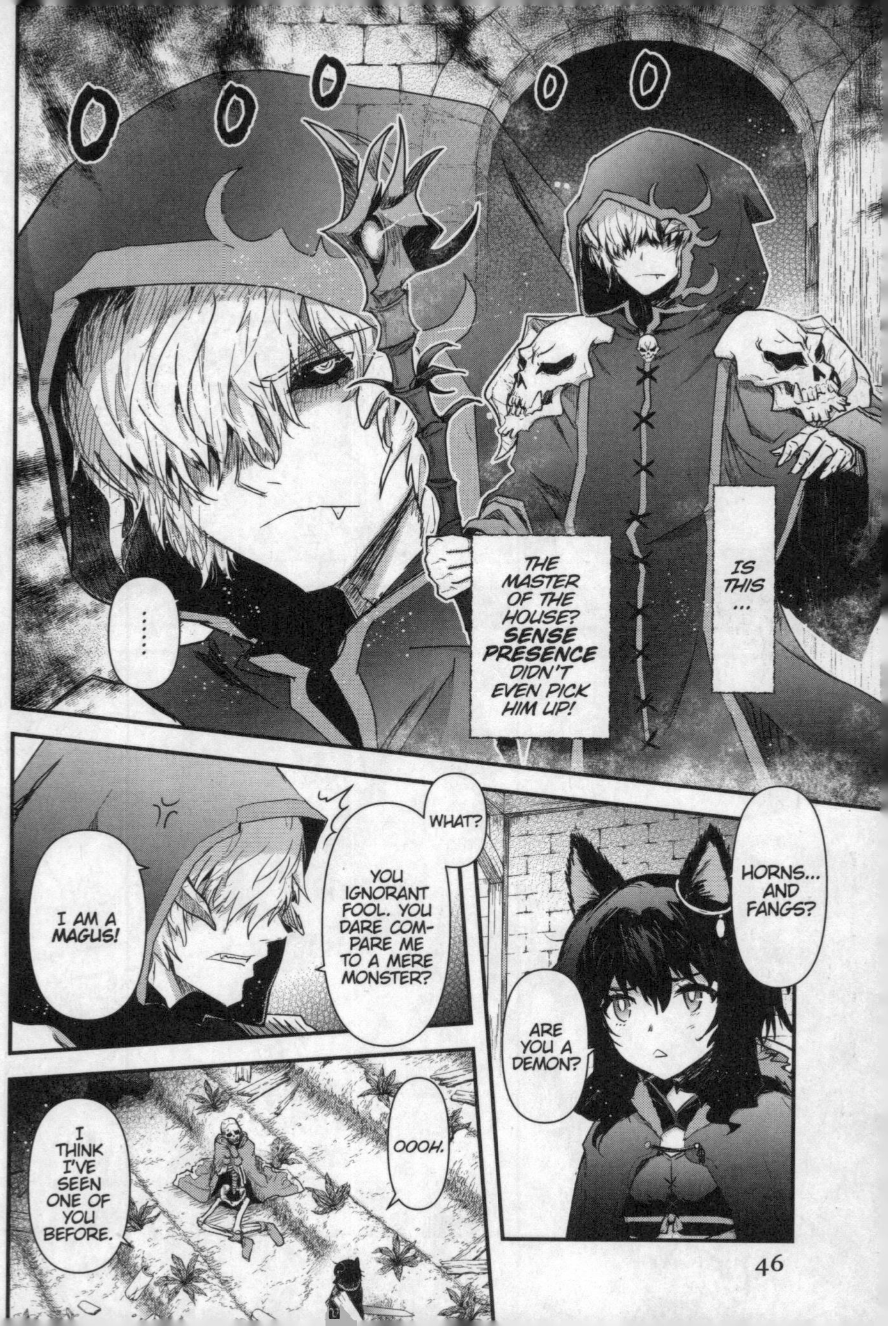
IS THIS...
THE MASTER OF THE HOUSE? SENSE PRESENCE DIDN'T EVEN PICK HIM UP!
......
HORNS... AND FANGS?
ARE YOU A DEMON?
WHAT?
YOU IGNORANT FOOL. YOU DARE COMPARE ME TO A MERE MONSTER?
I AM A MAGUS!
OOOH.
I THINK I'VE SEEN ONE OF YOU BEFORE.

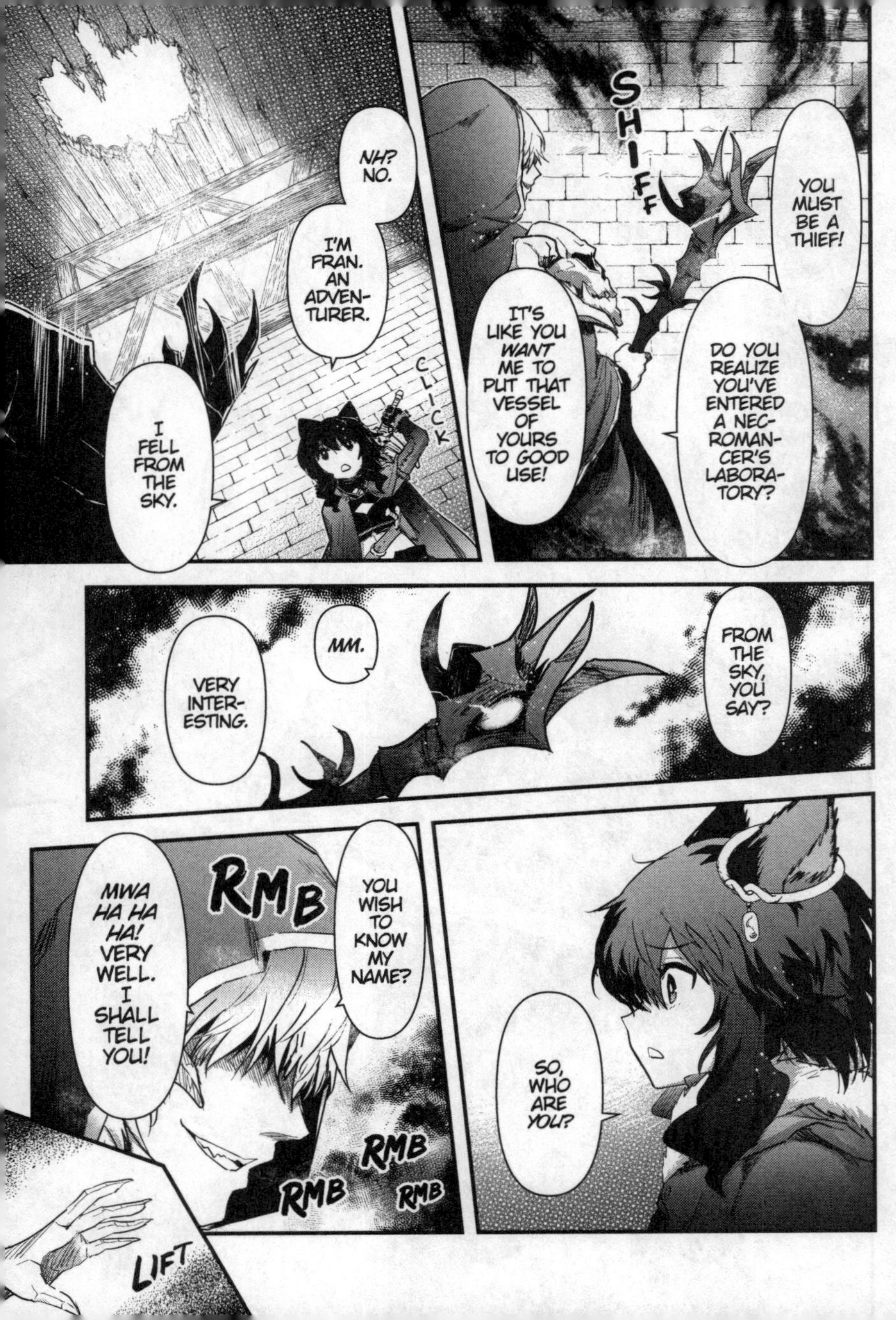
SHIFF
YOU MUST BE A THIEF!
DO YOU REALIZE YOU'VE ENTERED A NECROMANCER'S LABORATORY?
IT'S LIKE YOU *WANT* ME TO PUT THAT VESSEL OF YOURS TO GOOD USE!
NH? NO.
I'M FRAN. AN ADVENTURER.
CLICK
I FELL FROM THE SKY.
FROM THE SKY, YOU SAY?
MM.
VERY INTERESTING.
SO, WHO ARE *YOU*?
YOU WISH TO KNOW MY NAME?
RMB
MWA HA HA HA! VERY WELL. I SHALL TELL YOU!
RMB
RMB
RMB
LIFT

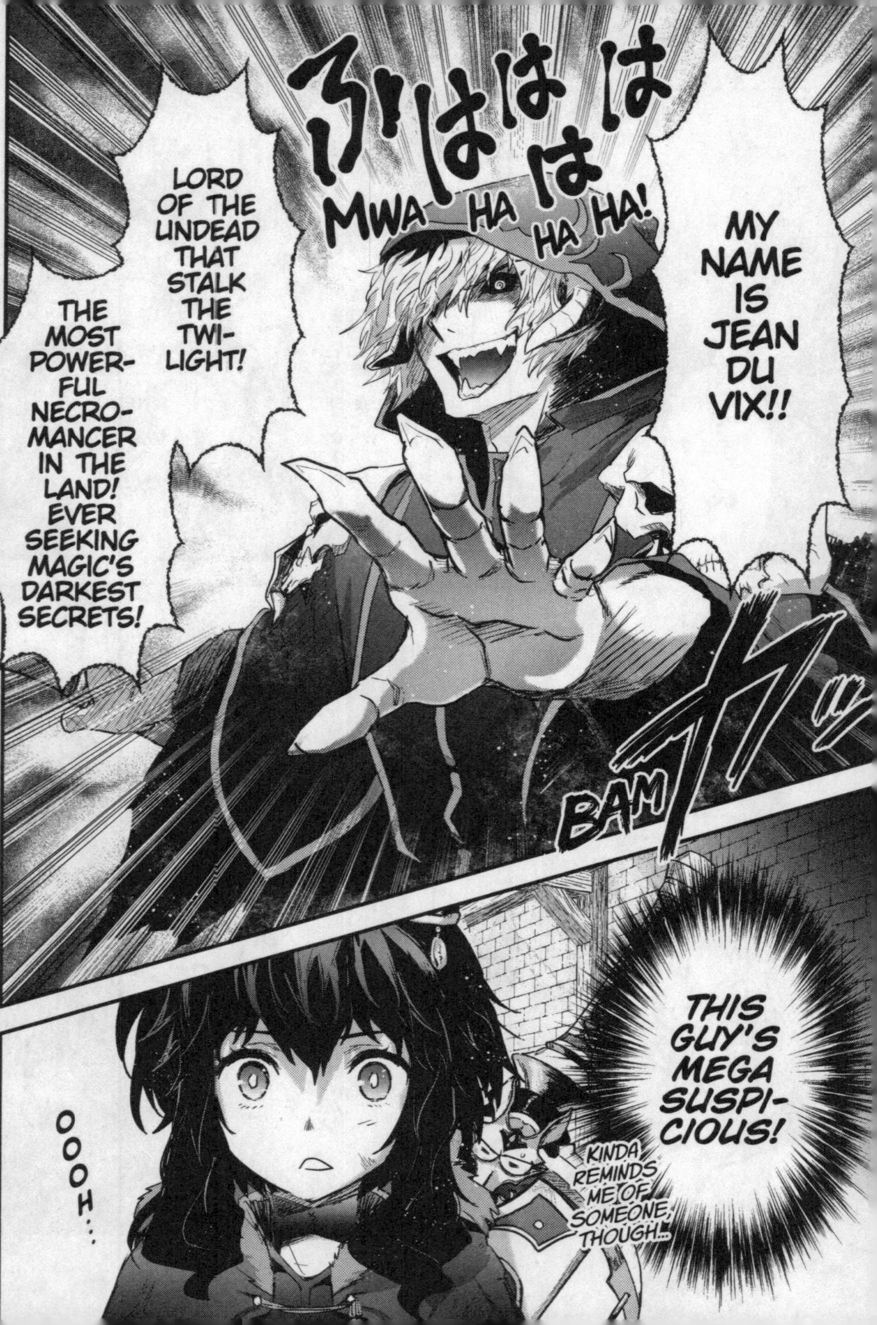
ふ!ははははは
MWA HA HA HA!
MY NAME IS JEAN DU VIX!!
LORD OF THE UNDEAD THAT STALK THE TWI-LIGHT!
THE MOST POWER-FUL NECRO-MANCER IN THE LAND! EVER SEEKING MAGIC'S DARKEST SECRETS!
BAM
THIS GUY'S MEGA SUSPI-CIOUS!
KINDA REMINDS ME OF SOMEONE, THOUGH...
OOOH...

Reincarnated
as a sword

Reincarnated
as a sword

Chapter 30: Slaughterfield Necromancer

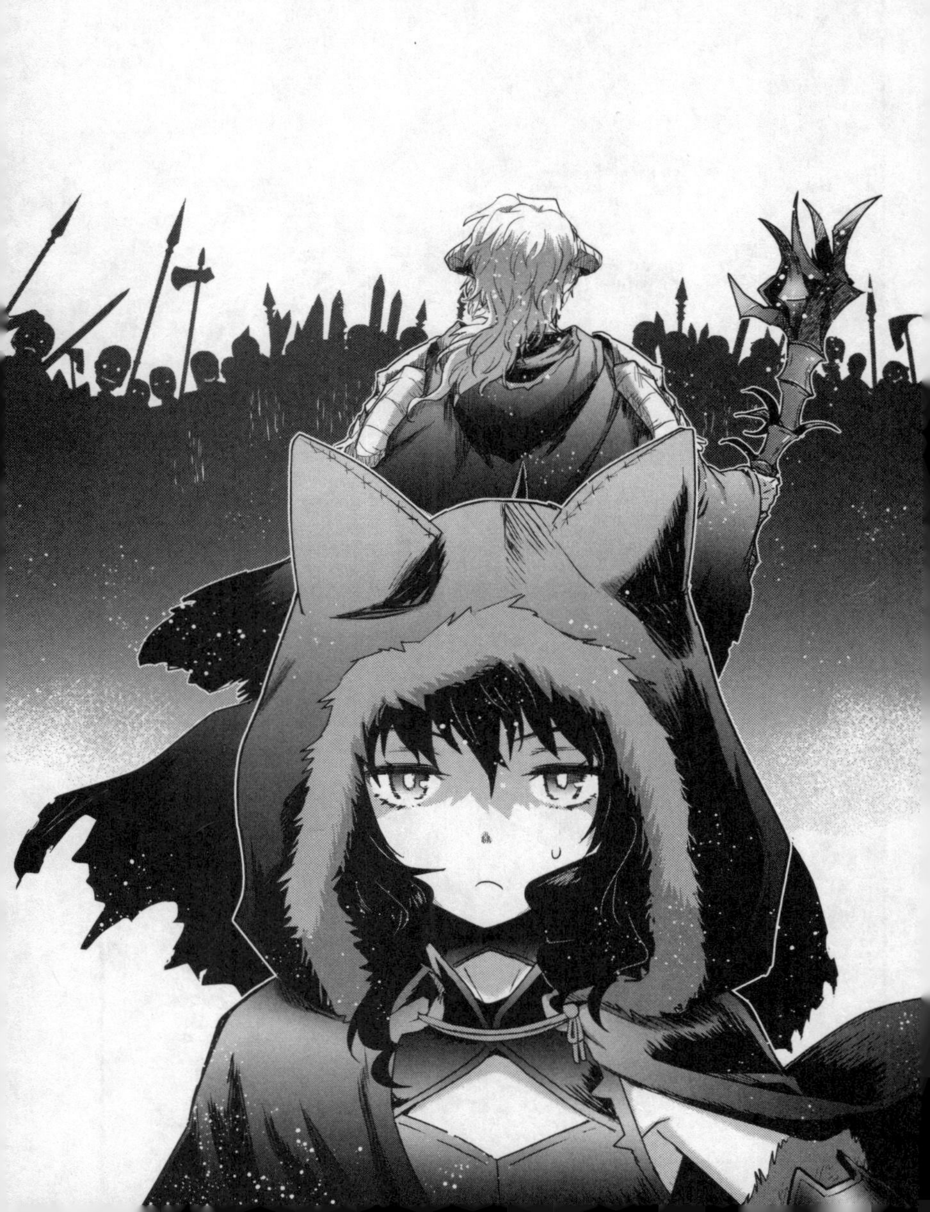

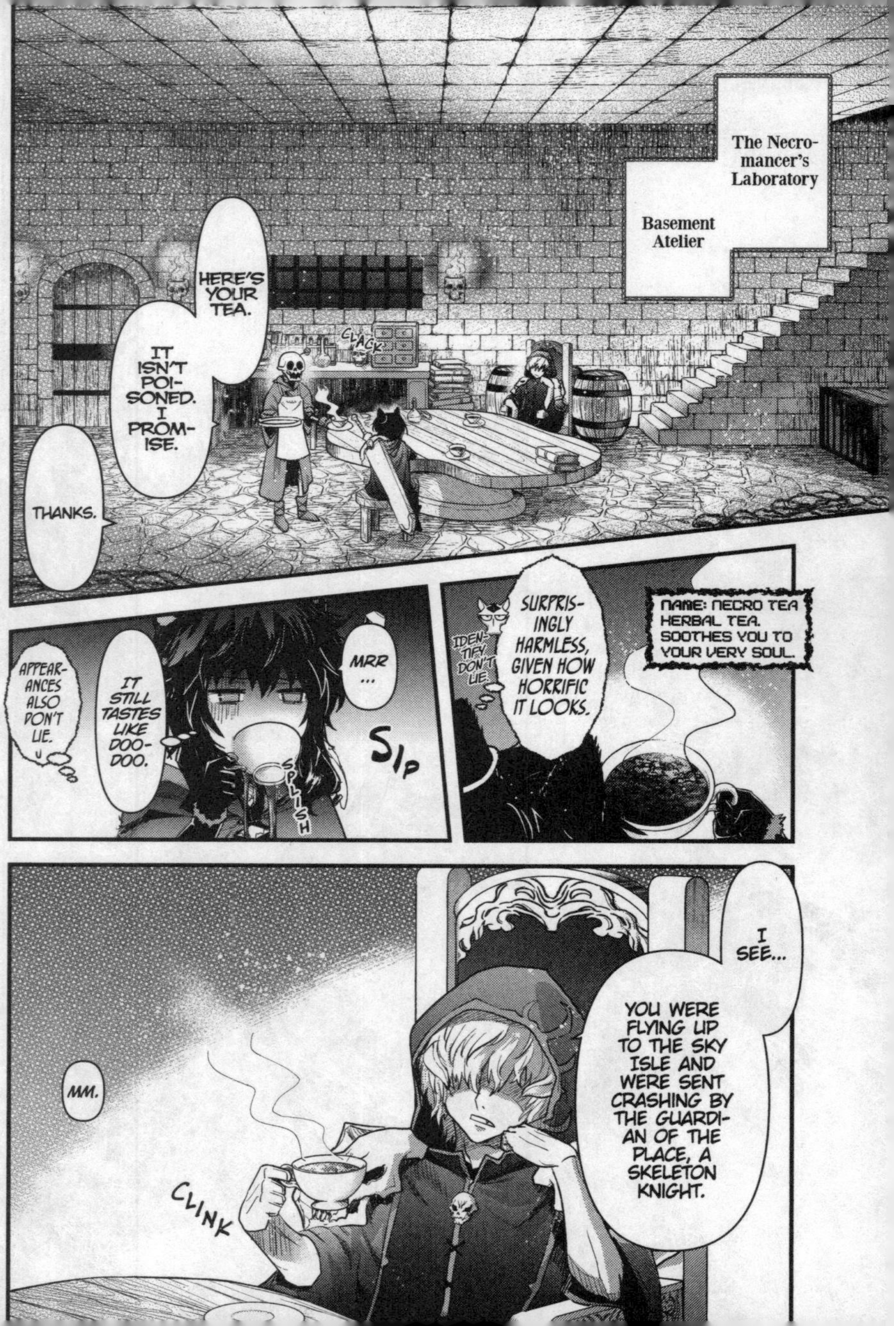
The Necromancer's Laboratory
Basement Atelier
HERE'S YOUR TEA.
CLACK
IT ISN'T POISONED. I PROMISE.
THANKS.
NAME: NECRO TEA HERBAL TEA. SOOTHES YOU TO YOUR VERY SOUL.
SURPRISINGLY HARMLESS, GIVEN HOW HORRIFIC IT LOOKS.
IDENTIFY DON'T LIE.
SIP
MRR ...
IT STILL TASTES LIKE DOO-DOO.
SPLISH
APPEARANCES ALSO DON'T LIE.
I SEE...
YOU WERE FLYING UP TO THE SKY ISLE AND WERE SENT CRASHING BY THE GUARDIAN OF THE PLACE, A SKELETON KNIGHT.
MM.
CLINK

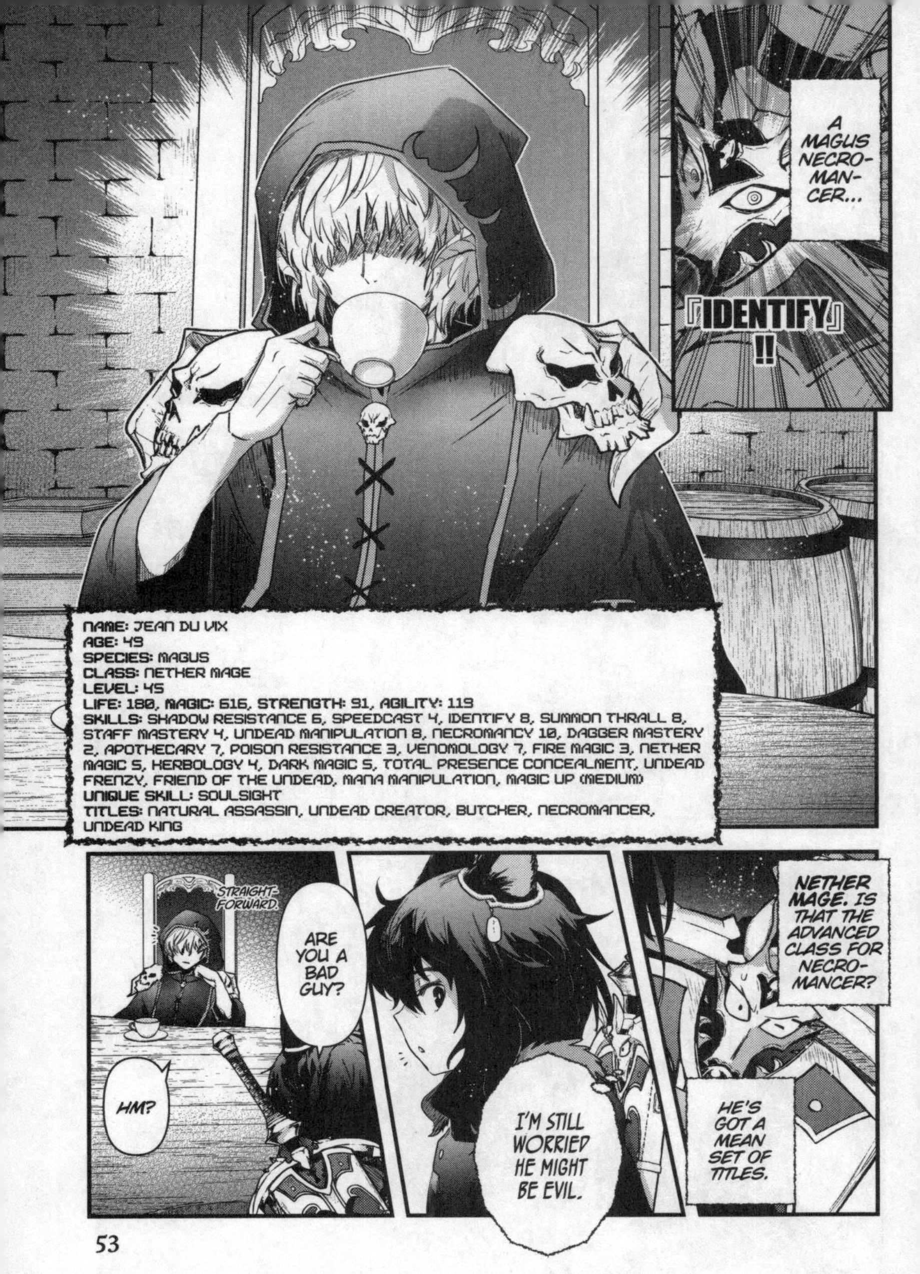
A MAGUS NECRO-MAN-CER...
『IDENTIFY』!!
NAME: JEAN DU VIX
AGE: 49
SPECIES: MAGUS
CLASS: NETHER MAGE
LEVEL: 45
LIFE: 180, MAGIC: 616, STRENGTH: 91, AGILITY: 119
SKILLS: SHADOW RESISTANCE 6, SPEEDCAST 4, IDENTIFY 8, SUMMON THRALL 8, STAFF MASTERY 4, UNDEAD MANIPULATION 8, NECROMANCY 10, DAGGER MASTERY 2, APOTHECARY 7, POISON RESISTANCE 3, VENOMOLOGY 7, FIRE MAGIC 3, NETHER MAGIC 5, HERBOLOGY 4, DARK MAGIC 5, TOTAL PRESENCE CONCEALMENT, UNDEAD FRENZY, FRIEND OF THE UNDEAD, MANA MANIPULATION, MAGIC UP (MEDIUM)
UNIQUE SKILL: SOULSIGHT
TITLES: NATURAL ASSASSIN, UNDEAD CREATOR, BUTCHER, NECROMANCER, UNDEAD KING
NETHER MAGE. IS THAT THE ADVANCED CLASS FOR NECRO-MANCER?
HE'S GOT A MEAN SET OF TITLES.
I'M STILL WORRIED HE MIGHT BE EVIL.
STRAIGHT-FORWARD.
ARE YOU A BAD GUY?
HM?

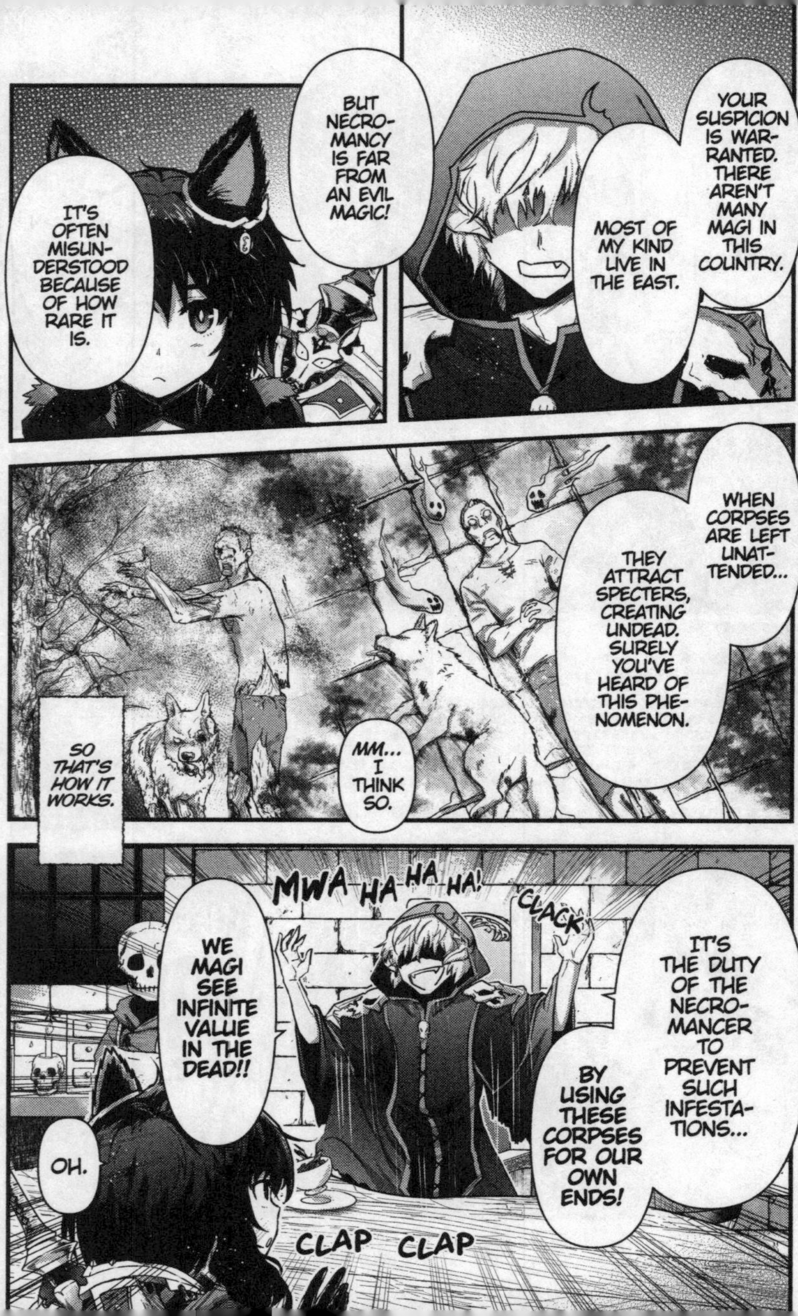
YOUR SUSPICION IS WARRANTED. THERE AREN'T MANY MAGI IN THIS COUNTRY.
MOST OF MY KIND LIVE IN THE EAST.
BUT NECROMANCY IS FAR FROM AN EVIL MAGIC!
IT'S OFTEN MISUNDERSTOOD BECAUSE OF HOW RARE IT IS.
WHEN CORPSES ARE LEFT UNATTENDED...
THEY ATTRACT SPECTERS, CREATING UNDEAD. SURELY YOU'VE HEARD OF THIS PHENOMENON.
MM... I THINK SO.
SO THAT'S HOW IT WORKS.
IT'S THE DUTY OF THE NECROMANCER TO PREVENT SUCH INFESTATIONS...
BY USING THESE CORPSES FOR OUR OWN ENDS!
MWA HA HA HA!
CLACK
WE MAGI SEE INFINITE VALUE IN THE DEAD!!
OH.
CLAP CLAP

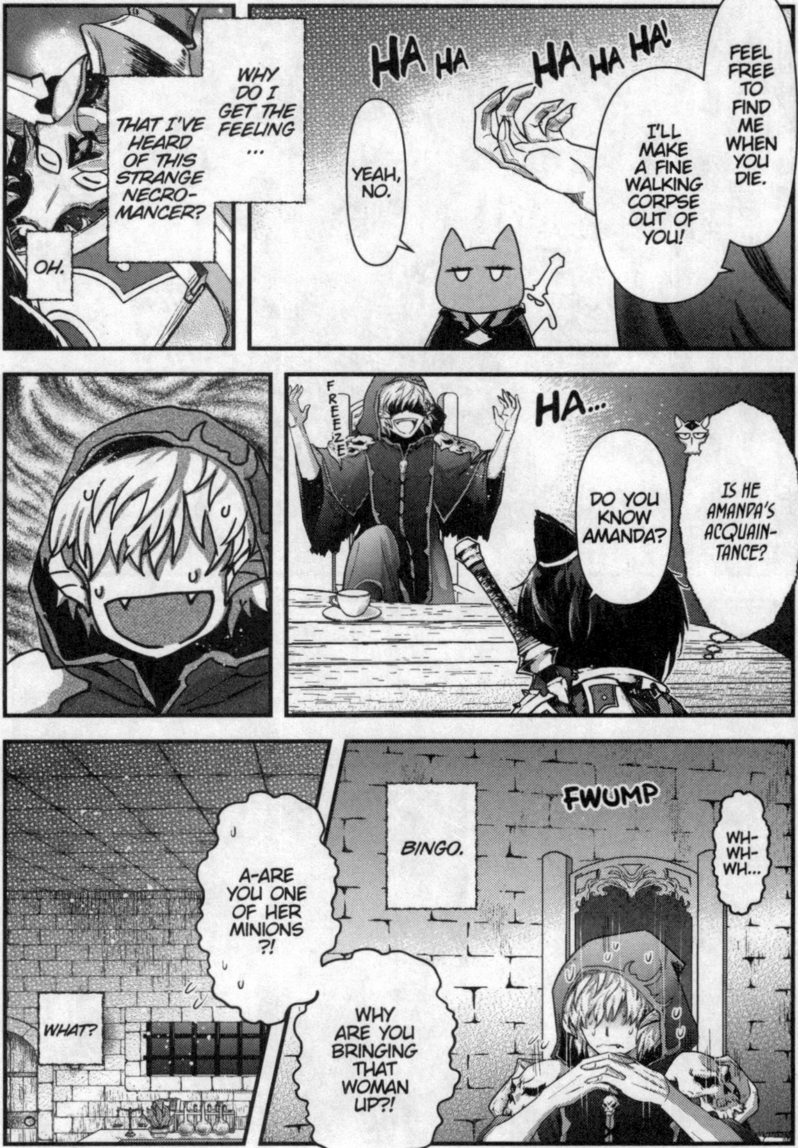
FEEL FREE TO FIND ME WHEN YOU DIE.
HA HA HA!
I'LL MAKE A FINE WALKING CORPSE OUT OF YOU!
HA HA
YEAH, NO.
WHY DO I GET THE FEELING ...
THAT I'VE HEARD OF THIS STRANGE NECRO-MANCER?
OH.
HA...
IS HE AMANDA'S ACQUAIN-TANCE?
DO YOU KNOW AMANDA?
FREEZE
FWUMP
WH-WH-WH...
BINGO.
A-ARE YOU ONE OF HER MINIONS ?!
WHY ARE YOU BRINGING THAT WOMAN UP?!
WHAT?

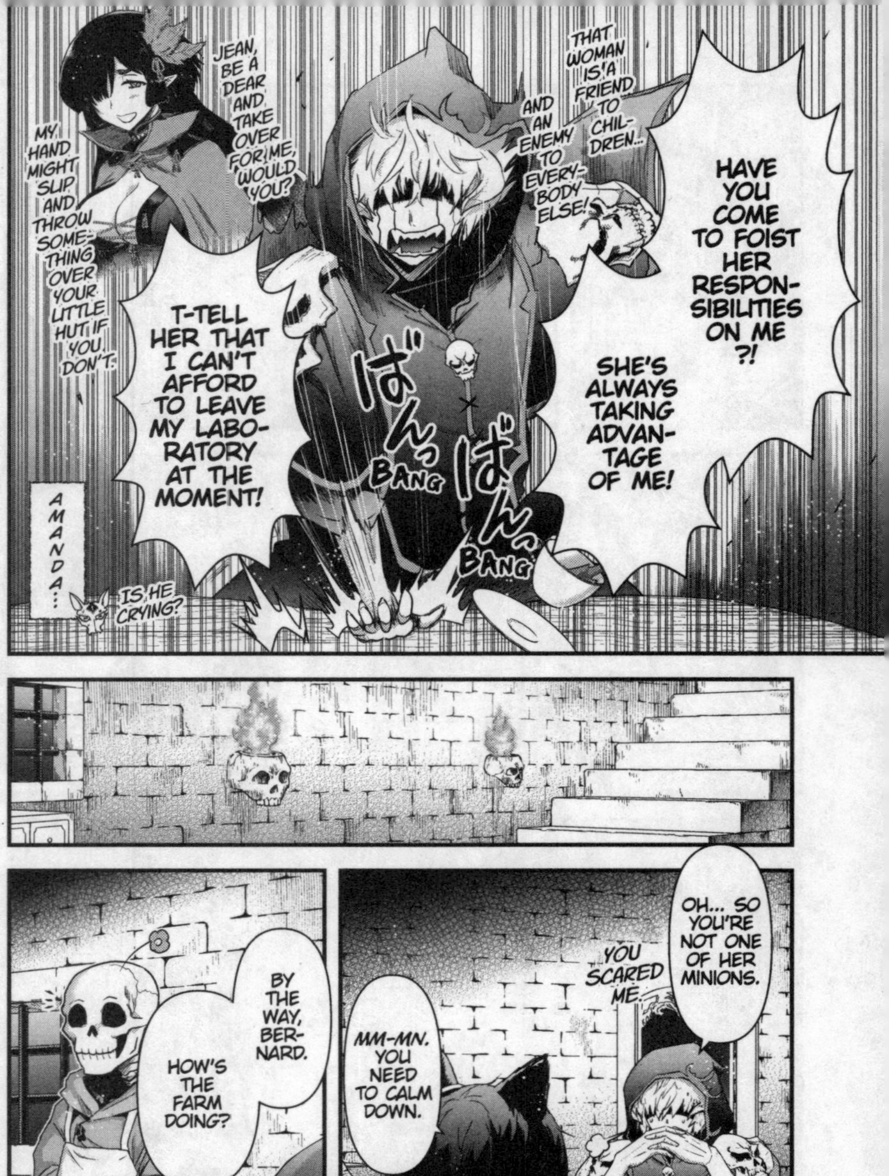
HAVE YOU COME TO FOIST HER RESPONSIBILITIES ON ME?!
THAT WOMAN IS A FRIEND TO CHILDREN...
AND AN ENEMY TO EVERYBODY ELSE!
SHE'S ALWAYS TAKING ADVANTAGE OF ME!
JEAN, BE A DEAR AND TAKE OVER FOR ME, WOULD YOU?
MY HAND MIGHT SLIP AND THROW SOMETHING OVER YOUR LITTLE HUT IF YOU DON'T.
T-TELL HER THAT I CAN'T AFFORD TO LEAVE MY LABORATORY AT THE MOMENT!
ばんっ BANG
ばんっ BANG
AMANDA...
IS HE CRYING?
OH... SO YOU'RE NOT ONE OF HER MINIONS.
YOU SCARED ME.
MM-MN. YOU NEED TO CALM DOWN.
BY THE WAY, BERNARD.
HOW'S THE FARM DOING?

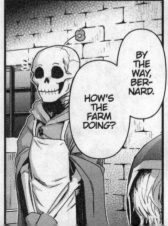

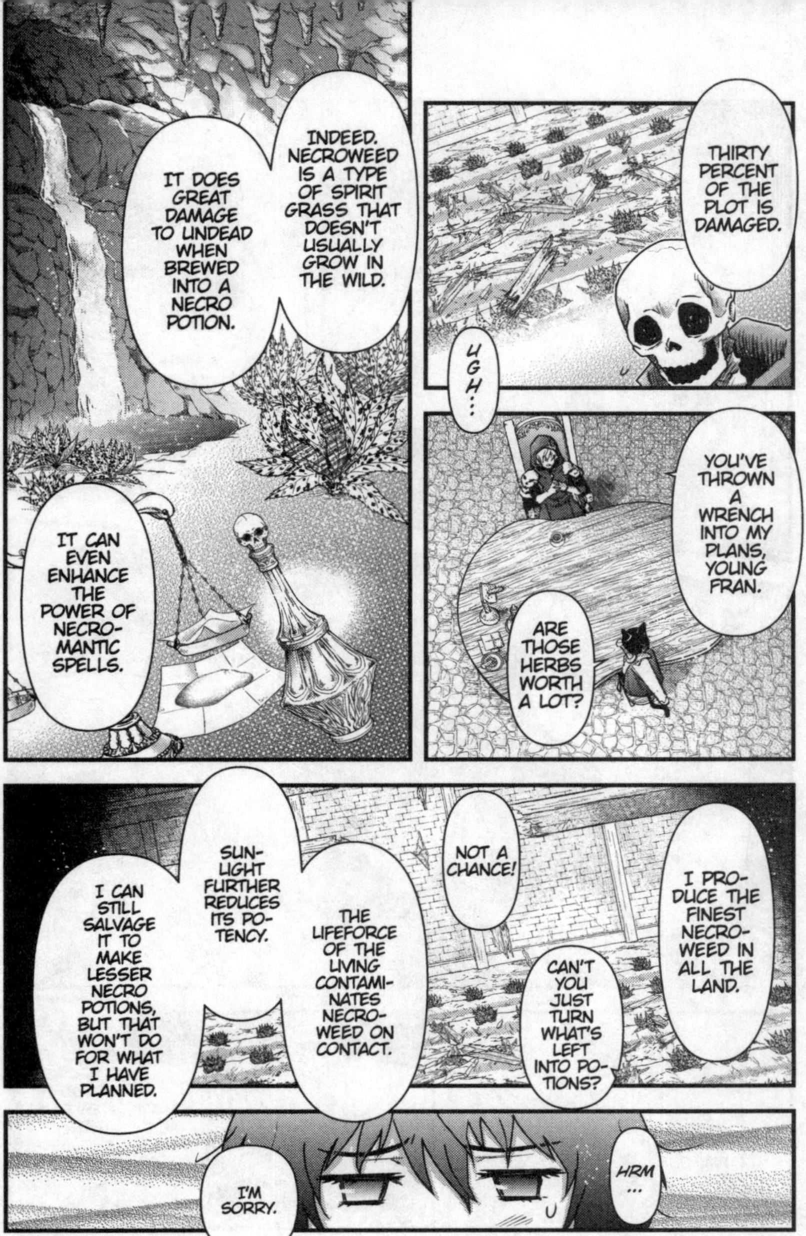
THIRTY PERCENT OF THE PLOT IS DAMAGED.
UGH...
YOU'VE THROWN A WRENCH INTO MY PLANS, YOUNG FRAN.
ARE THOSE HERBS WORTH A LOT?
INDEED. NECROWEED IS A TYPE OF SPIRIT GRASS THAT DOESN'T USUALLY GROW IN THE WILD.
IT DOES GREAT DAMAGE TO UNDEAD WHEN BREWED INTO A NECRO POTION.
IT CAN EVEN ENHANCE THE POWER OF NECROMANTIC SPELLS.
I PRODUCE THE FINEST NECROWEED IN ALL THE LAND.
CAN'T YOU JUST TURN WHAT'S LEFT INTO POTIONS?
NOT A CHANCE!
THE LIFEFORCE OF THE LIVING CONTAMINATES NECROWEED ON CONTACT.
SUNLIGHT FURTHER REDUCES ITS POTENCY.
I CAN STILL SALVAGE IT TO MAKE LESSER NECRO POTIONS, BUT THAT WON'T DO FOR WHAT I HAVE PLANNED.
HRM...
I'M SORRY.

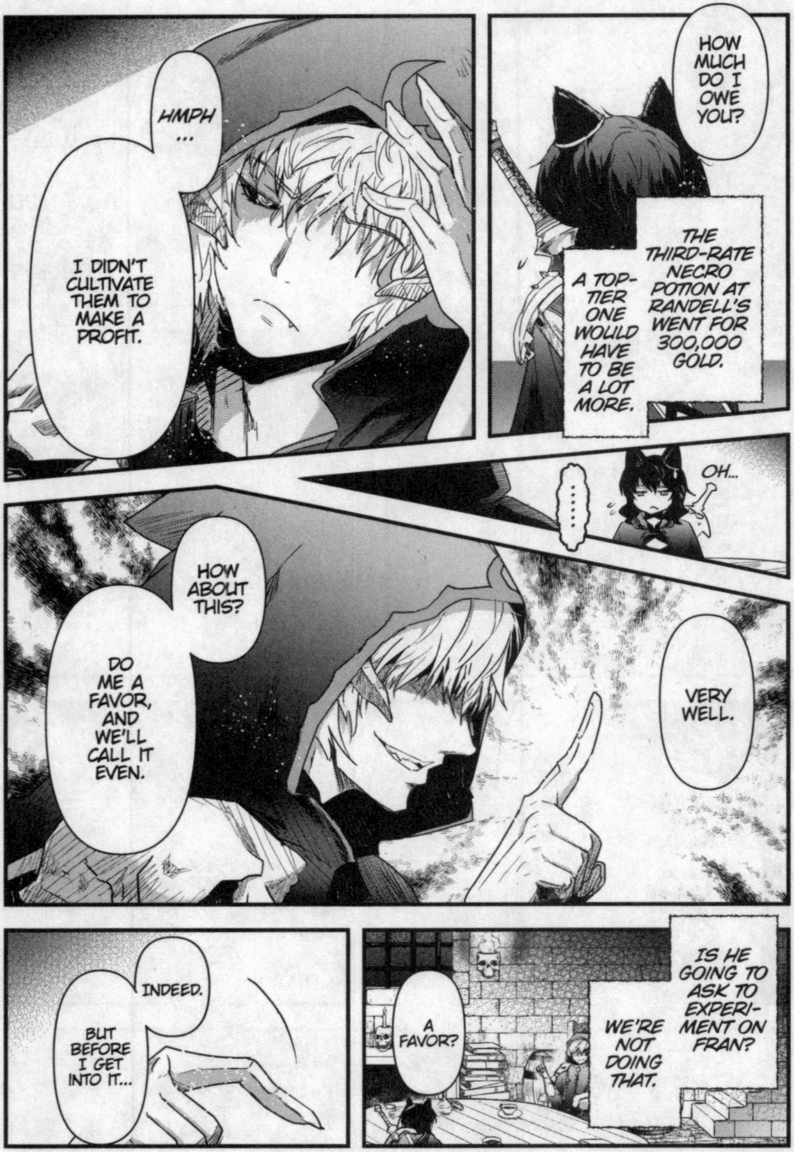
HOW MUCH DO I OWE YOU?
THE THIRD-RATE NECRO POTION AT RANDELL'S WENT FOR 300,000 GOLD.
A TOP-TIER ONE WOULD HAVE TO BE A LOT MORE.
HMPH ...
I DIDN'T CULTIVATE THEM TO MAKE A PROFIT.
OH...
......
VERY WELL.
HOW ABOUT THIS?
DO ME A FAVOR, AND WE'LL CALL IT EVEN.
IS HE GOING TO ASK TO EXPERIMENT ON FRAN?
WE'RE NOT DOING THAT.
A FAVOR?
INDEED.
BUT BEFORE I GET INTO IT...

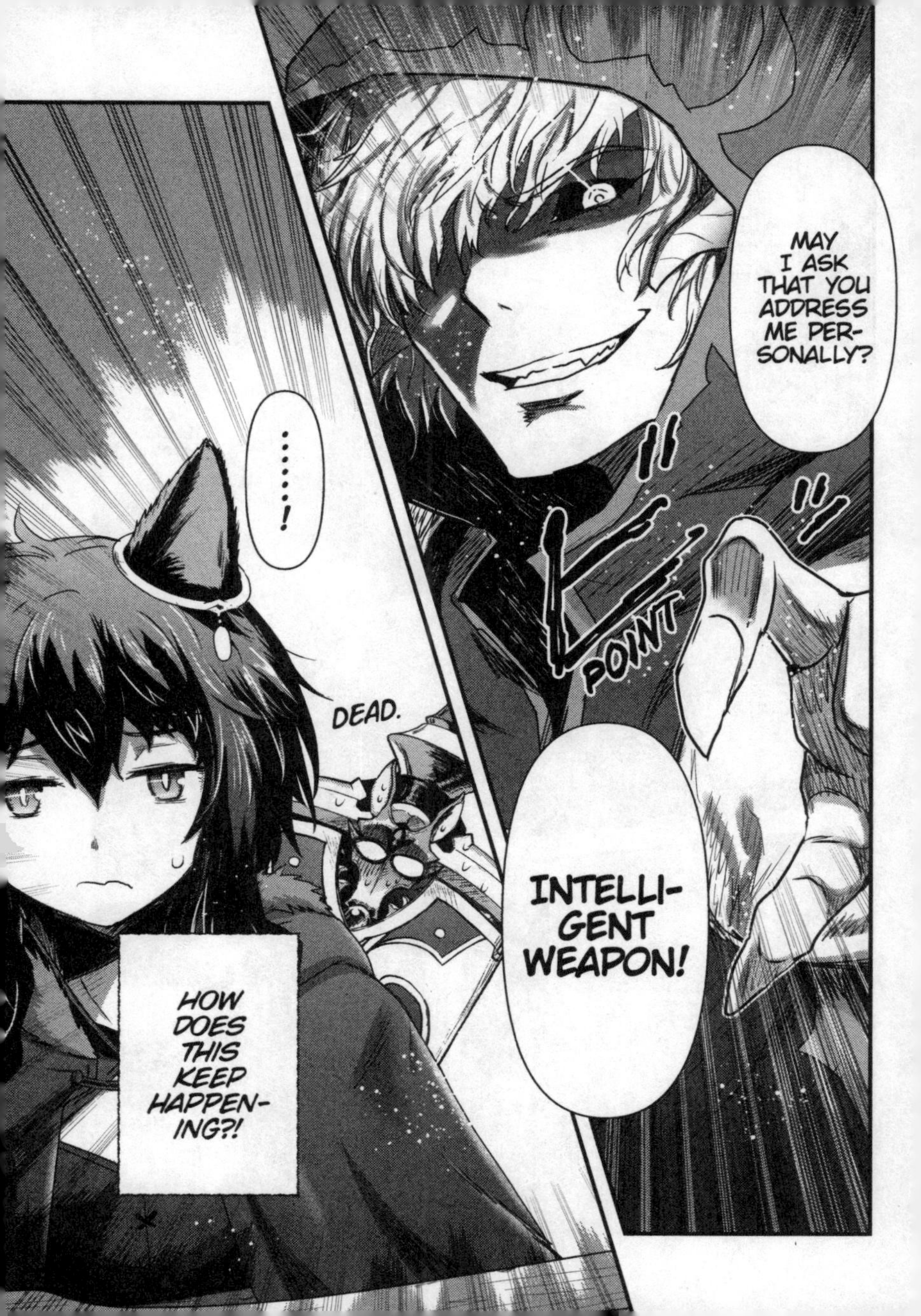
MAY I ASK THAT YOU ADDRESS ME PER-SONALLY?
POINT
INTELLI-GENT WEAPON!
......!
DEAD.
HOW DOES THIS KEEP HAPPEN-ING?!

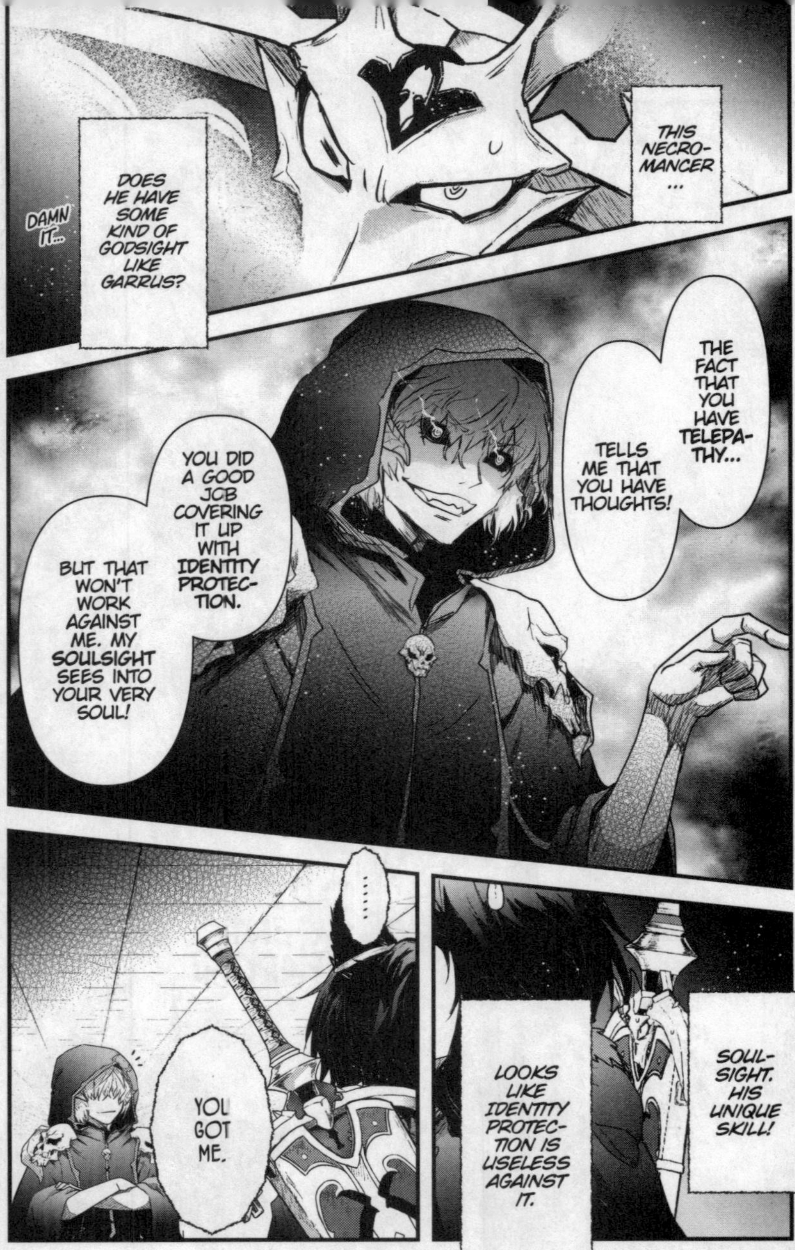
THIS NECRO-MANCER ...
DOES HE HAVE SOME KIND OF GODSIGHT LIKE GARRUS?
DAMN IT...
THE FACT THAT YOU HAVE TELEPA-THY...
TELLS ME THAT YOU HAVE THOUGHTS!
YOU DID A GOOD JOB COVERING IT UP WITH IDENTITY PROTEC-TION.
BUT THAT WON'T WORK AGAINST ME. MY SOULSIGHT SEES INTO YOUR VERY SOUL!
SOUL-SIGHT. HIS UNIQUE SKILL!
LOOKS LIKE IDENTITY PROTEC-TION IS USELESS AGAINST IT.
......
YOU GOT ME.

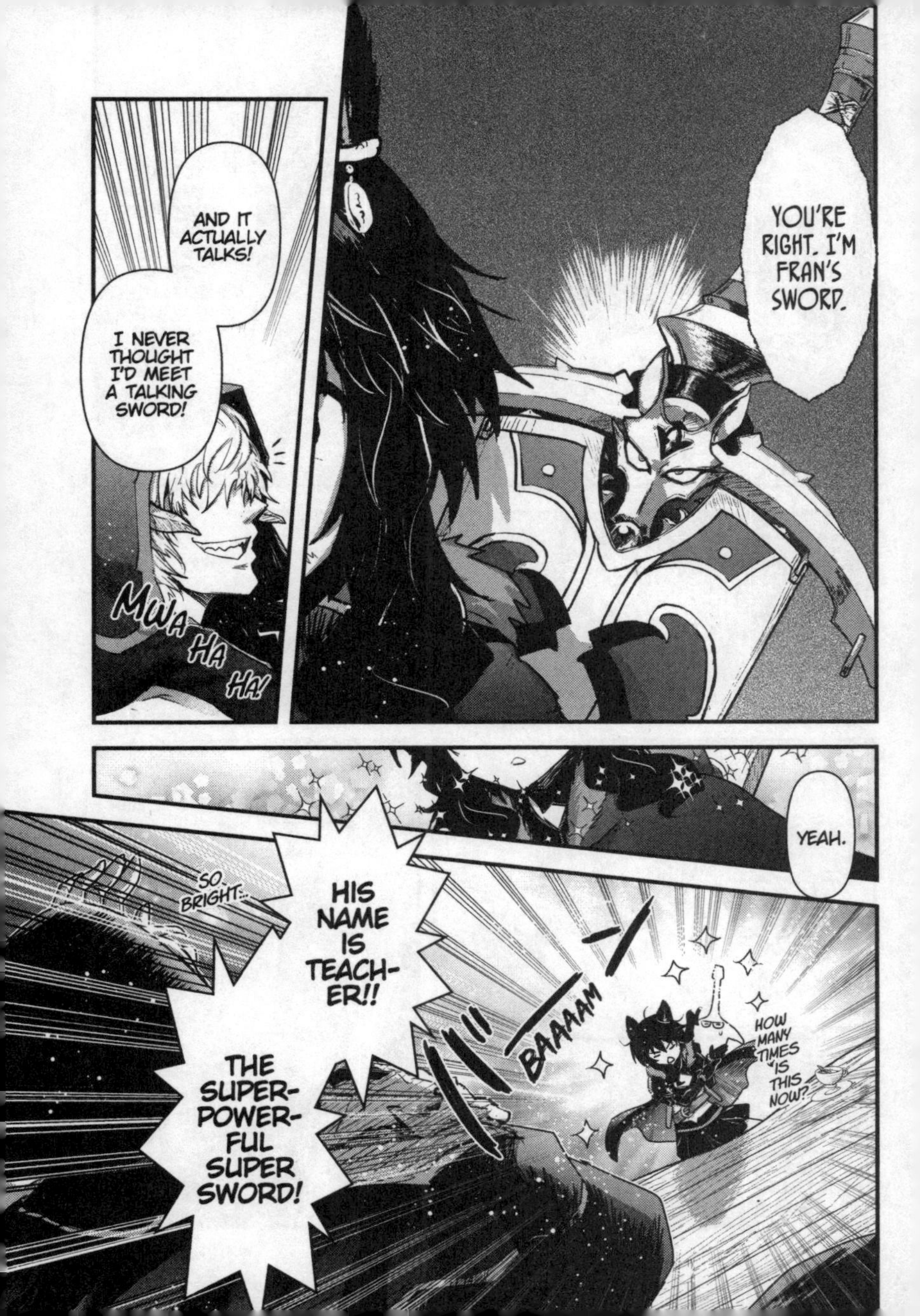
YOU'RE RIGHT. I'M FRAN'S SWORD.
AND IT ACTUALLY TALKS!
I NEVER THOUGHT I'D MEET A TALKING SWORD!
MWA HA HA HA!
YEAH.
HIS NAME IS TEACHER!!
BAAAAM
HOW MANY TIMES IS THIS NOW?
SO BRIGHT...
THE SUPER-POWERFUL SUPER SWORD!

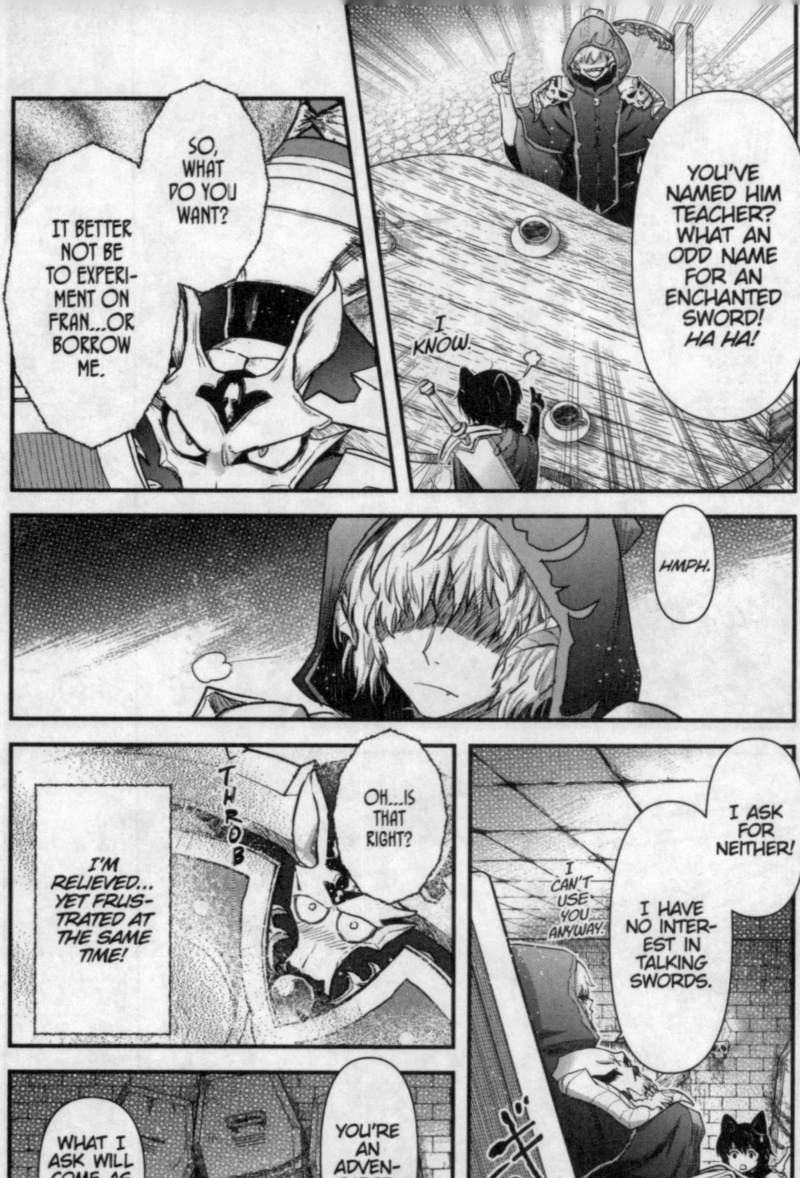
YOU'VE NAMED HIM TEACHER? WHAT AN ODD NAME FOR AN ENCHANTED SWORD! HA HA!
I KNOW.
SO, WHAT DO YOU WANT?
IT BETTER NOT BE TO EXPERIMENT ON FRAN...OR BORROW ME.
HMPH.
I ASK FOR NEITHER!
I HAVE NO INTEREST IN TALKING SWORDS.
I CAN'T USE YOU ANYWAY.
CREAK
THROB
OH...IS THAT RIGHT?
I'M RELIEVED... YET FRUSTRATED AT THE SAME TIME!
YOU'RE AN ADVENTURER.
WHAT I ASK WILL COME AS NO SURPRISE.

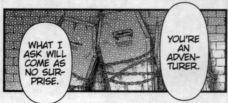

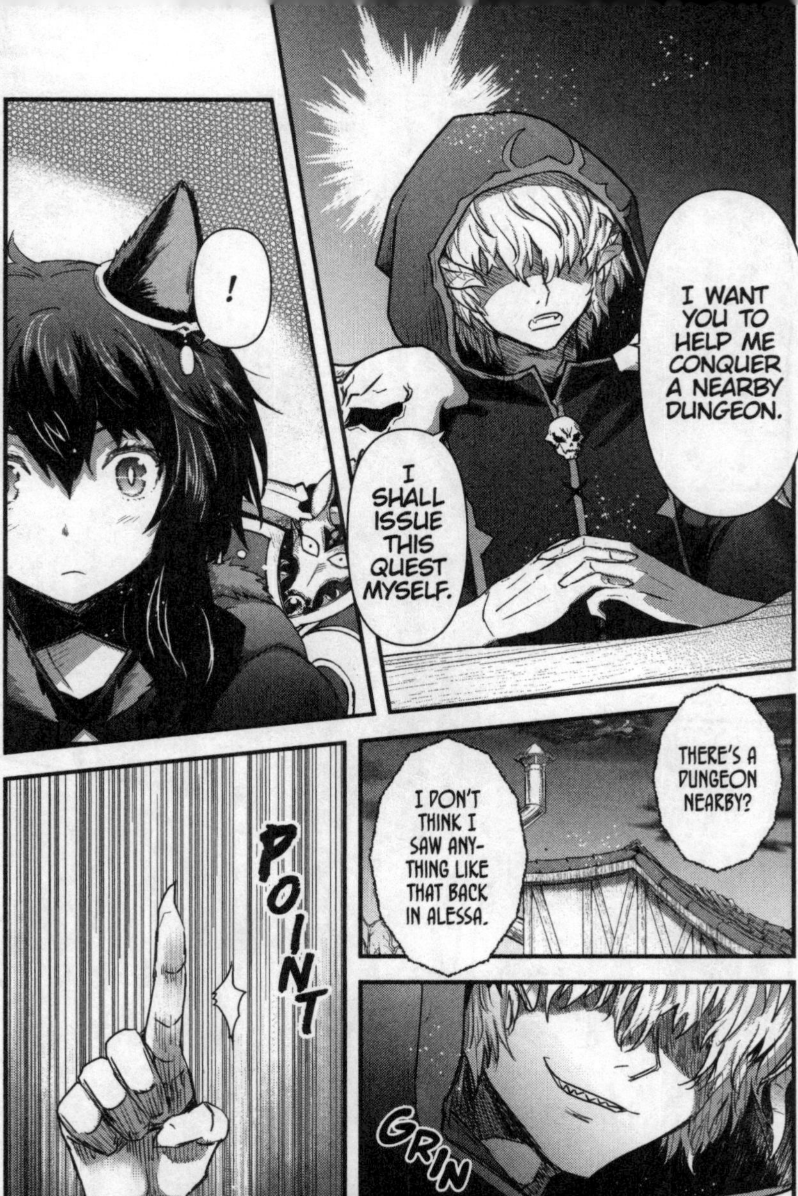
I WANT YOU TO HELP ME CONQUER A NEARBY DUNGEON.
I SHALL ISSUE THIS QUEST MYSELF.
!
THERE'S A DUNGEON NEARBY?
I DON'T THINK I SAW ANY-THING LIKE THAT BACK IN ALESSA.
GRIN
POINT

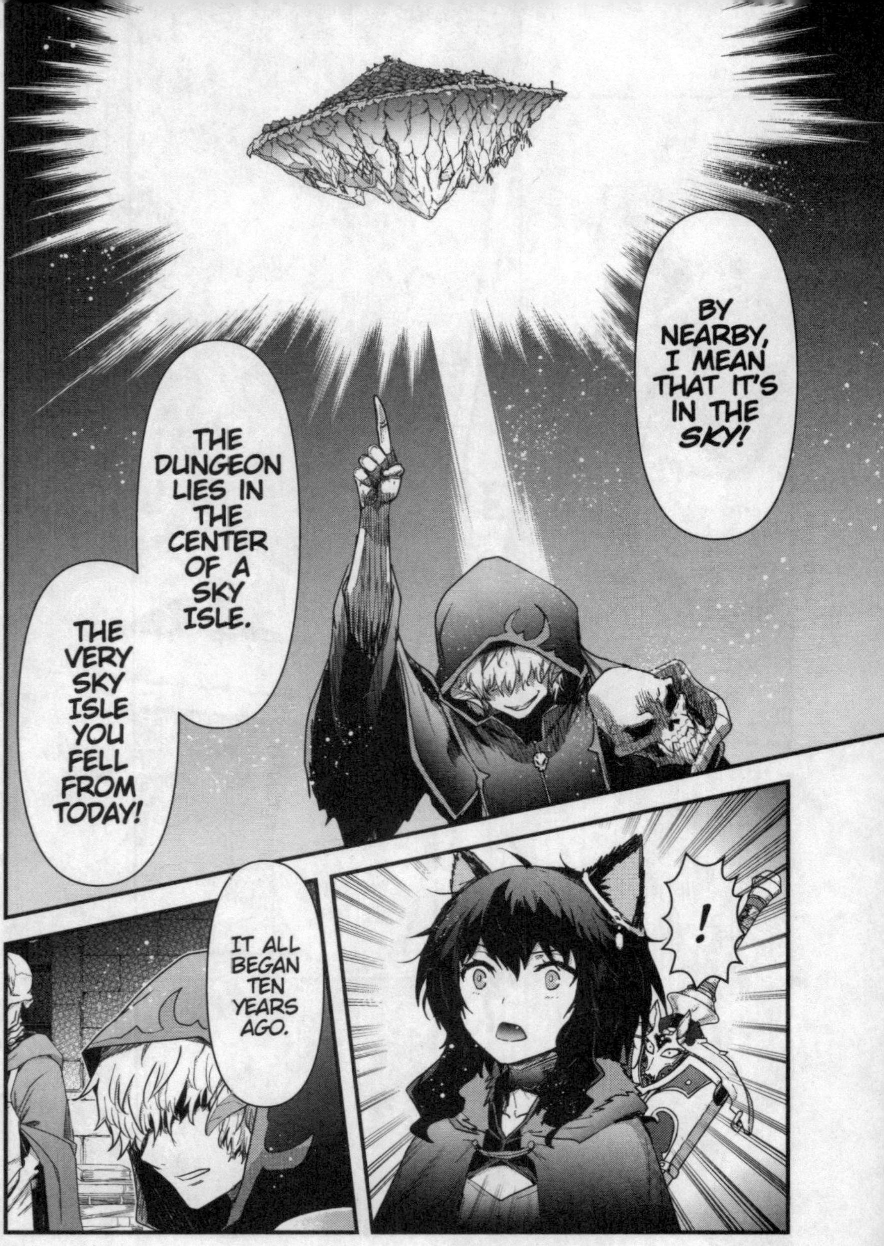
BY NEARBY, I MEAN THAT IT'S IN THE *SKY!*
THE DUNGEON LIES IN THE CENTER OF A SKY ISLE.
THE VERY SKY ISLE YOU FELL FROM TODAY!
!
IT ALL BEGAN TEN YEARS AGO.

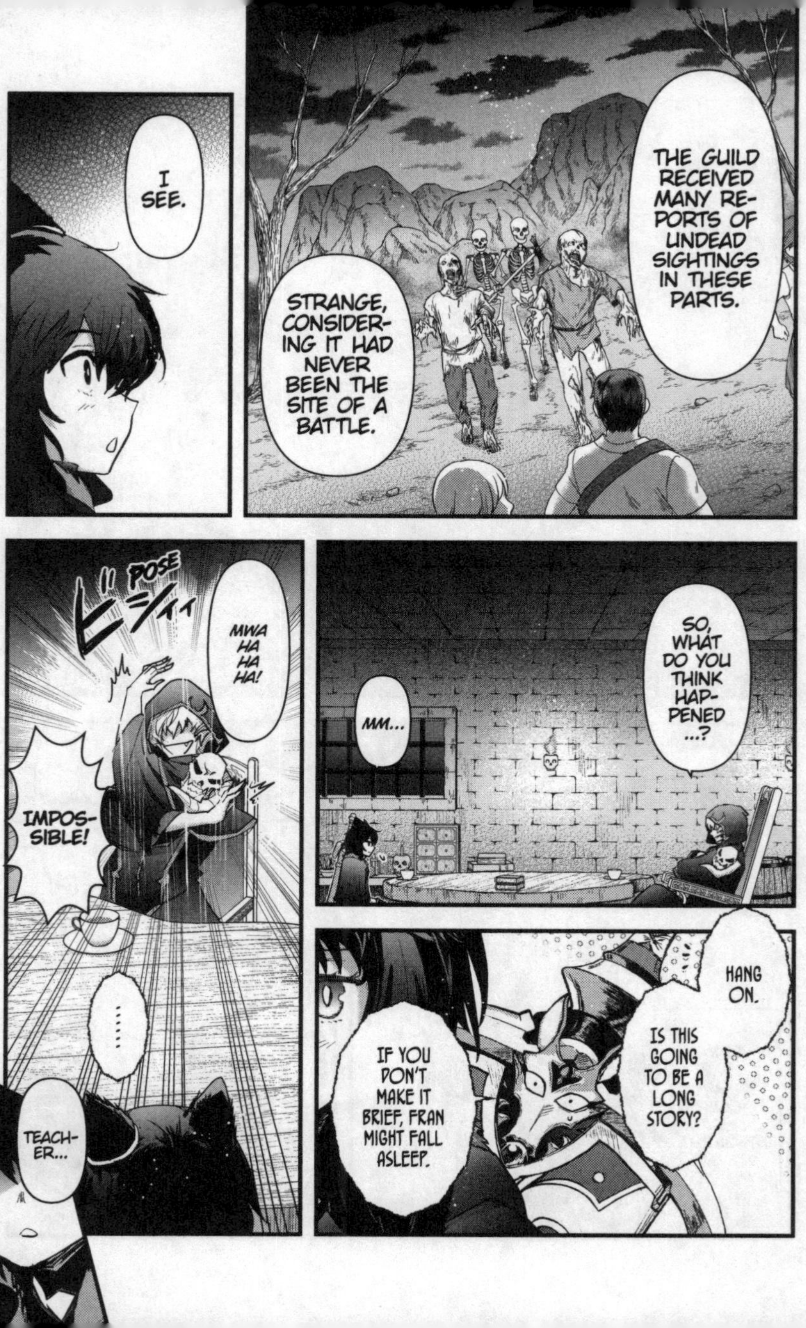
THE GUILD RECEIVED MANY REPORTS OF UNDEAD SIGHTINGS IN THESE PARTS.
STRANGE, CONSIDERING IT HAD NEVER BEEN THE SITE OF A BATTLE.
I SEE.
SO, WHAT DO YOU THINK HAPPENED ...?
MM...
HANG ON.
IS THIS GOING TO BE A LONG STORY?
IF YOU DON'T MAKE IT BRIEF, FRAN MIGHT FALL ASLEEP.
POSE
ビシィィ
MWA HA HA HA!
IMPOSSIBLE!
......
TEACHER...

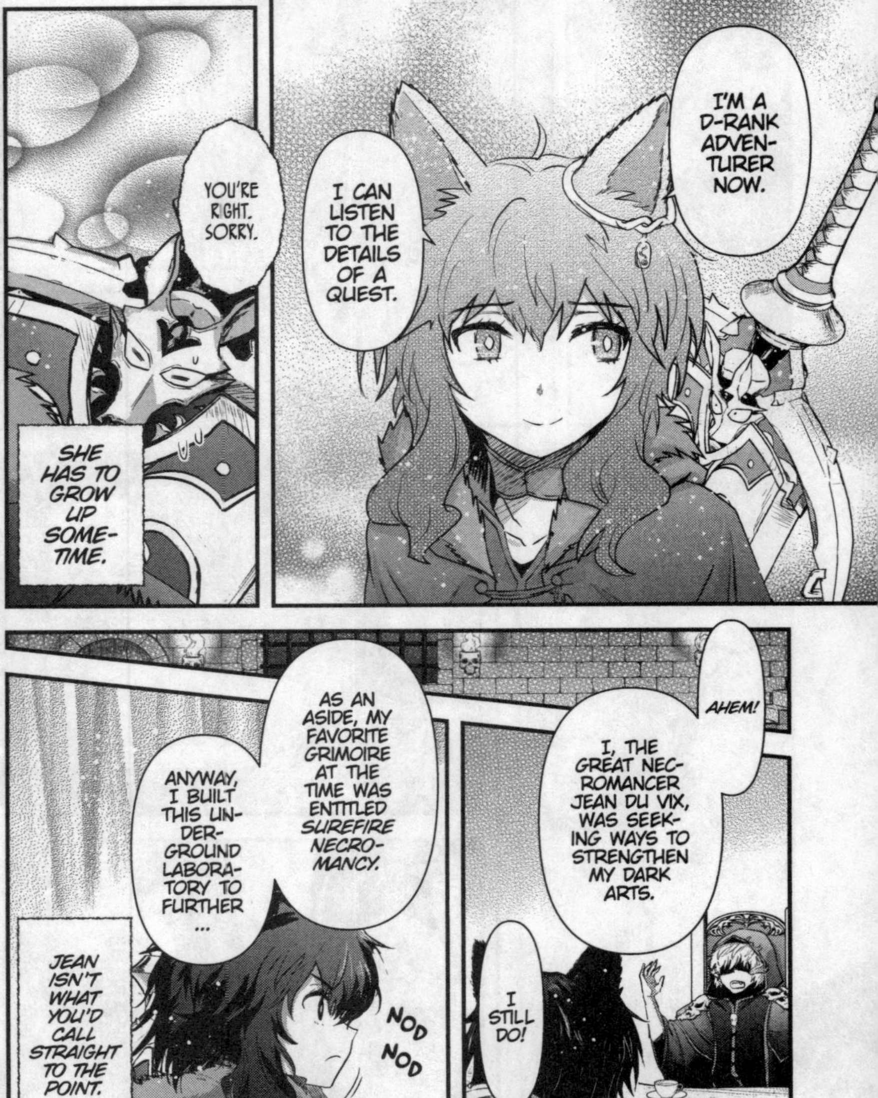
I'M A D-RANK ADVEN-TURER NOW.
I CAN LISTEN TO THE DETAILS OF A QUEST.
YOU'RE RIGHT. SORRY.
SHE HAS TO GROW UP SOME-TIME.
AHEM!
I, THE GREAT NEC-ROMANCER JEAN DU VIX, WAS SEEK-ING WAYS TO STRENGTHEN MY DARK ARTS.
AS AN ASIDE, MY FAVORITE GRIMOIRE AT THE TIME WAS ENTITLED *SUREFIRE NECRO-MANCY.*
I STILL DO!
ANYWAY, I BUILT THIS UN-DER-GROUND LABORA-TORY TO FURTHER ...
NOD NOD
JEAN ISN'T WHAT YOU'D CALL STRAIGHT TO THE POINT.

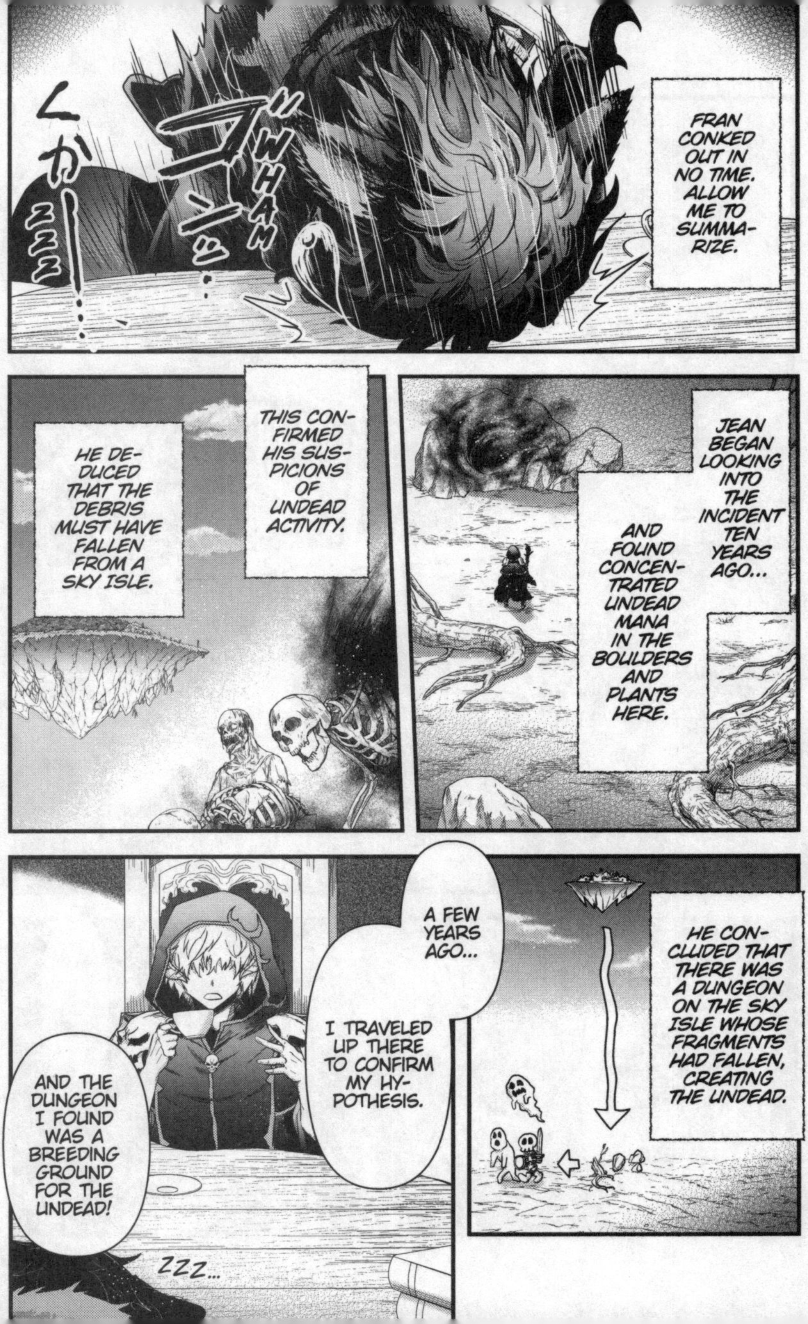
FRAN CONKED OUT IN NO TIME. ALLOW ME TO SUMMA-RIZE.
WHAM
ゴンッ
くかー
ZZZ
JEAN BEGAN LOOKING INTO THE INCIDENT TEN YEARS AGO...
AND FOUND CONCEN-TRATED UNDEAD MANA IN THE BOULDERS AND PLANTS HERE.
THIS CON-FIRMED HIS SUS-PICIONS OF UNDEAD ACTIVITY.
HE DE-DUCED THAT THE DEBRIS MUST HAVE FALLEN FROM A SKY ISLE.
HE CON-CLUDED THAT THERE WAS A DUNGEON ON THE SKY ISLE WHOSE FRAGMENTS HAD FALLEN, CREATING THE UNDEAD.
A FEW YEARS AGO...
I TRAVELED UP THERE TO CONFIRM MY HY-POTHESIS.
AND THE DUNGEON I FOUND WAS A BREEDING GROUND FOR THE UNDEAD!
ZZZ...

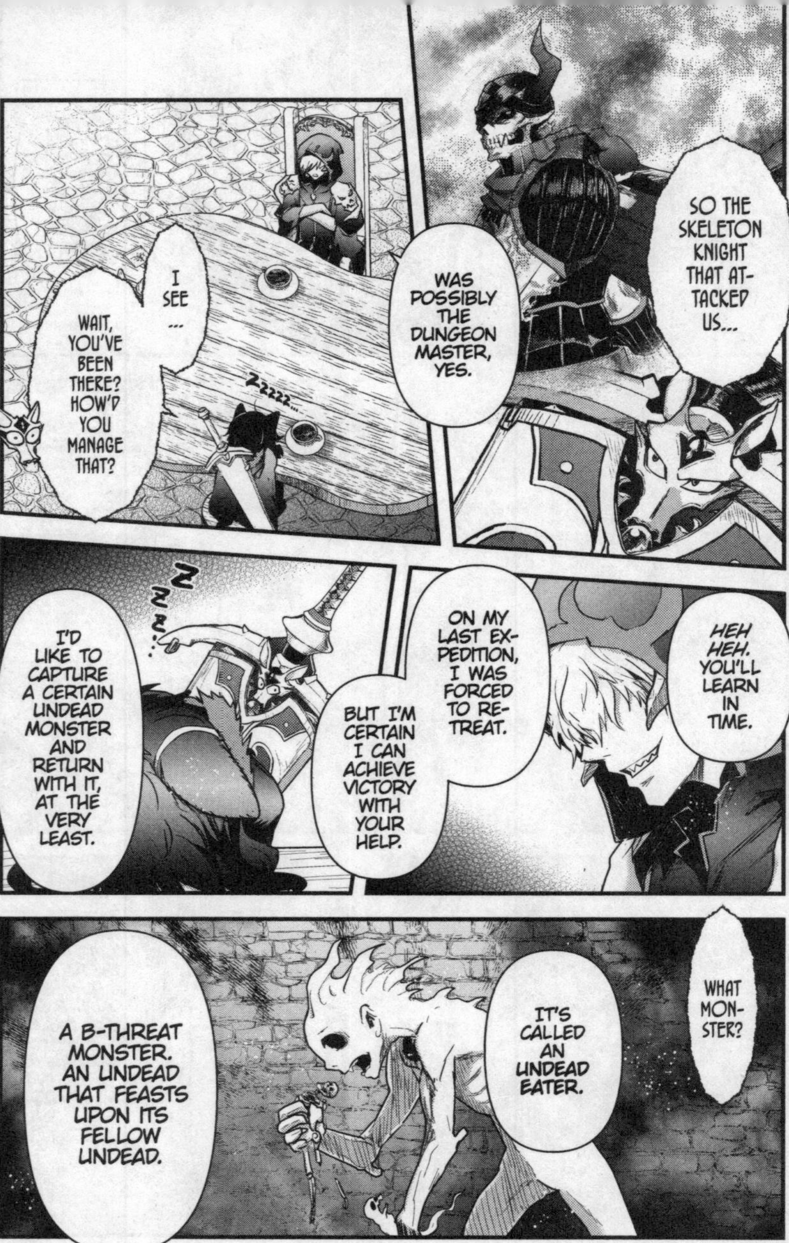
SO THE SKELETON KNIGHT THAT ATTACKED US...
WAS POSSIBLY THE DUNGEON MASTER, YES.
I SEE ...
WAIT, YOU'VE BEEN THERE? HOW'D YOU MANAGE THAT?
Zzzzz...
HEH HEH. YOU'LL LEARN IN TIME.
ON MY LAST EXPEDITION, I WAS FORCED TO RETREAT.
BUT I'M CERTAIN I CAN ACHIEVE VICTORY WITH YOUR HELP.
Zzz...
I'D LIKE TO CAPTURE A CERTAIN UNDEAD MONSTER AND RETURN WITH IT, AT THE VERY LEAST.
WHAT MONSTER?
IT'S CALLED AN UNDEAD EATER.
A B-THREAT MONSTER. AN UNDEAD THAT FEASTS UPON ITS FELLOW UNDEAD.

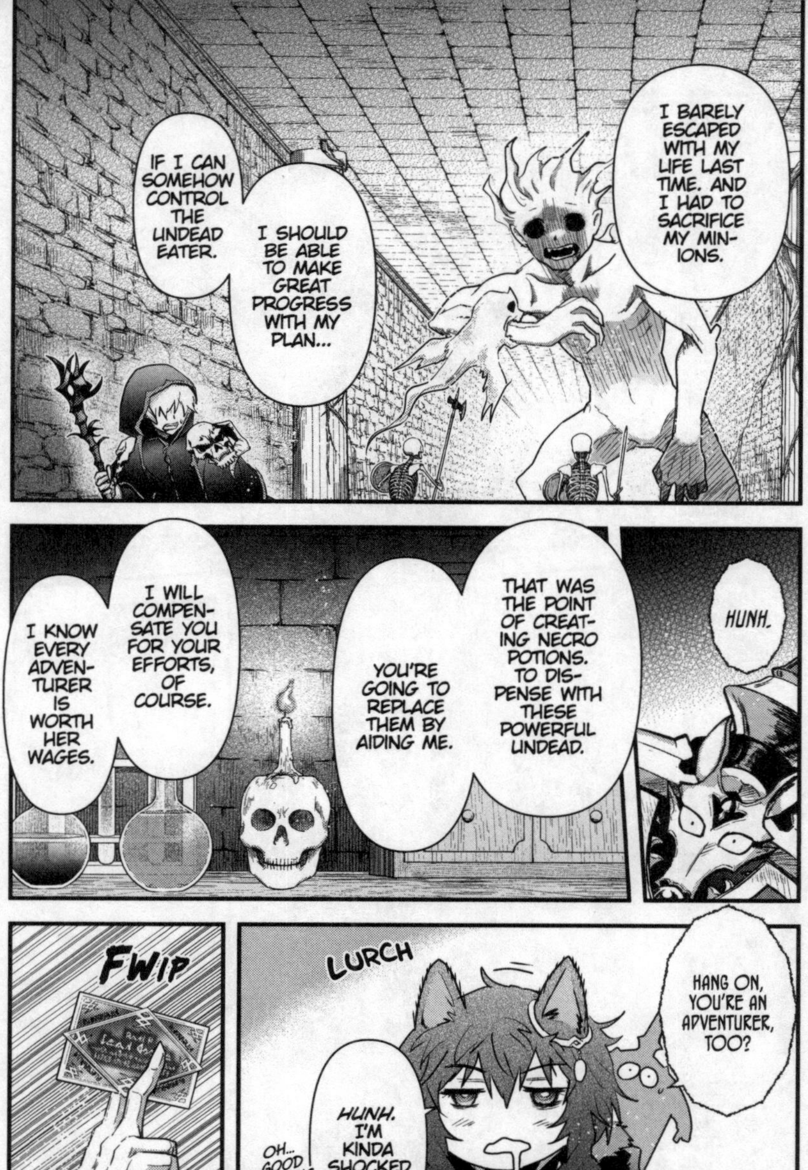

I BARELY ESCAPED WITH MY LIFE LAST TIME. AND I HAD TO SACRIFICE MY MIN-IONS.
IF I CAN SOMEHOW CONTROL THE UNDEAD EATER.
I SHOULD BE ABLE TO MAKE GREAT PROGRESS WITH MY PLAN...
HUNH.
THAT WAS THE POINT OF CREAT-ING NECRO POTIONS. TO DIS-PENSE WITH THESE POWERFUL UNDEAD.
YOU'RE GOING TO REPLACE THEM BY AIDING ME.
I WILL COMPEN-SATE YOU FOR YOUR EFFORTS, OF COURSE.
I KNOW EVERY ADVEN-TURER IS WORTH HER WAGES.
HANG ON, YOU'RE AN ADVENTURER, TOO?
LURCH
HUNH. I'M KINDA SHOCKED ...
OH... GOOD MORNING, FRAN.
FWIP

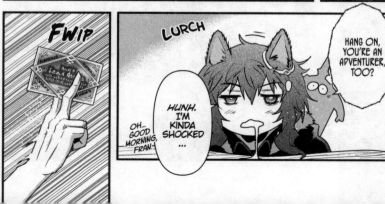

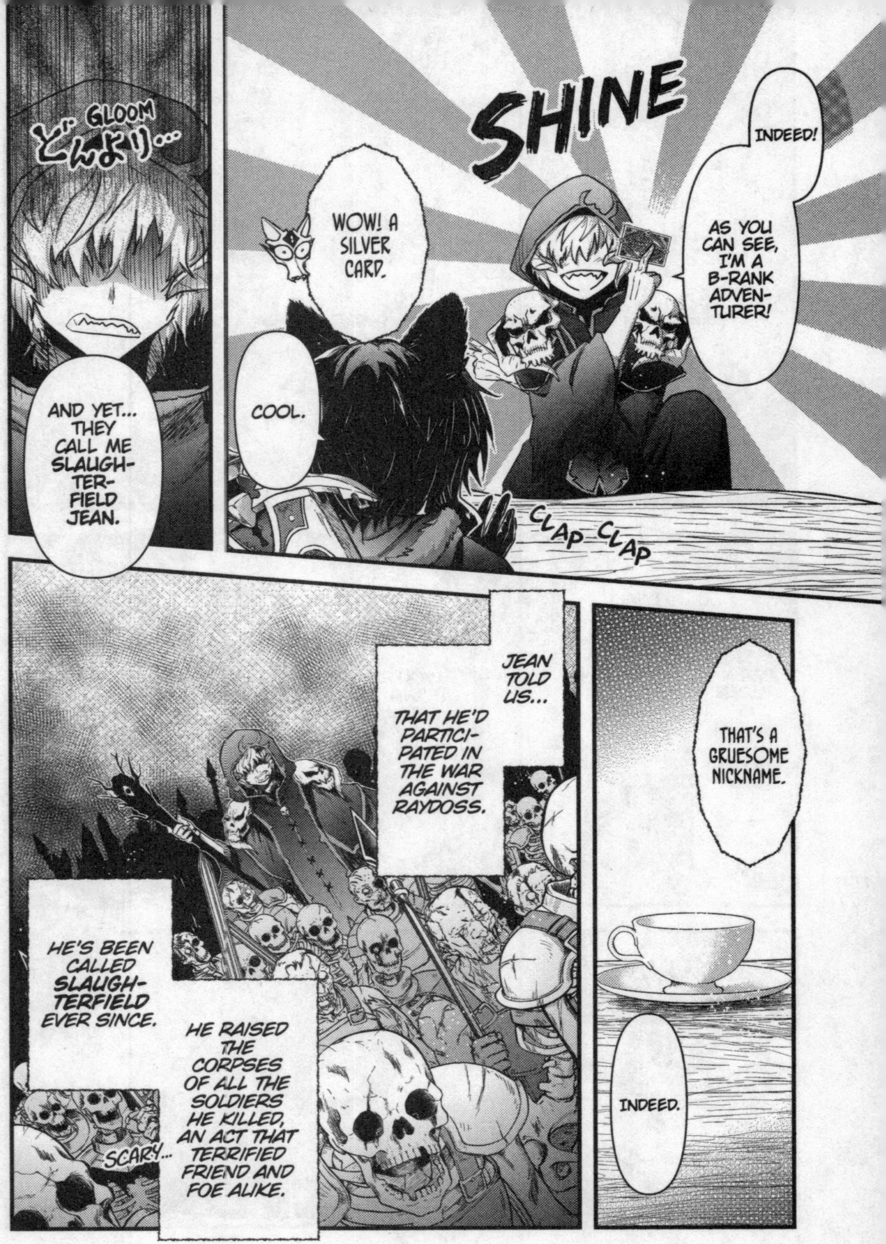

INDEED!
AS YOU CAN SEE, I'M A B-RANK ADVENTURER!
SHINE
WOW! A SILVER CARD.
COOL.
CLAP CLAP
GLOOM
どんより…
AND YET... THEY CALL ME SLAUGHTER-FIELD JEAN.
THAT'S A GRUESOME NICKNAME.
INDEED.
JEAN TOLD US...
THAT HE'D PARTICI-PATED IN THE WAR AGAINST RAYDOSS.
HE RAISED THE CORPSES OF ALL THE SOLDIERS HE KILLED, AN ACT THAT TERRIFIED FRIEND AND FOE ALIKE.
HE'S BEEN CALLED SLAUGH-TERFIELD EVER SINCE.
SCARY...

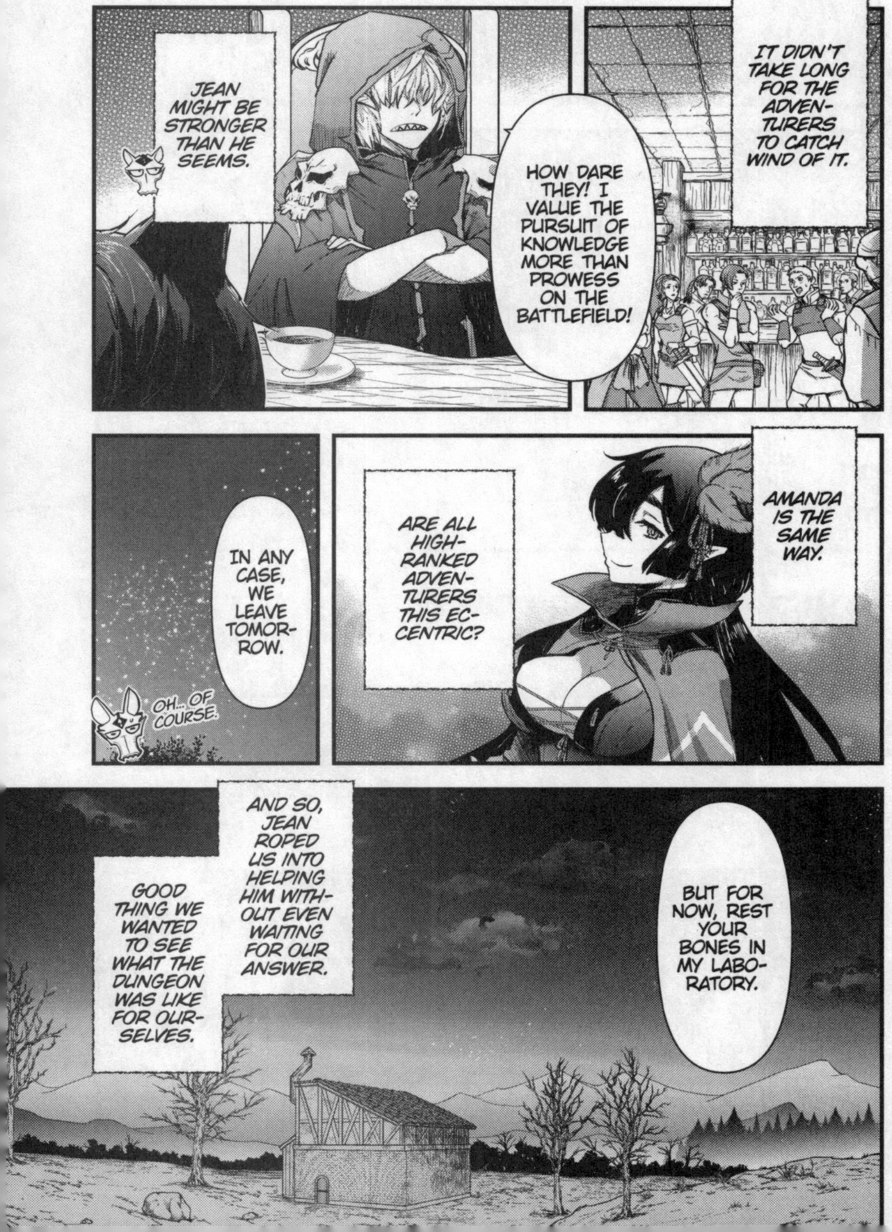
IT DIDN'T TAKE LONG FOR THE ADVEN-TURERS TO CATCH WIND OF IT.
HOW DARE THEY! I VALUE THE PURSUIT OF KNOWLEDGE MORE THAN PROWESS ON THE BATTLEFIELD!
JEAN MIGHT BE STRONGER THAN HE SEEMS.
AMANDA IS THE SAME WAY.
ARE ALL HIGH-RANKED ADVEN-TURERS THIS EC-CENTRIC?
IN ANY CASE, WE LEAVE TOMOR-ROW.
OH... OF COURSE.
BUT FOR NOW, REST YOUR BONES IN MY LABO-RATORY.
AND SO, JEAN ROPED US INTO HELPING HIM WITH-OUT EVEN WAITING FOR OUR ANSWER.
GOOD THING WE WANTED TO SEE WHAT THE DUNGEON WAS LIKE FOR OUR-SELVES.

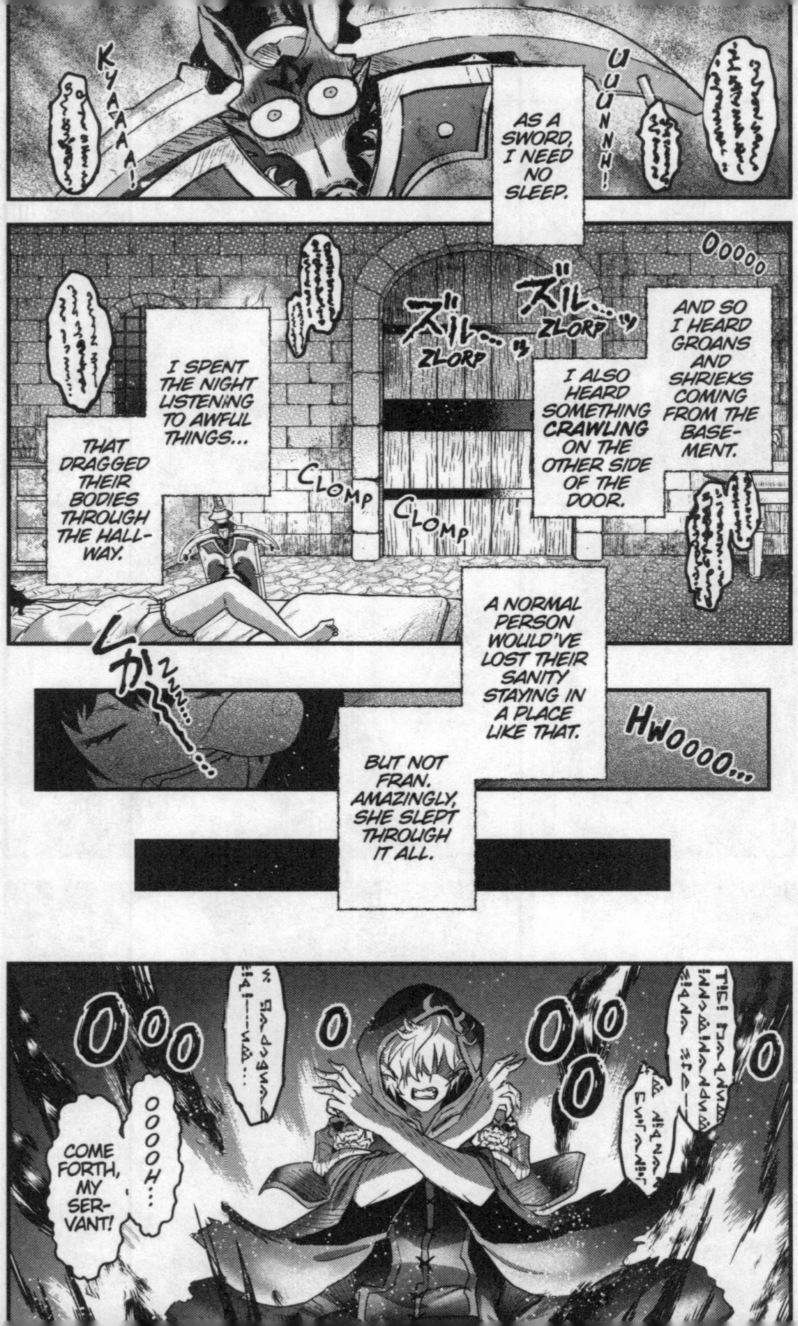
UUUNNH!
AS A SWORD, I NEED NO SLEEP.
KYAAAAA!
Ooooo
AND SO I HEARD GROANS AND SHRIEKS COMING FROM THE BASEMENT.
ズル… ZLORP
ズル… ZLORP
I ALSO HEARD SOMETHING CRAWLING ON THE OTHER SIDE OF THE DOOR.
CLOMP
CLOMP
I SPENT THE NIGHT LISTENING TO AWFUL THINGS...
THAT DRAGGED THEIR BODIES THROUGH THE HALLWAY.
HWOOOOO...
A NORMAL PERSON WOULD'VE LOST THEIR SANITY STAYING IN A PLACE LIKE THAT.
ZZNN...
BUT NOT FRAN. AMAZINGLY, SHE SLEPT THROUGH IT ALL.
OOOOOH...
COME FORTH, MY SERVANT!

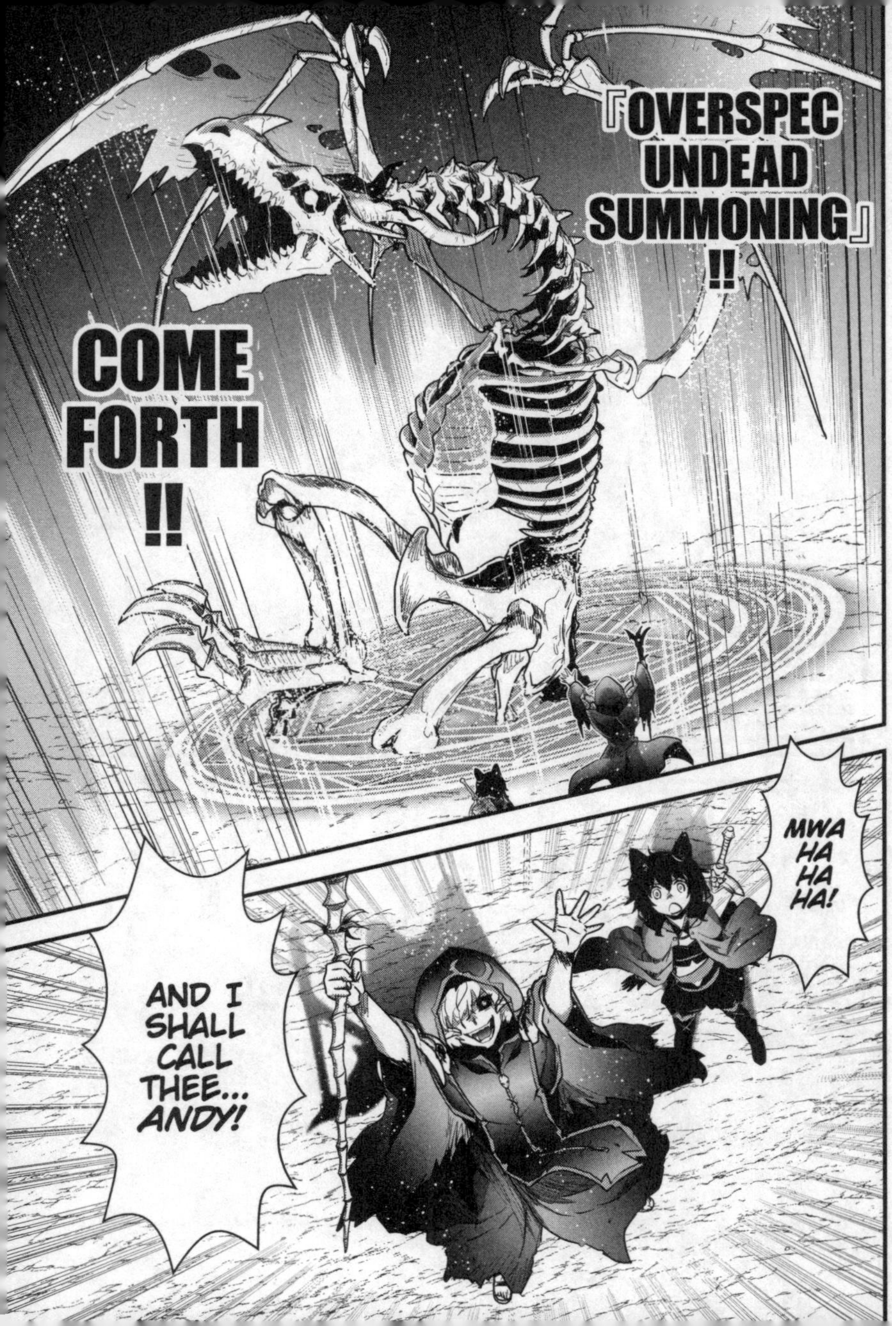

『OVERSPEC UNDEAD SUMMONING』!!
COME FORTH!!
MWA HA HA HA HA!
AND I SHALL CALL THEE... ANDY!

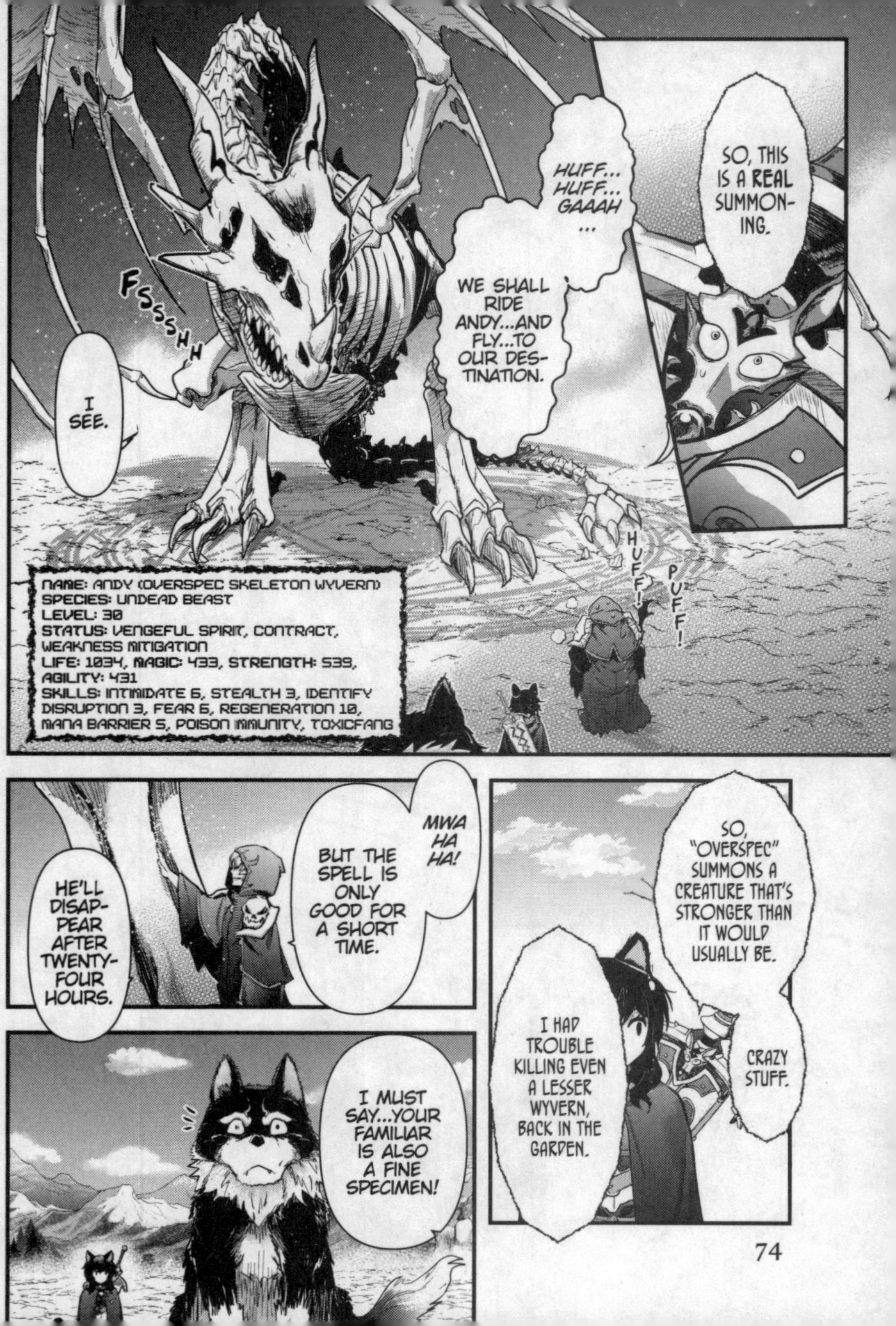
SO, THIS IS A REAL SUMMONING.
HUFF... HUFF... GAAAH...
WE SHALL RIDE ANDY...AND FLY...TO OUR DESTINATION.
FSSSHH
I SEE.
NAME: ANDY (OVERSPEC SKELETON WYVERN)
SPECIES: UNDEAD BEAST
LEVEL: 30
STATUS: VENGEFUL SPIRIT, CONTRACT, WEAKNESS MITIGATION
LIFE: 1034, MAGIC: 433, STRENGTH: 539, AGILITY: 431
SKILLS: INTIMIDATE 6, STEALTH 3, IDENTIFY DISRUPTION 3, FEAR 6, REGENERATION 10, MANA BARRIER 5, POISON IMMUNITY, TOXICFANG
HUFF! PUFF!
SO, "OVERSPEC" SUMMONS A CREATURE THAT'S STRONGER THAN IT WOULD USUALLY BE.
CRAZY STUFF.
I HAD TROUBLE KILLING EVEN A LESSER WYVERN, BACK IN THE GARDEN.
MWA HA HA!
BUT THE SPELL IS ONLY GOOD FOR A SHORT TIME.
HE'LL DISAPPEAR AFTER TWENTY-FOUR HOURS.
I MUST SAY...YOUR FAMILIAR IS ALSO A FINE SPECIMEN!

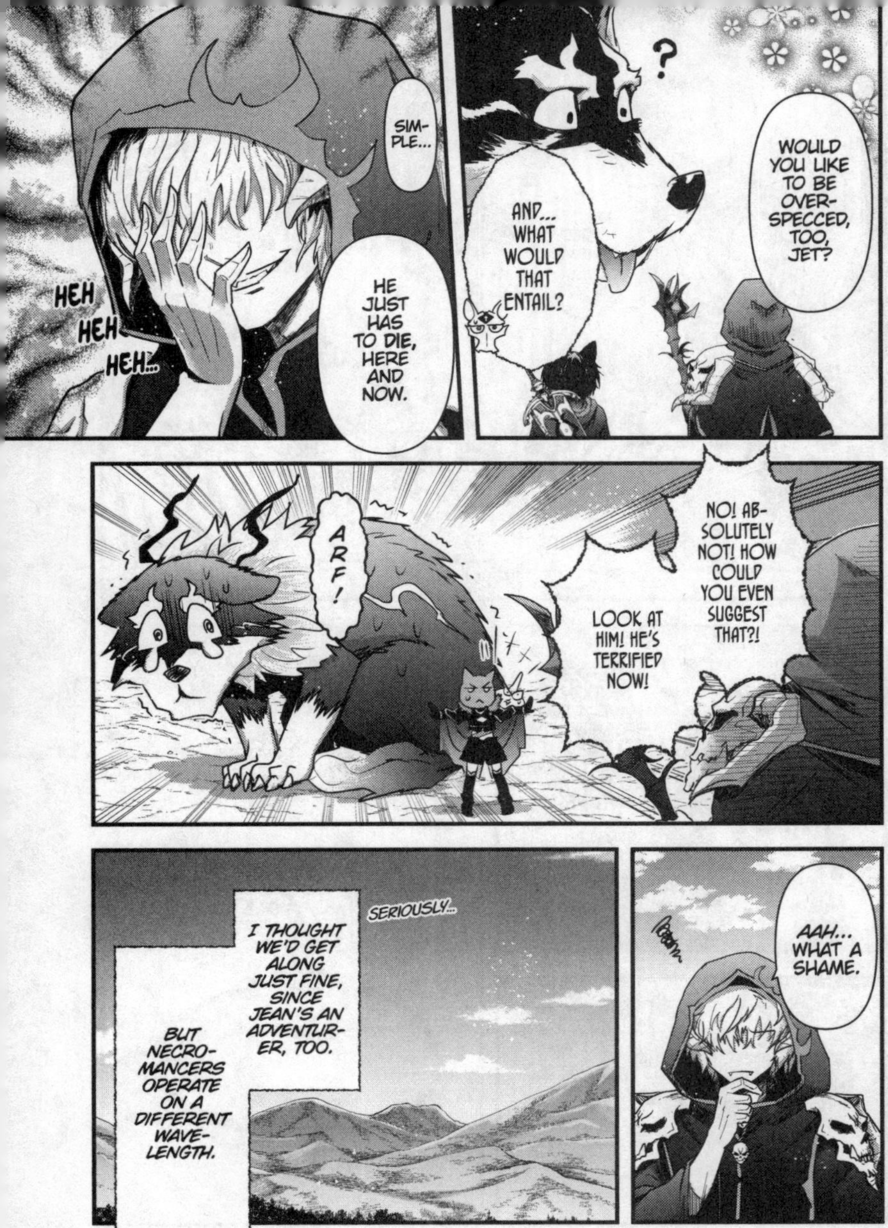
?
WOULD YOU LIKE TO BE OVER-SPECCED, TOO, JET?
AND... WHAT WOULD THAT ENTAIL?
SIMP-LE...
HE JUST HAS TO DIE, HERE AND NOW.
HEH HEH HEH...
NO! AB-SOLUTELY NOT! HOW COULD YOU EVEN SUGGEST THAT?!
LOOK AT HIM! HE'S TERRIFIED NOW!
ARF!
AAH... WHAT A SHAME.
SERIOUSLY...
I THOUGHT WE'D GET ALONG JUST FINE, SINCE JEAN'S AN ADVENTURER, TOO.
BUT NECROMANCERS OPERATE ON A DIFFERENT WAVELENGTH.

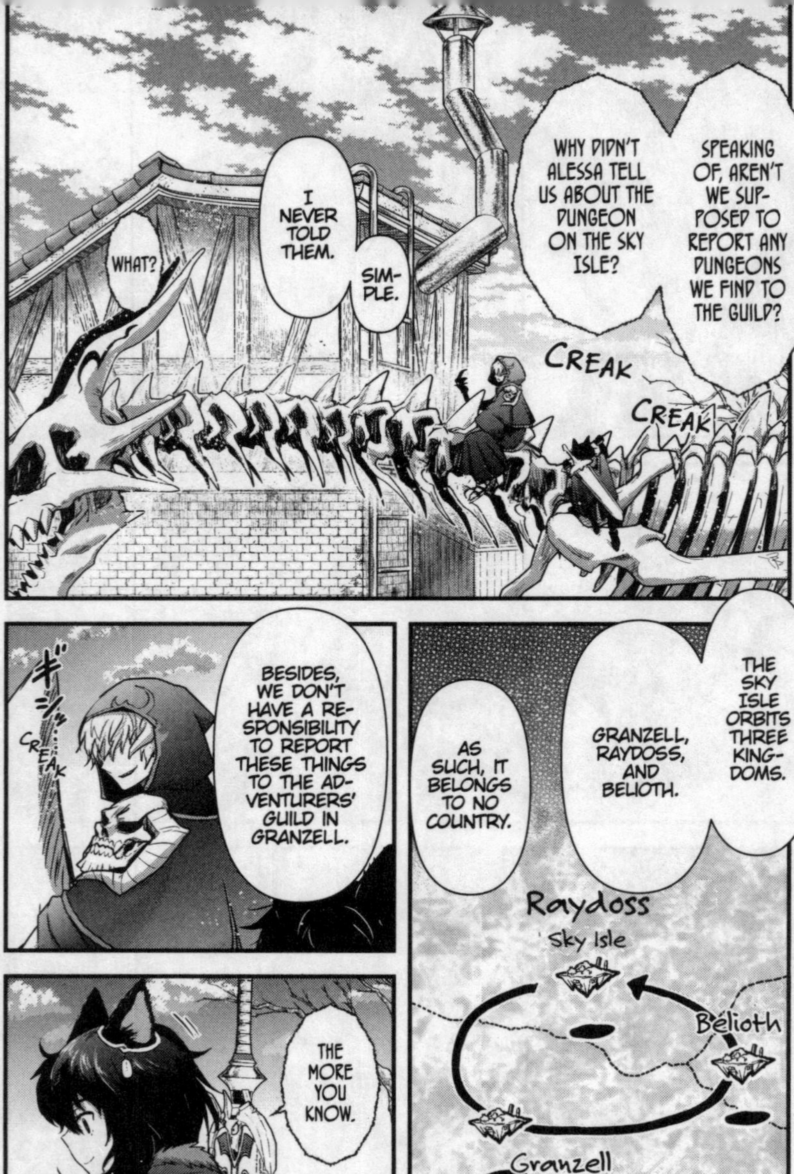

SPEAKING OF, AREN'T WE SUP-POSED TO REPORT ANY DUNGEONS WE FIND TO THE GUILD?
WHY DIDN'T ALESSA TELL US ABOUT THE DUNGEON ON THE SKY ISLE?
SIMPLE.
I NEVER TOLD THEM.
WHAT?
CREAK
CREAK
THE SKY ISLE ORBITS THREE KING-DOMS.
GRANZELL, RAYDOSS, AND BELIOTH.
AS SUCH, IT BELONGS TO NO COUNTRY.
Raydoss
Sky Isle
Belioth
Granzell
BESIDES, WE DON'T HAVE A RE-SPONSIBILITY TO REPORT THESE THINGS TO THE AD-VENTURERS' GUILD IN GRANZELL.
CREAK
THE MORE YOU KNOW.

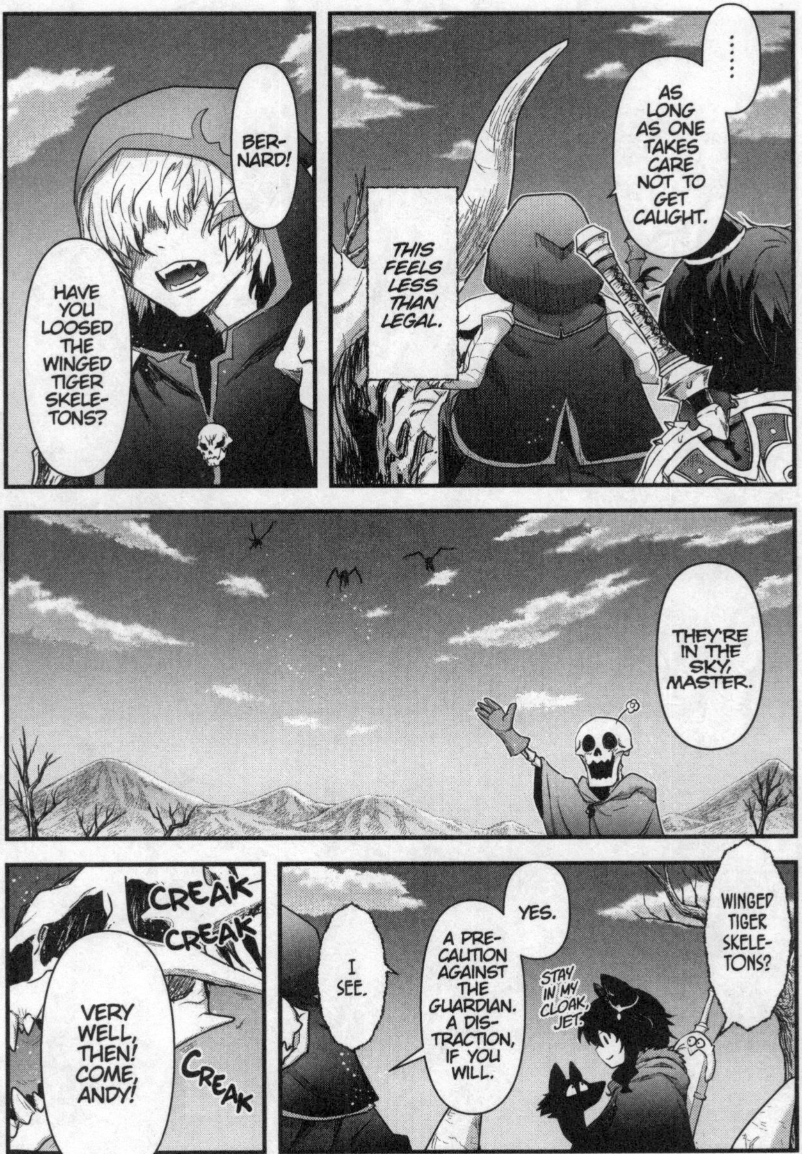
......
AS LONG AS ONE TAKES CARE NOT TO GET CAUGHT.
THIS FEELS LESS THAN LEGAL.
BER-NARD!
HAVE YOU LOOSED THE WINGED TIGER SKELE-TONS?
THEY'RE IN THE SKY, MASTER.
WINGED TIGER SKELE-TONS?
STAY IN MY CLOAK, JET.
YES.
A PRE-CAUTION AGAINST THE GUARDIAN. A DIS-TRACTION, IF YOU WILL.
I SEE.
CREAK
CREAK
VERY WELL, THEN! COME, ANDY!
CREAK

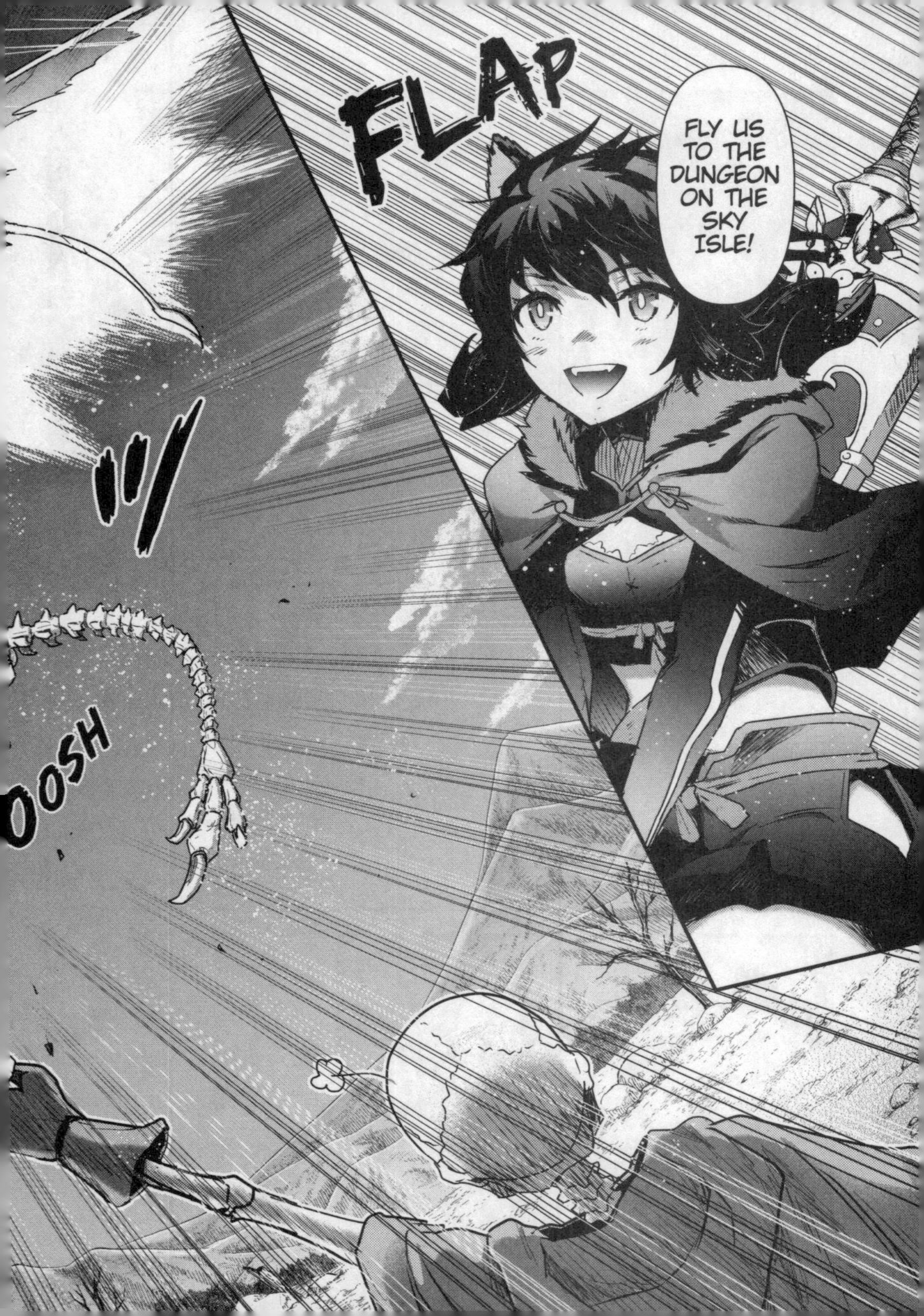
FLAP
FLY US TO THE DUNGEON ON THE SKY ISLE!
OOSH

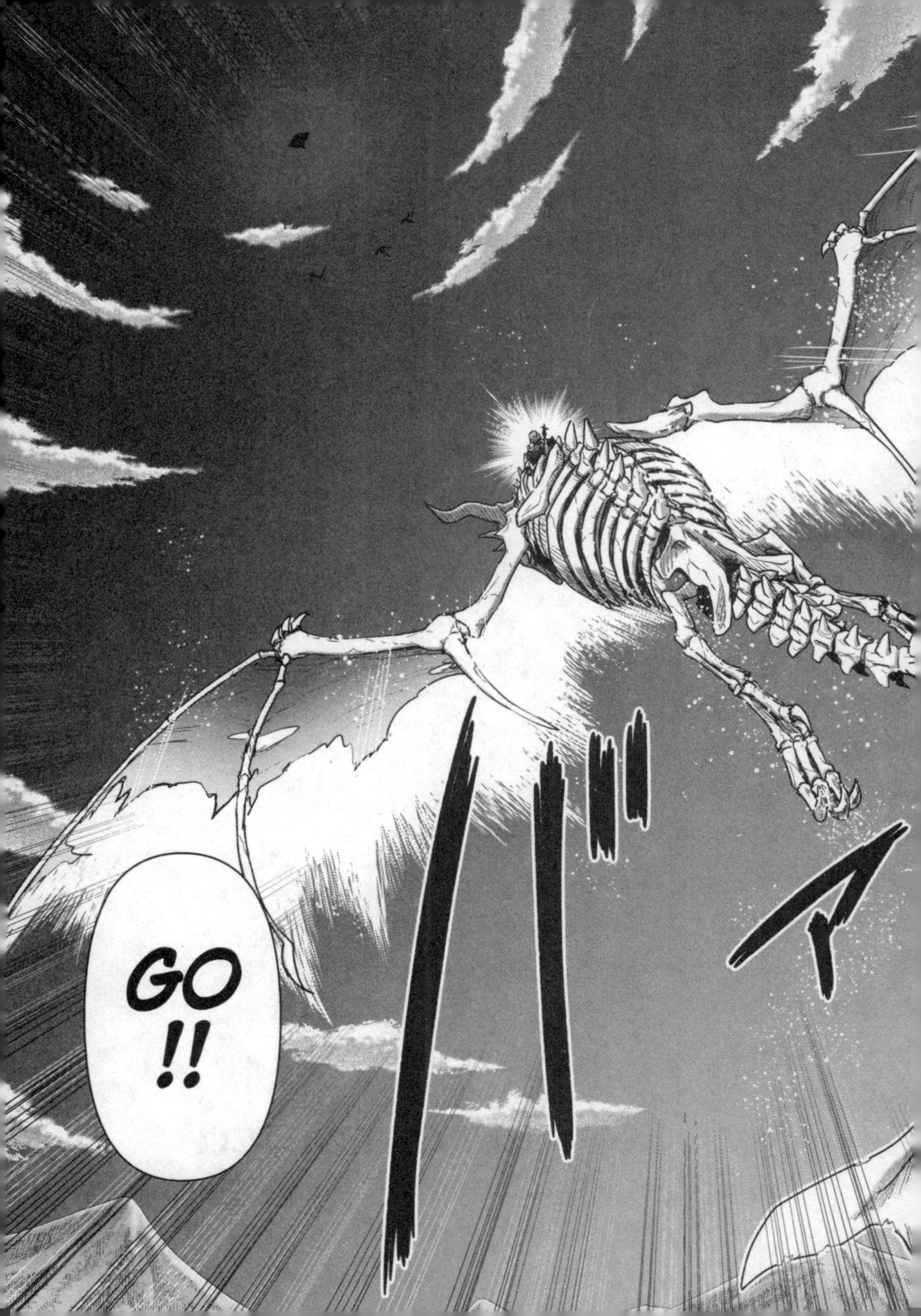
GO !!
バア

Reincarnated
as a Sword

Chapter 31: Nameless's Diary and Aerial Defenses

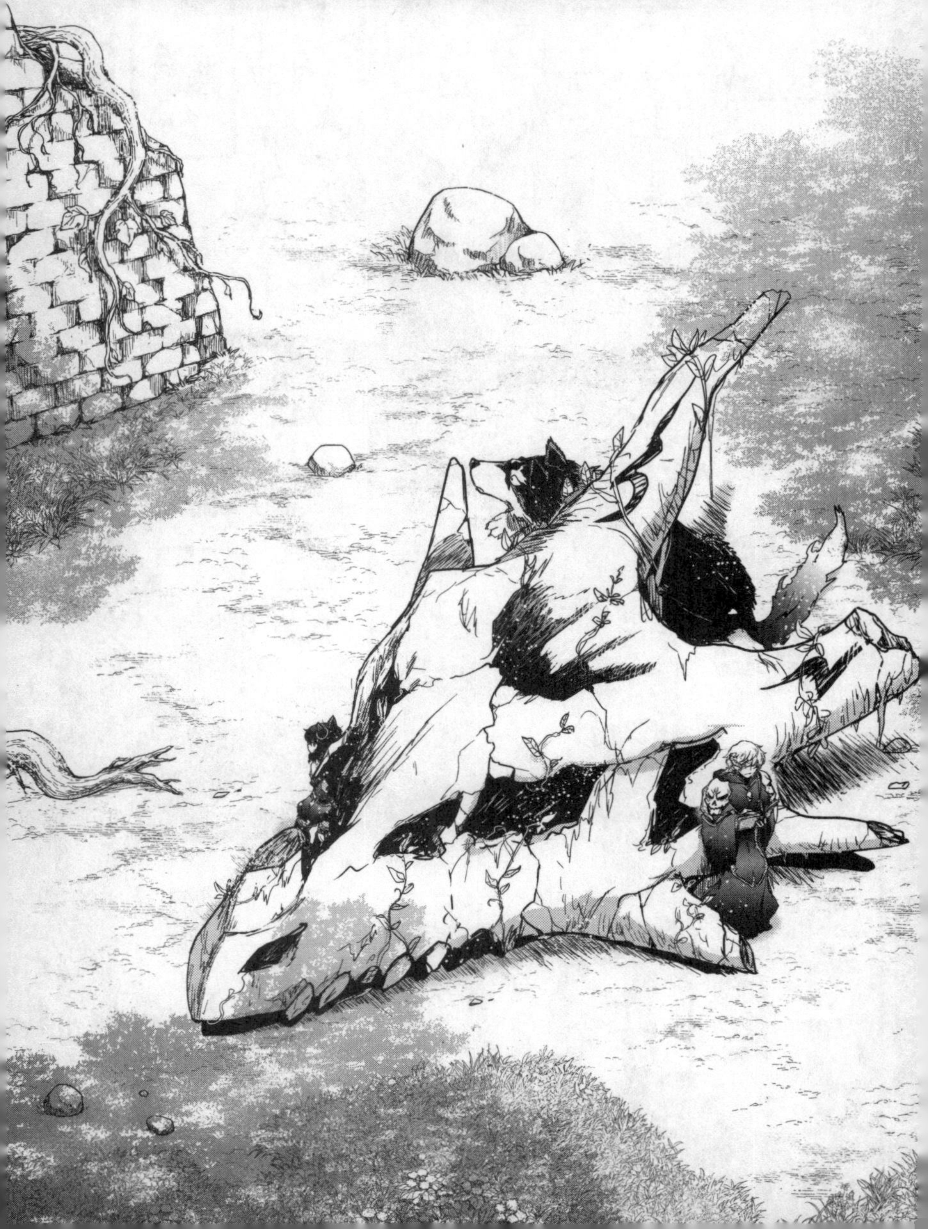

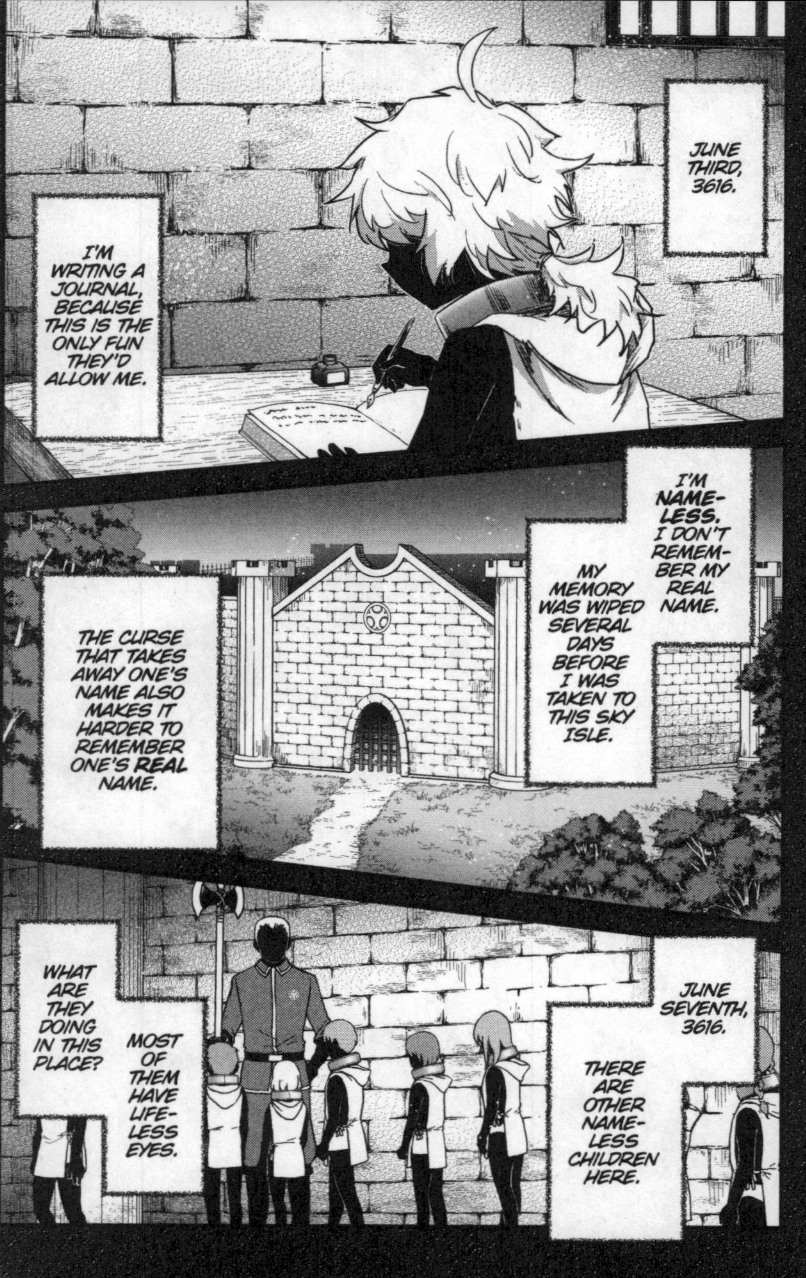
JUNE THIRD, 3616.
I'M WRITING A JOURNAL, BECAUSE THIS IS THE ONLY FUN THEY'D ALLOW ME.
I'M NAMELESS. I DON'T REMEMBER MY REAL NAME.
MY MEMORY WAS WIPED SEVERAL DAYS BEFORE I WAS TAKEN TO THIS SKY ISLE.
THE CURSE THAT TAKES AWAY ONE'S NAME ALSO MAKES IT HARDER TO REMEMBER ONE'S **REAL** NAME.
JUNE SEVENTH, 3616.
THERE ARE OTHER NAMELESS CHILDREN HERE.
MOST OF THEM HAVE LIFELESS EYES.
WHAT ARE THEY DOING IN THIS PLACE?

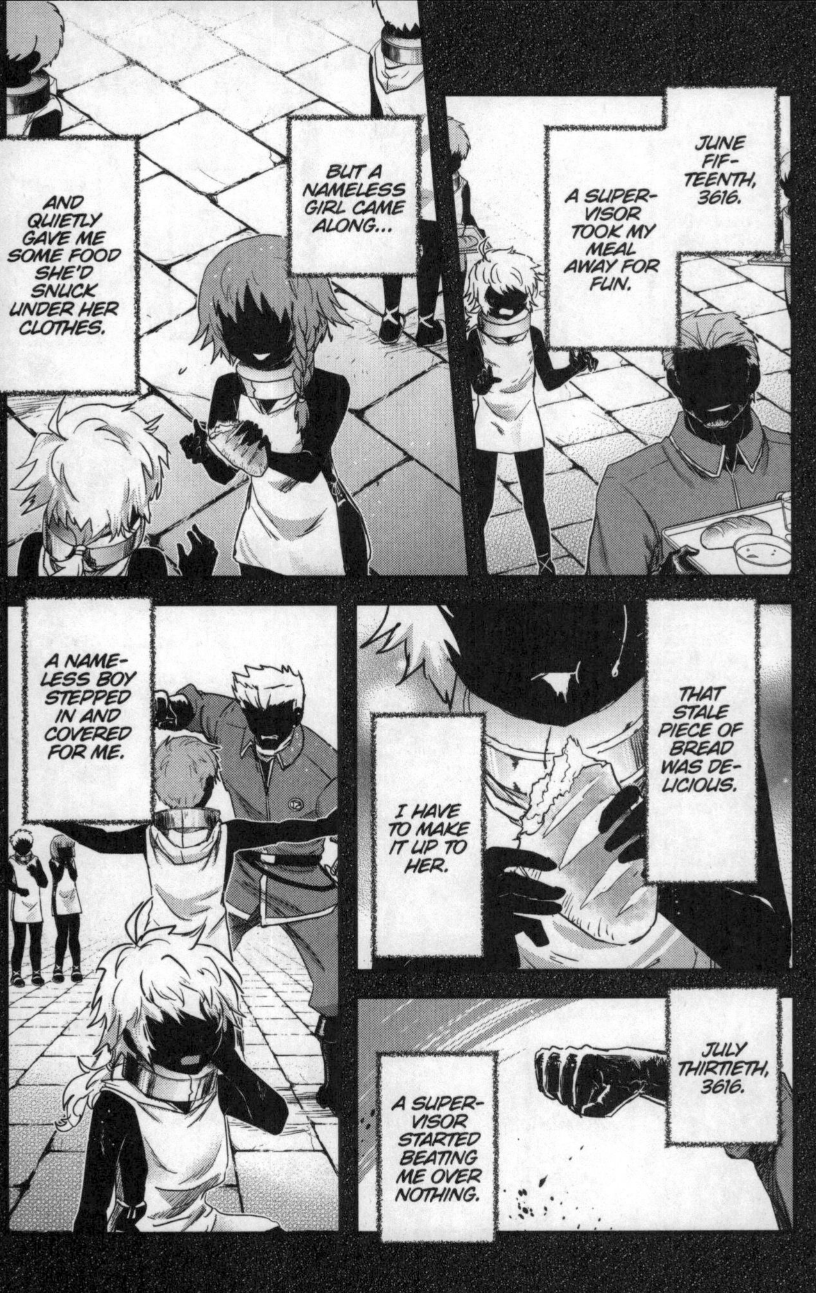
JUNE FIFTEENTH, 3616.
A SUPERVISOR TOOK MY MEAL AWAY FOR FUN.
BUT A NAMELESS GIRL CAME ALONG...
AND QUIETLY GAVE ME SOME FOOD SHE'D SNUCK UNDER HER CLOTHES.
THAT STALE PIECE OF BREAD WAS DELICIOUS.
I HAVE TO MAKE IT UP TO HER.
JULY THIRTIETH, 3616.
A SUPERVISOR STARTED BEATING ME OVER NOTHING.
A NAMELESS BOY STEPPED IN AND COVERED FOR ME.

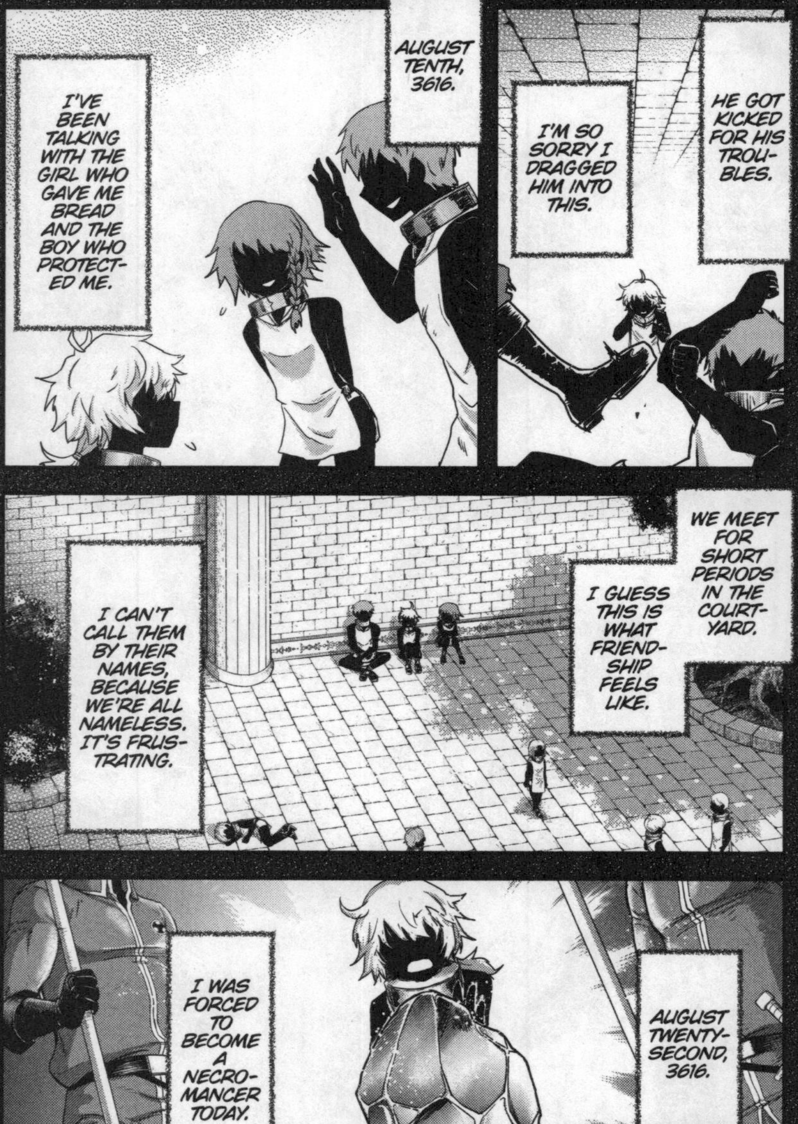
HE GOT KICKED FOR HIS TROUBLES.
I'M SO SORRY I DRAGGED HIM INTO THIS.
AUGUST TENTH, 3616.
I'VE BEEN TALKING WITH THE GIRL WHO GAVE ME BREAD AND THE BOY WHO PROTECTED ME.
WE MEET FOR SHORT PERIODS IN THE COURTYARD.
I GUESS THIS IS WHAT FRIENDSHIP FEELS LIKE.
I CAN'T CALL THEM BY THEIR NAMES, BECAUSE WE'RE ALL NAMELESS. IT'S FRUSTRATING.
AUGUST TWENTY-SECOND, 3616.
I WAS FORCED TO BECOME A NECROMANCER TODAY.

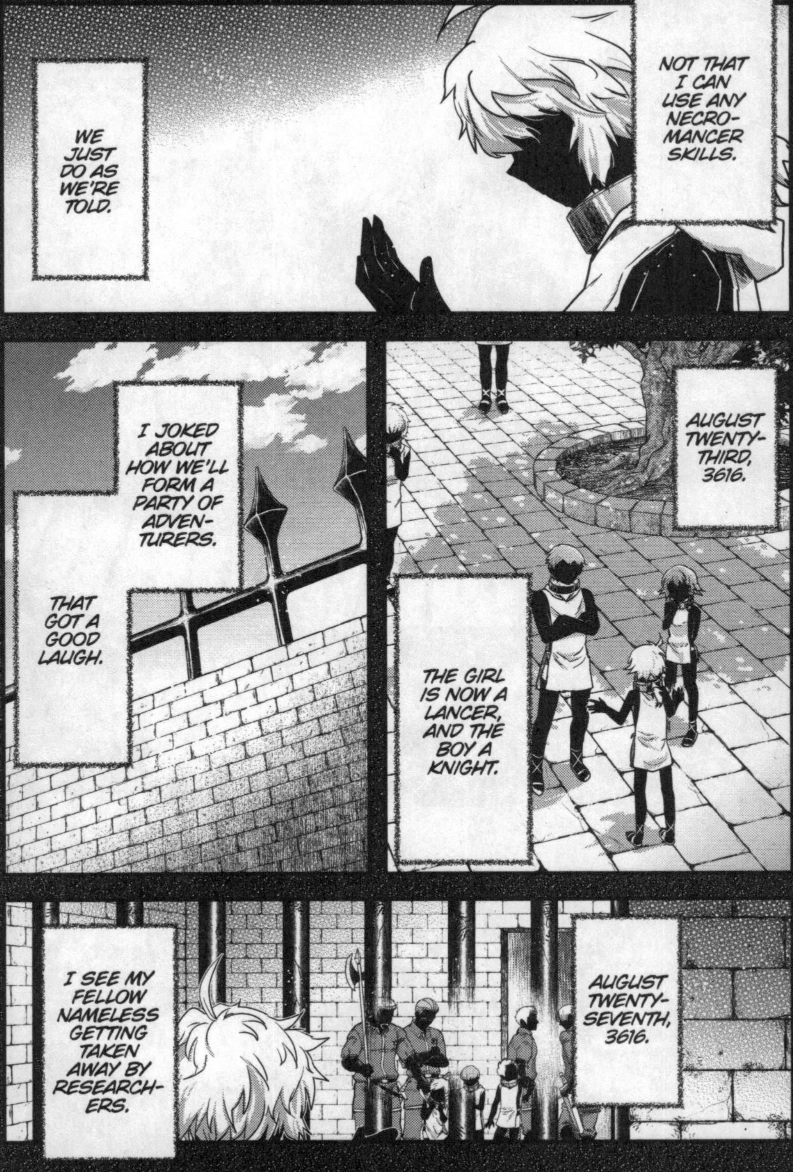
NOT THAT I CAN USE ANY NECRO-MANCER SKILLS.
WE JUST DO AS WE'RE TOLD.
AUGUST TWENTY-THIRD, 3616.
THE GIRL IS NOW A LANCER, AND THE BOY A KNIGHT.
I JOKED ABOUT HOW WE'LL FORM A PARTY OF ADVEN-TURERS.
THAT GOT A GOOD LAUGH.
AUGUST TWENTY-SEVENTH, 3616.
I SEE MY FELLOW NAMELESS GETTING TAKEN AWAY BY RESEARCH-ERS.

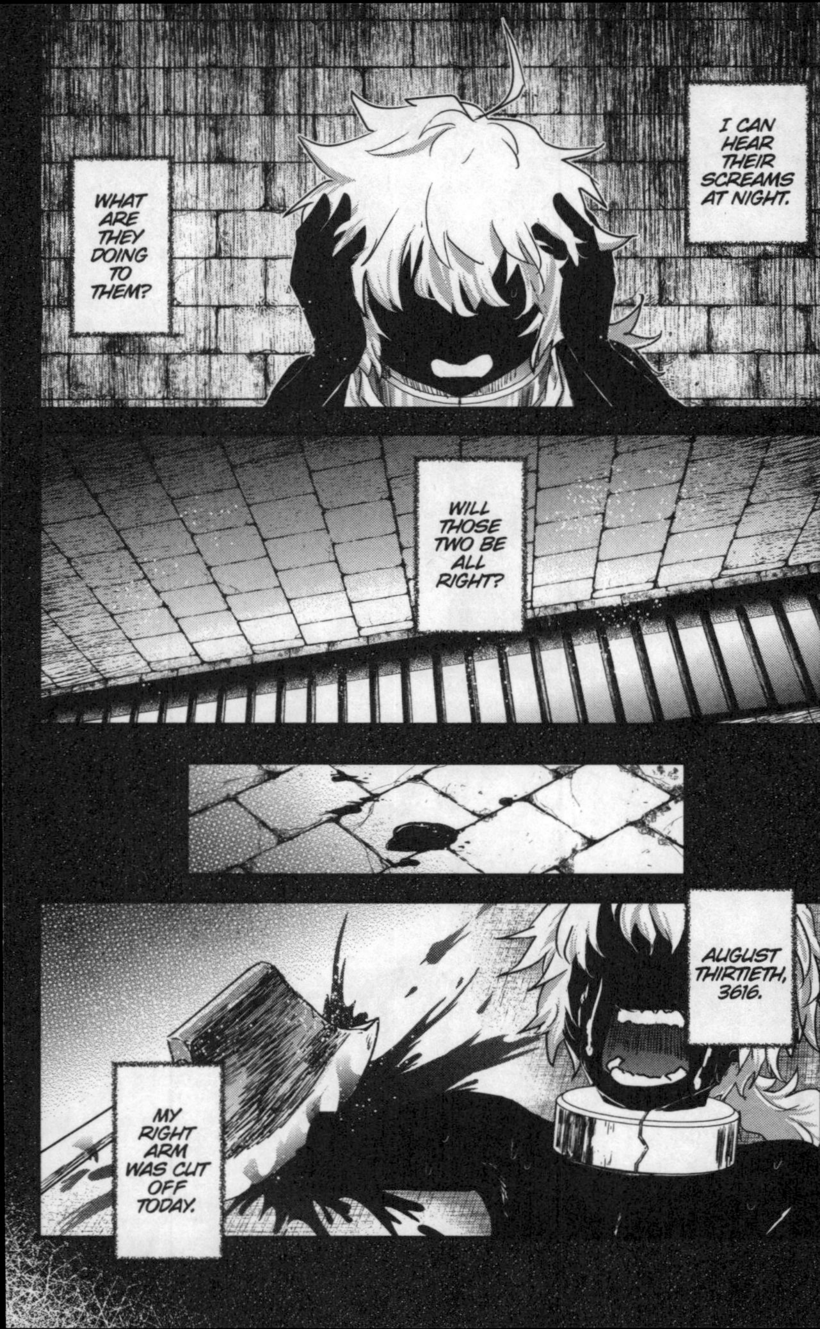
I CAN HEAR THEIR SCREAMS AT NIGHT.
WHAT ARE THEY DOING TO THEM?
WILL THOSE TWO BE ALL RIGHT?
AUGUST THIRTIETH, 3616.
MY RIGHT ARM WAS CUT OFF TODAY.

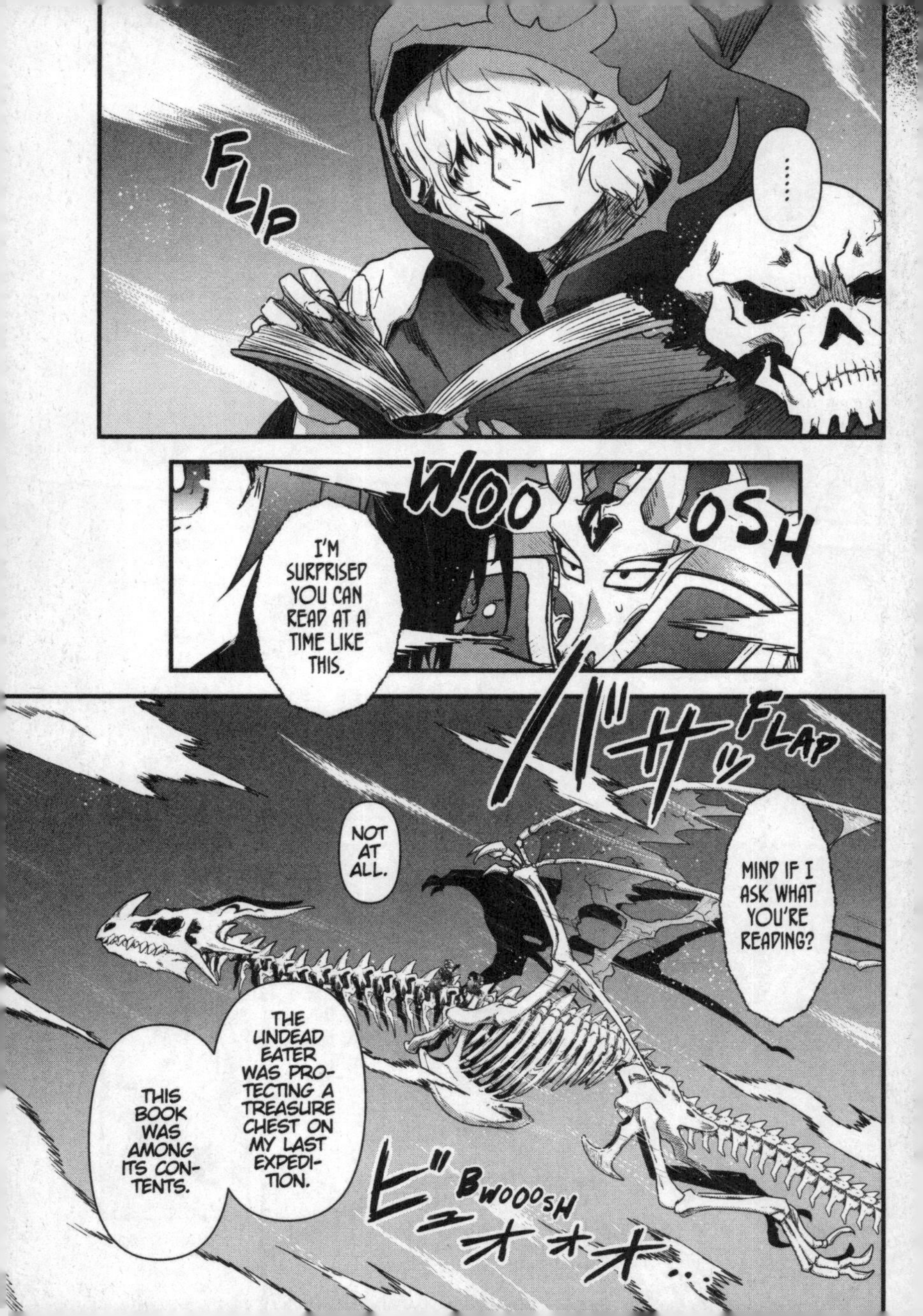
FLIP
......
WOOOSH
I'M SURPRISED YOU CAN READ AT A TIME LIKE THIS.
バサッ
FLAP
MIND IF I ASK WHAT YOU'RE READING?
NOT AT ALL.
THE UNDEAD EATER WAS PRO-TECTING A TREASURE CHEST ON MY LAST EXPEDI-TION.
THIS BOOK WAS AMONG ITS CON-TENTS.
ビュオオオ...
BWOOOSH

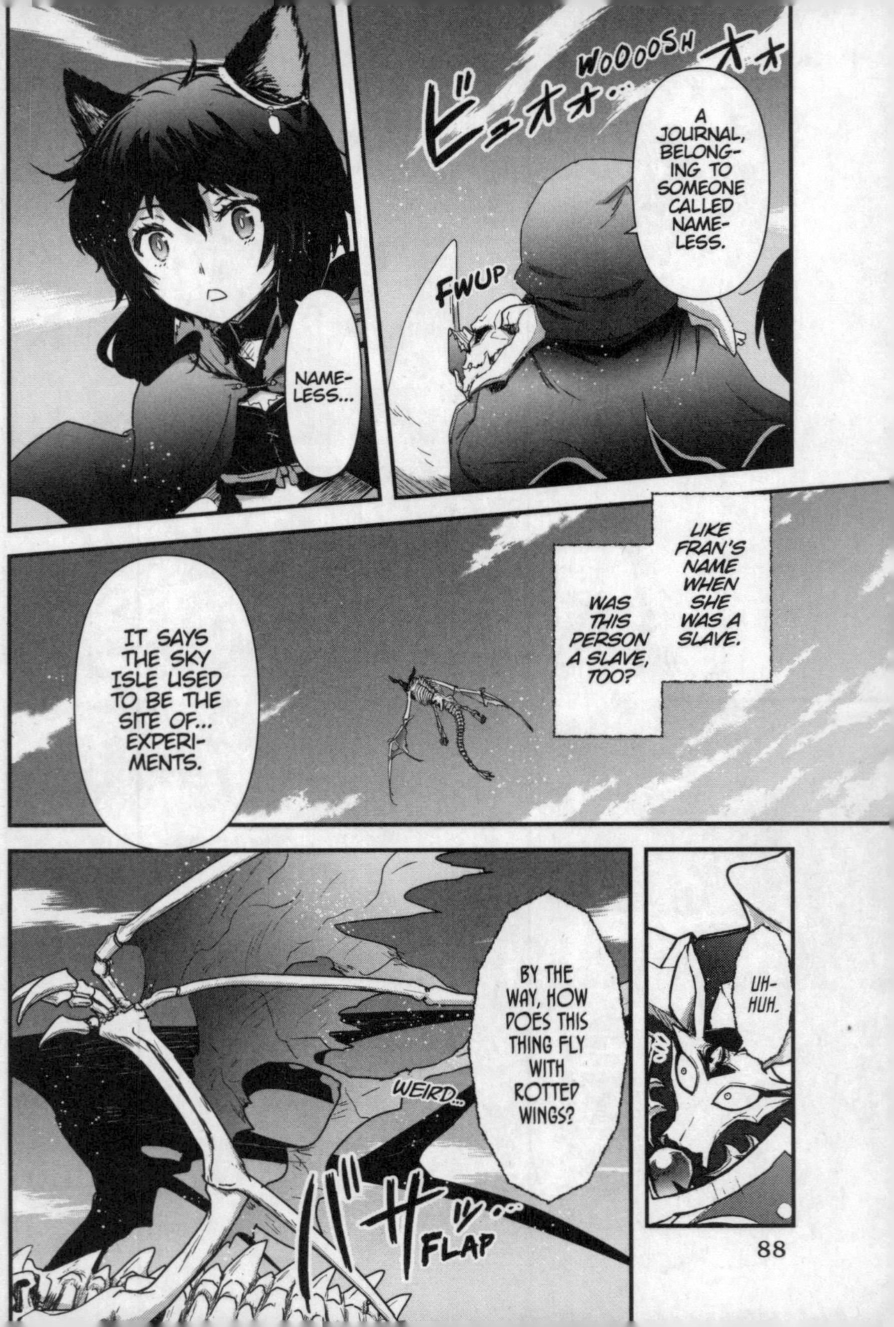
ビュオオ…オォ
WOOOOSH
A JOURNAL, BELONGING TO SOMEONE CALLED NAMELESS.
FWUP
NAME-LESS...
LIKE FRAN'S NAME WHEN SHE WAS A SLAVE.
WAS THIS PERSON A SLAVE, TOO?
IT SAYS THE SKY ISLE USED TO BE THE SITE OF... EXPERIMENTS.
UH-HUH.
BY THE WAY, HOW DOES THIS THING FLY WITH ROTTED WINGS?
WEIRD...
バサッ…
FLAP

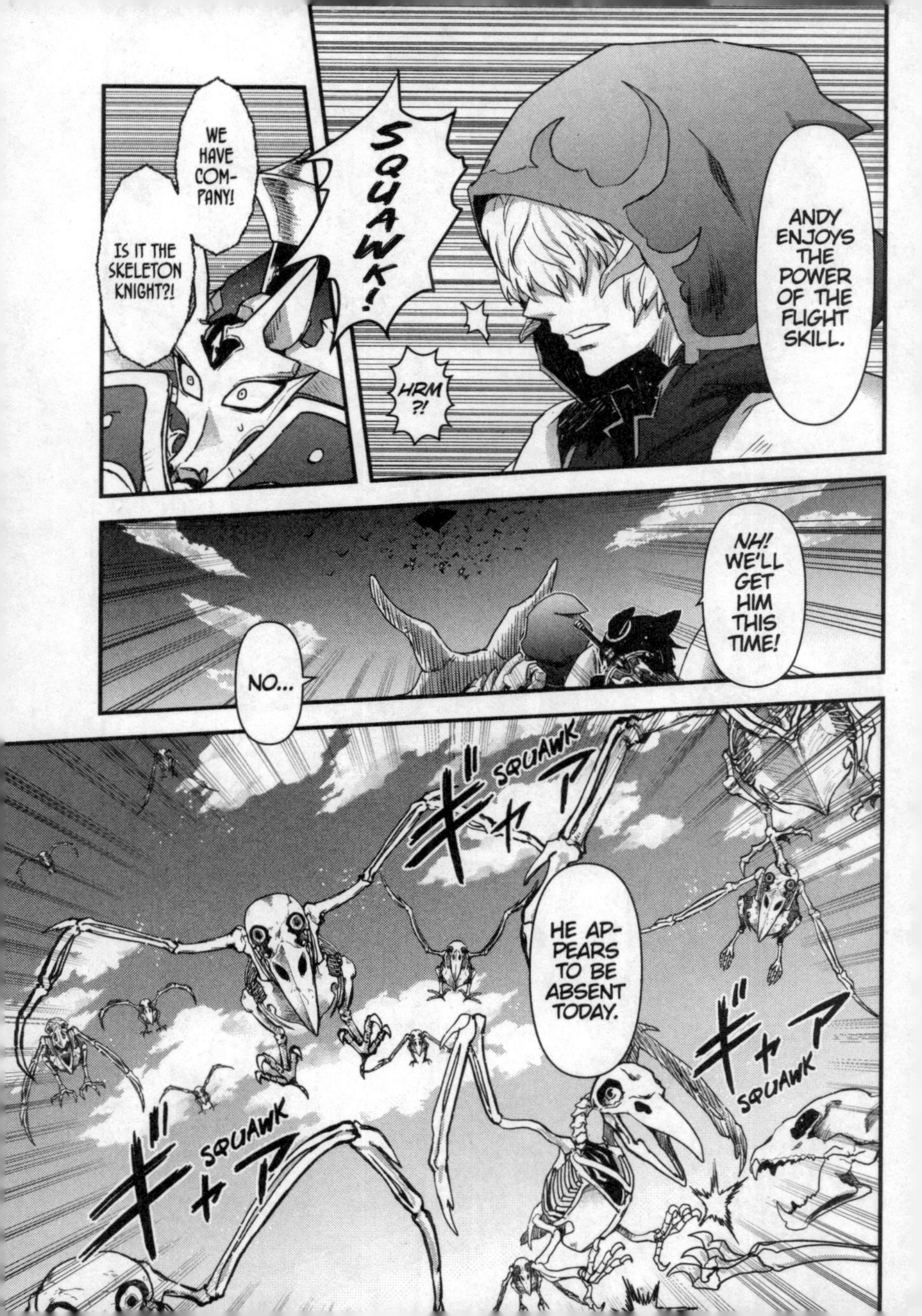
ANDY ENJOYS THE POWER OF THE FLIGHT SKILL.
HRM ?!
SQUAWK!
WE HAVE COM-PANY!
IS IT THE SKELETON KNIGHT?!
NH! WE'LL GET HIM THIS TIME!
NO...
HE AP-PEARS TO BE ABSENT TODAY.
SQUAWK
SQUAWK
SQUAWK

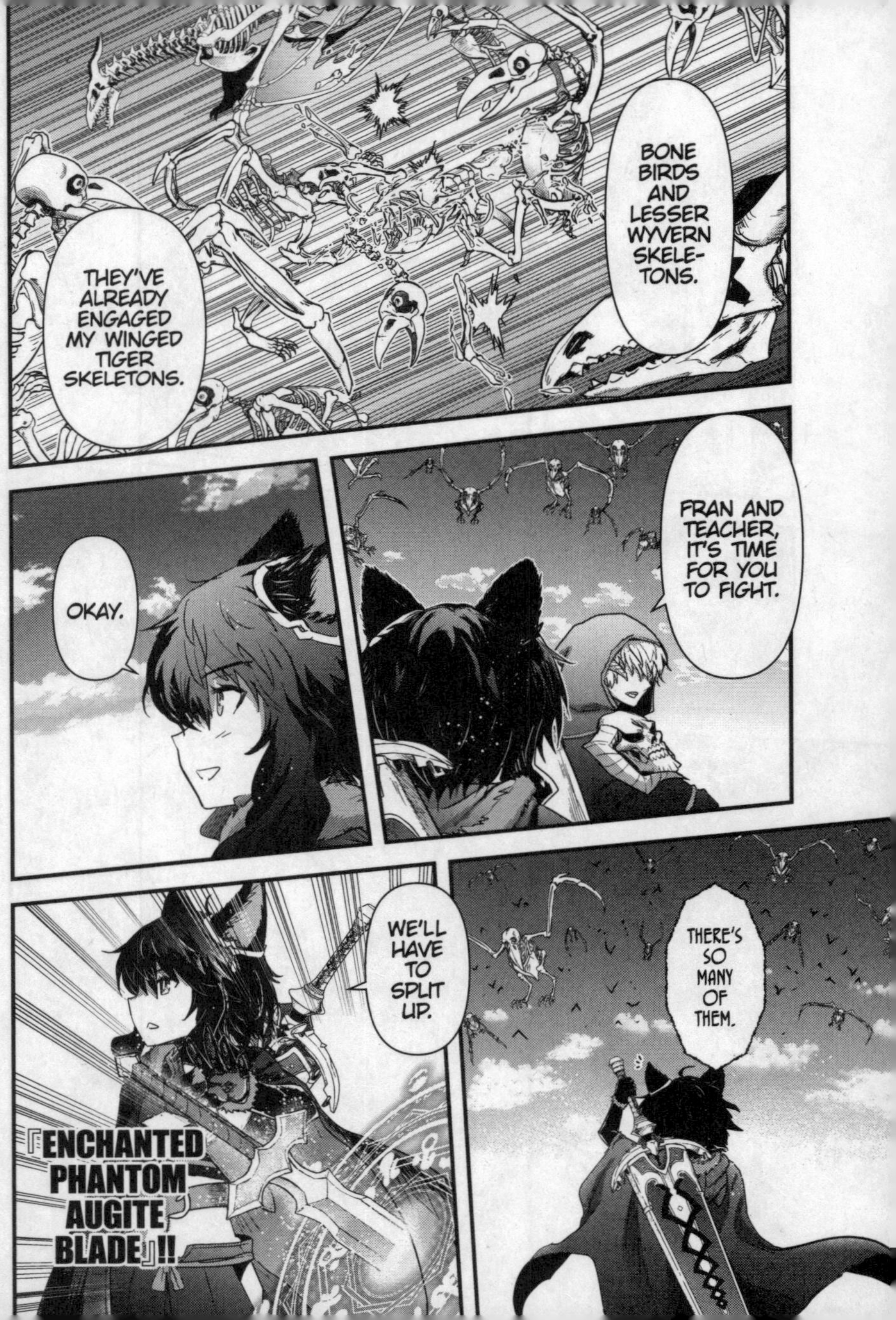
BONE BIRDS AND LESSER WYVERN SKELETONS.
THEY'VE ALREADY ENGAGED MY WINGED TIGER SKELETONS.
FRAN AND TEACHER, IT'S TIME FOR YOU TO FIGHT.
OKAY.
THERE'S SO MANY OF THEM.
WE'LL HAVE TO SPLIT UP.
『ENCHANTED PHANTOM AUGITE BLADE』!!

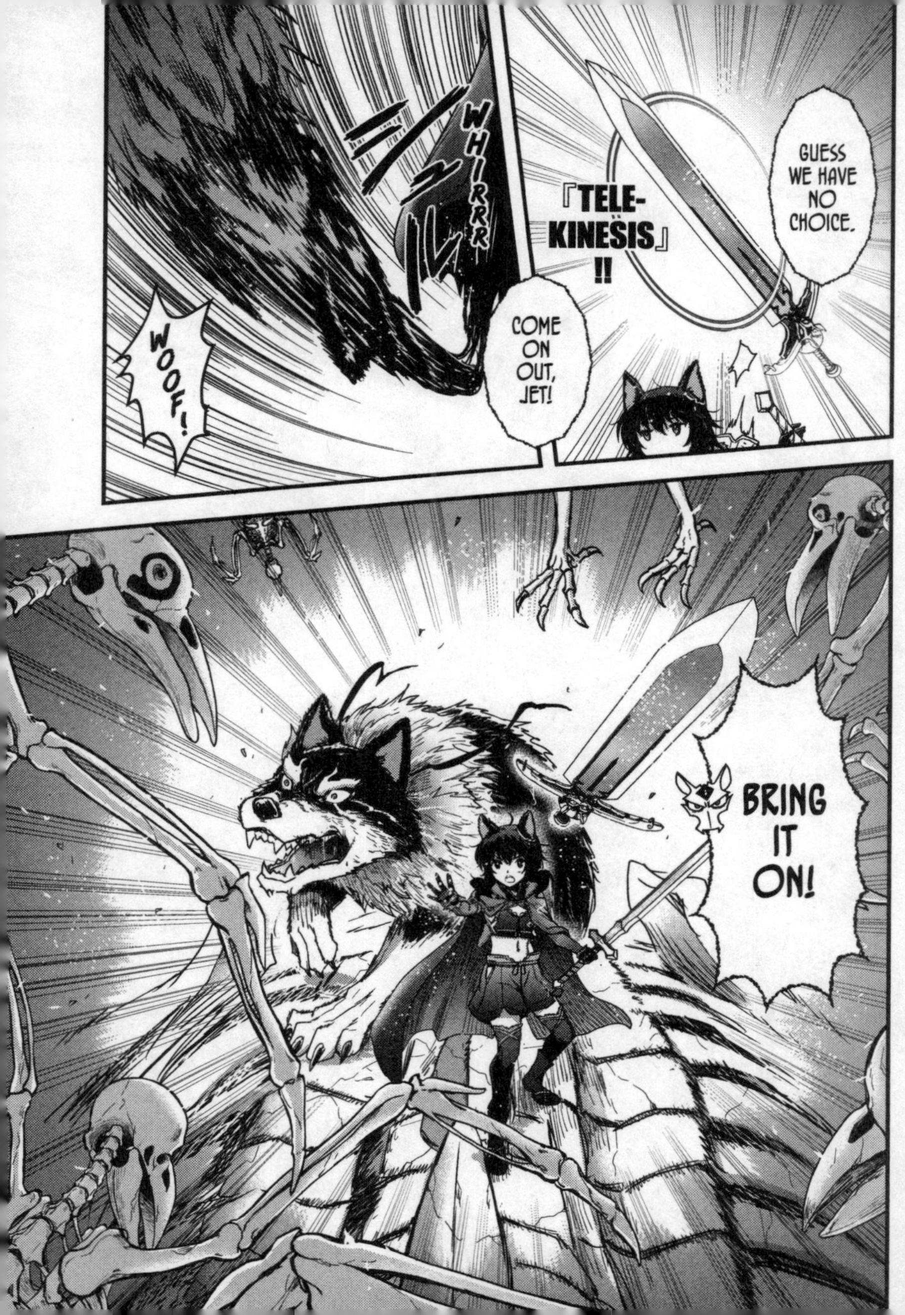
GUESS WE HAVE NO CHOICE.
『TELE-KINESIS』!!
COME ON OUT, JET!
WHIRRR
WOOF!
BRING IT ON!

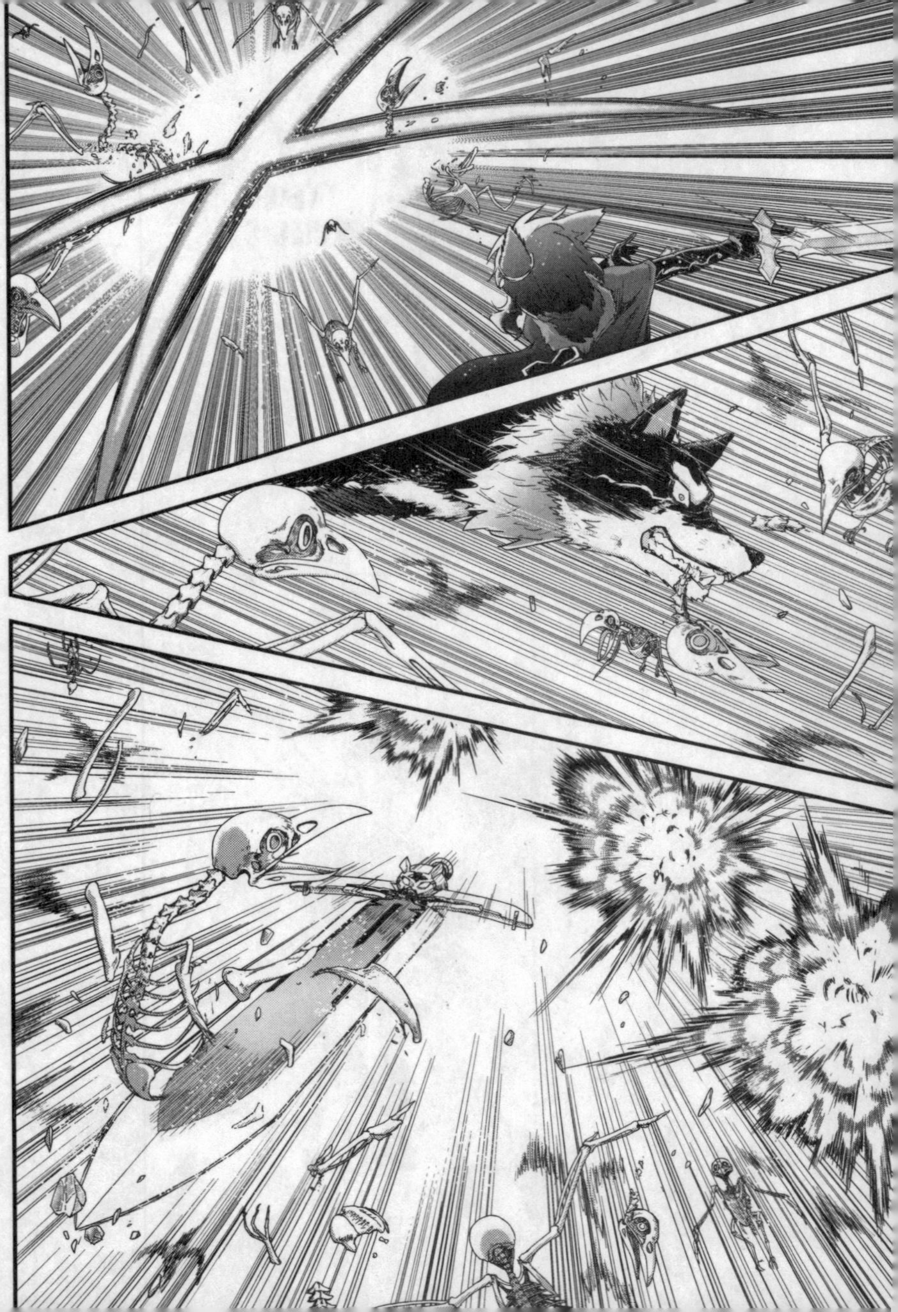

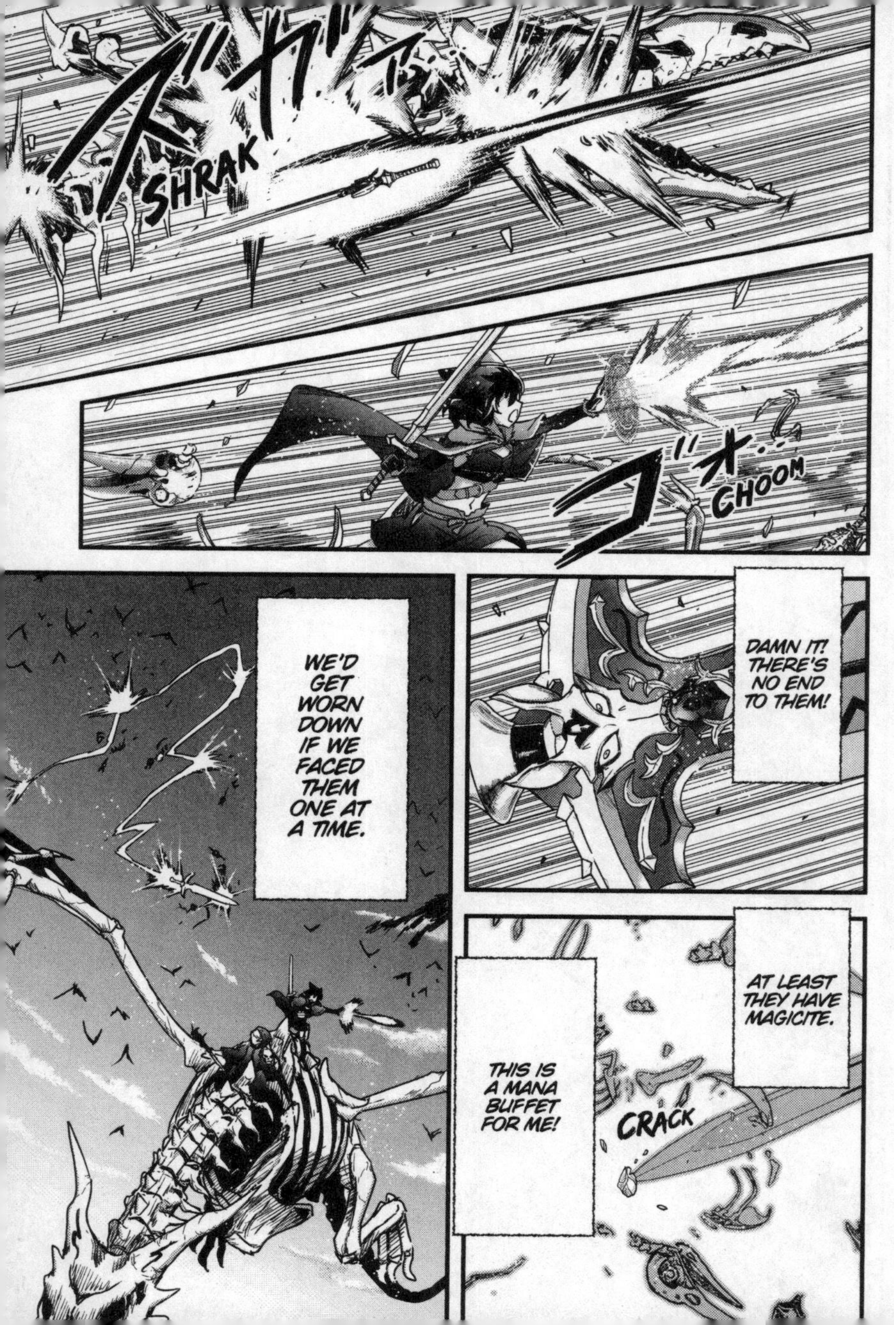
SHRAK
CHOOM
DAMN IT! THERE'S NO END TO THEM!
AT LEAST THEY HAVE MAGICITE.
THIS IS A MANA BUFFET FOR ME!
CRACK
WE'D GET WORN DOWN IF WE FACED THEM ONE AT A TIME.

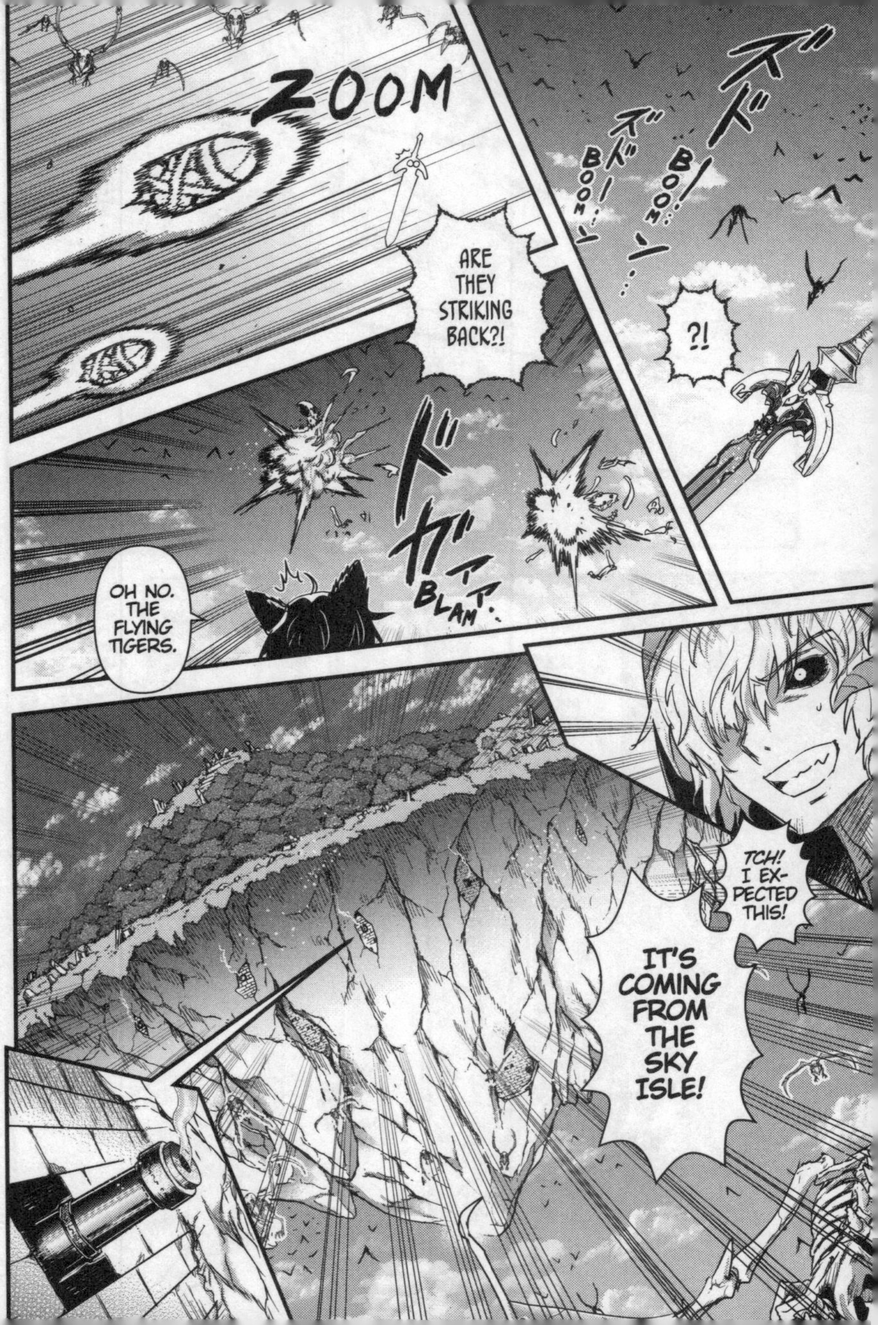
BOOM...
BOOM...
?!
ZOOM
ARE THEY STRIKING BACK?!
BLAM...
OH NO. THE FLYING TIGERS.
TCH! I EXPECTED THIS!
IT'S COMING FROM THE SKY ISLE!

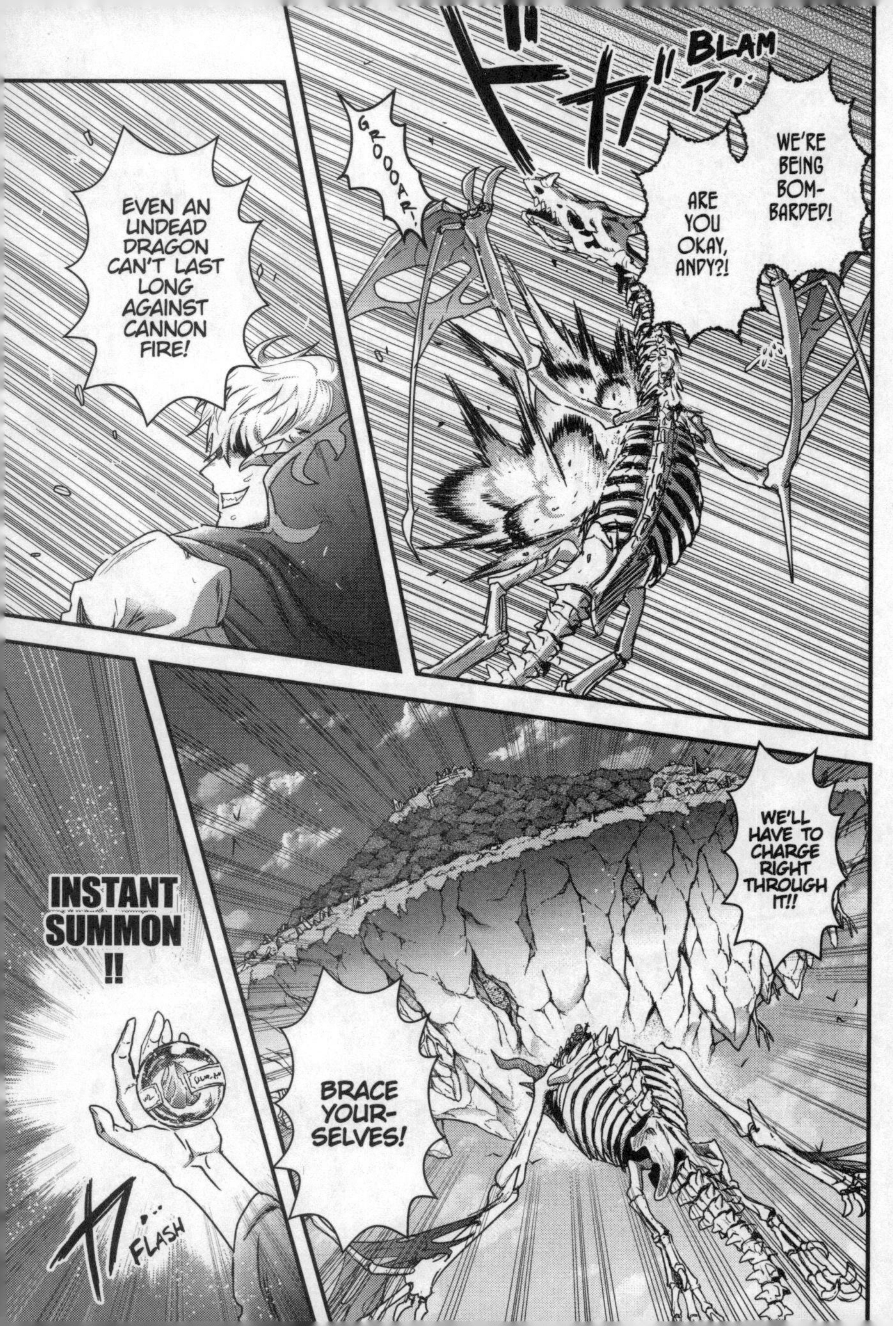
BLAM
WE'RE BEING BOM-BARDED!
ARE YOU OKAY, ANDY?!
GROOOAR!
EVEN AN UNDEAD DRAGON CAN'T LAST LONG AGAINST CANNON FIRE!
WE'LL HAVE TO CHARGE RIGHT THROUGH IT!!
BRACE YOUR-SELVES!
INSTANT SUMMON !!
FLASH

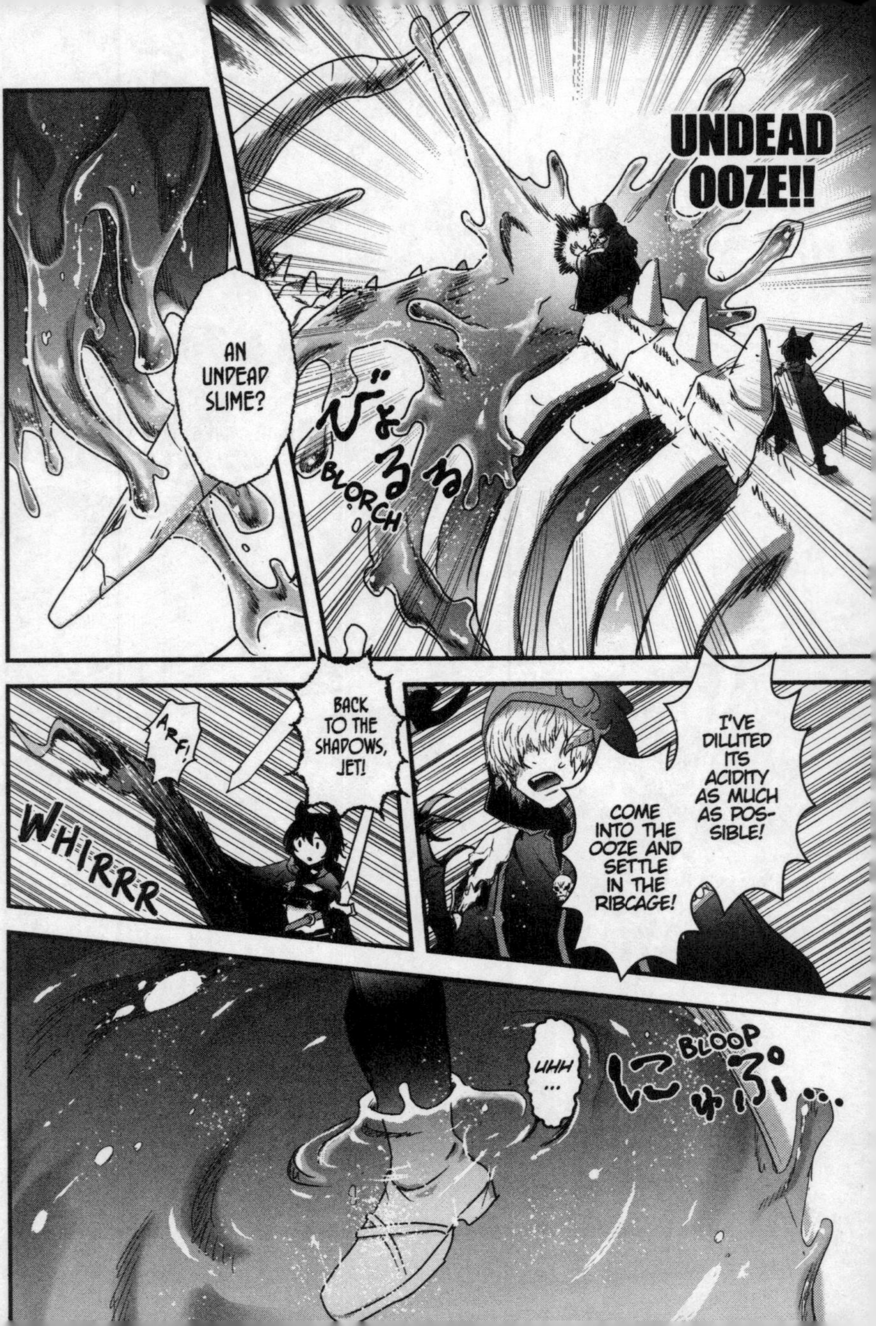
UNDEAD OOZE!!
びよるる
BLORCH
AN UNDEAD SLIME?
I'VE DILLUTED ITS ACIDITY AS MUCH AS POS-SIBLE!
COME INTO THE OOZE AND SETTLE IN THE RIBCAGE!
BACK TO THE SHADOWS, JET!
ARF!
WHIRRR
にゅぷ…
BLOOP
UHH...

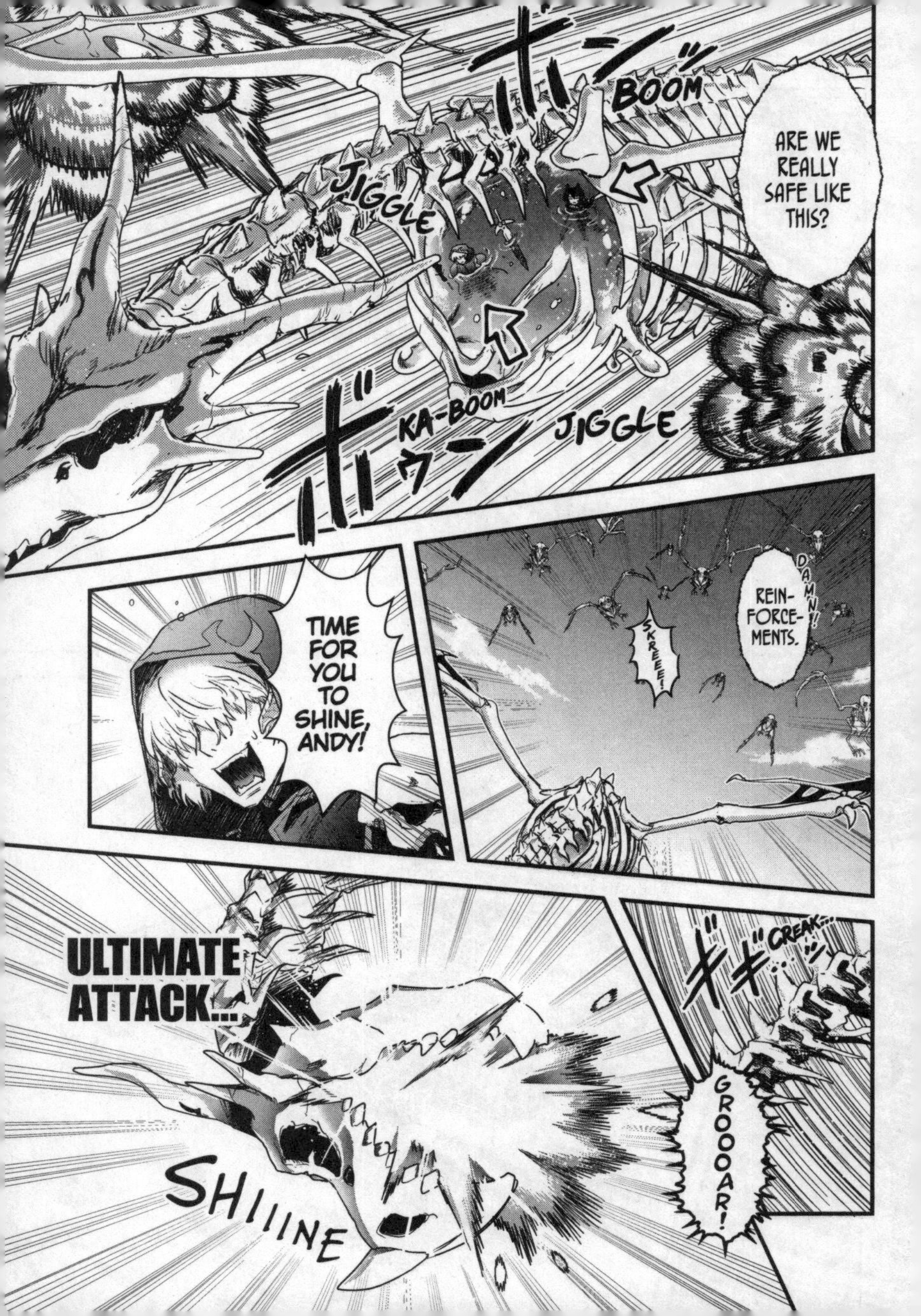
BOOM
ARE WE REALLY SAFE LIKE THIS?
JIGGLE
KA-BOOM
JIGGLE
DAMN!
REIN-FORCEMENTS.
SKREEEE!
TIME FOR YOU TO SHINE, ANDY!
CREAK...
ULTIMATE ATTACK...
GROOOAR!
SHIIINE

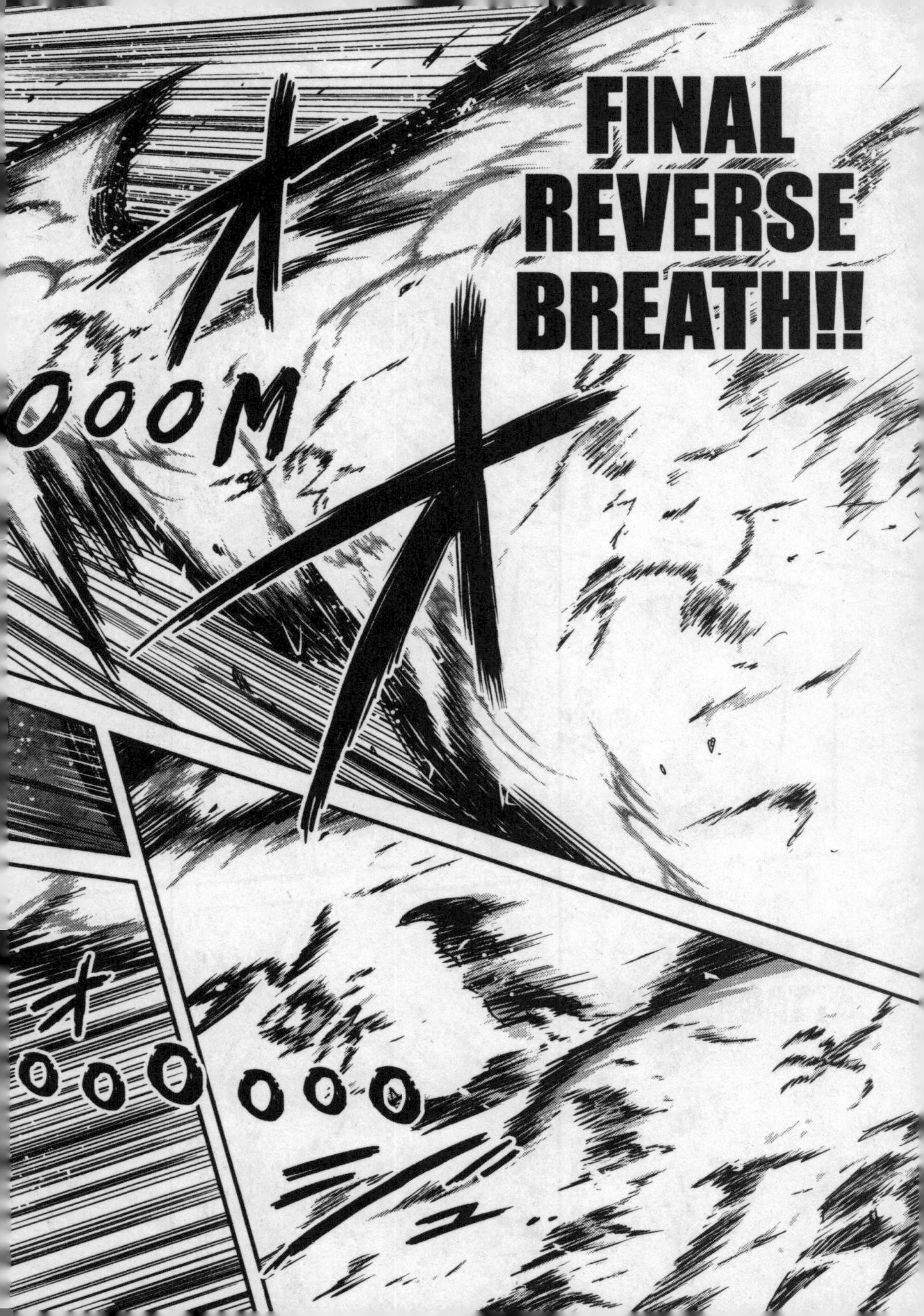
FINAL REVERSE BREATH!!
OOOM
OOOOOO...

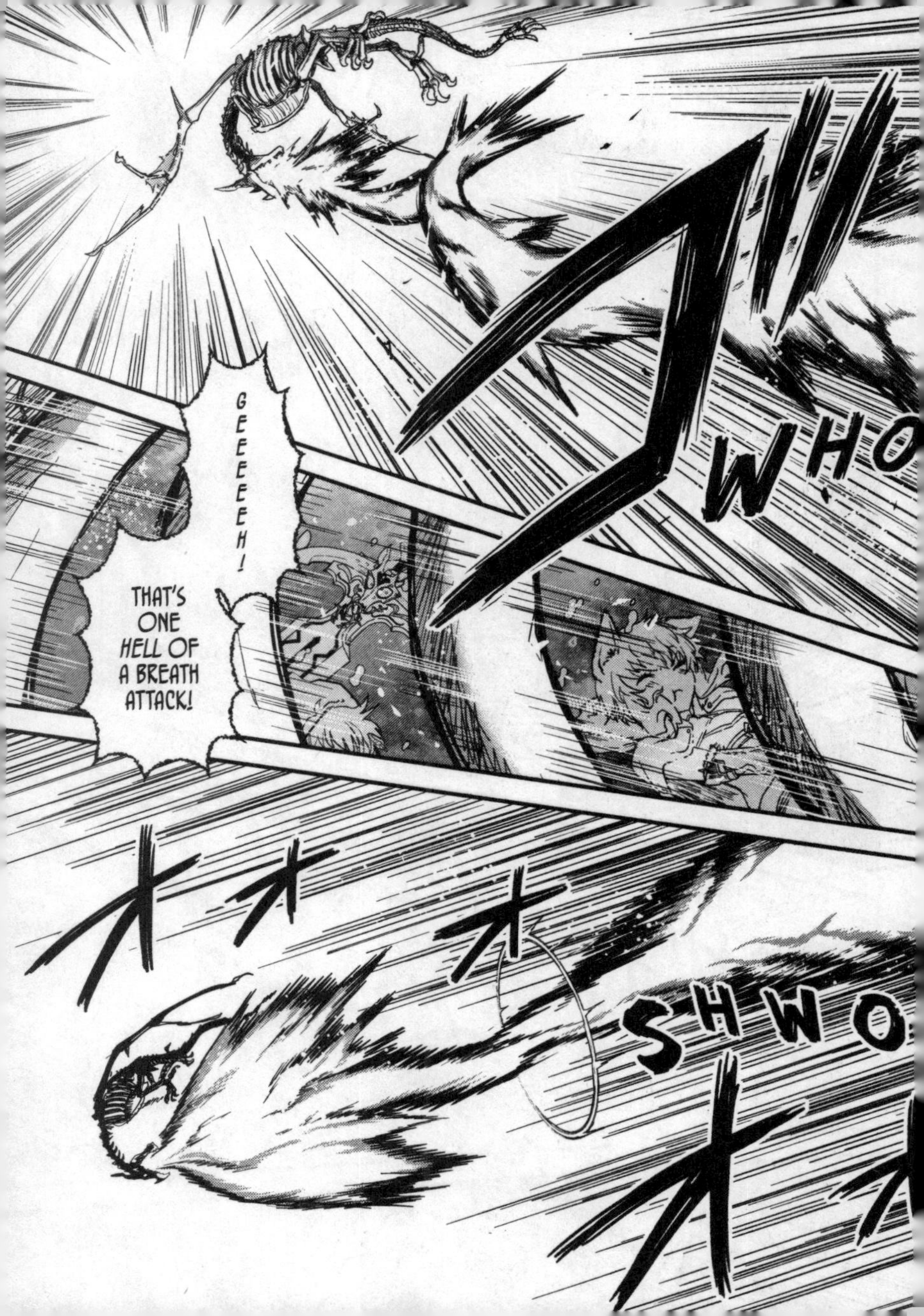
WHO
GEEEEEEH!
THAT'S ONE *HELL* OF A BREATH ATTACK!
SHWO

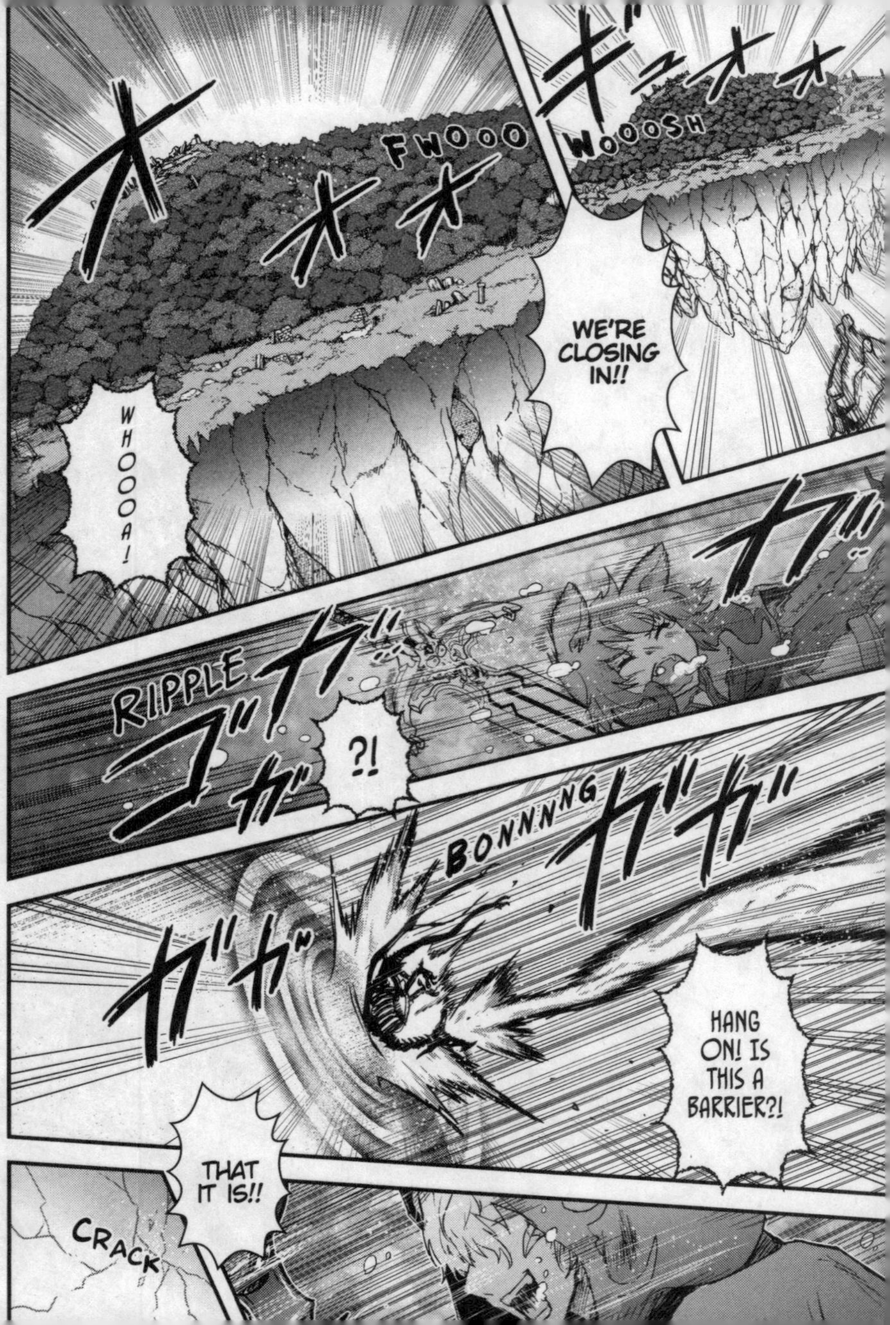
ギュオオ
WOOOSH
WE'RE CLOSING IN!!
オオオオ
FWOOO
WHOOOOA!
ブ
RIPPLE
ゴガ
?!
BONNNNG
ガガガ
ガガ
HANG ON! IS THIS A BARRIER?!
THAT IT IS!!
CRACK

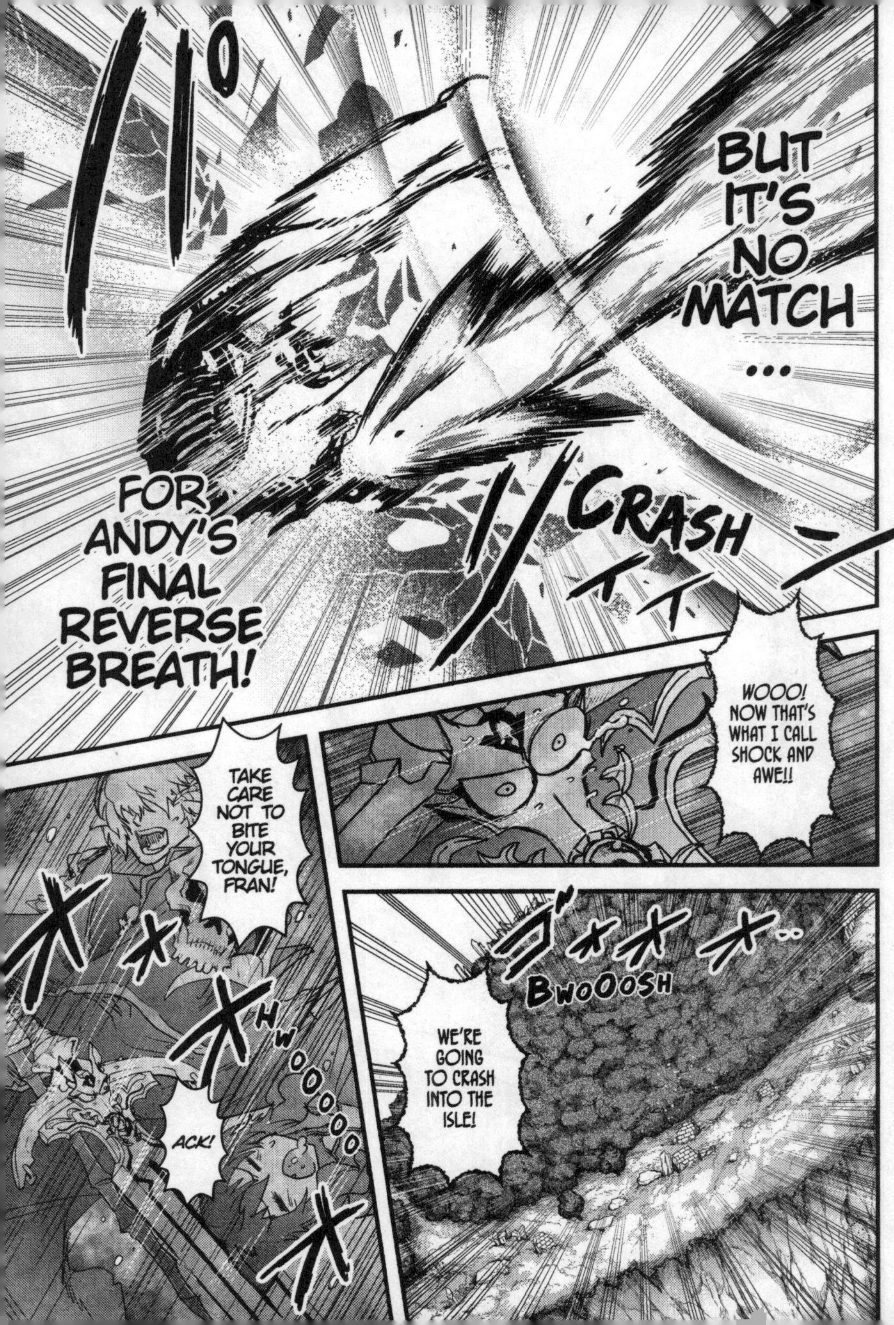
BUT IT'S NO MATCH...
CRASH
FOR ANDY'S FINAL REVERSE BREATH!
WOOO! NOW THAT'S WHAT I CALL SHOCK AND AWE!!
BWOOOSH
WE'RE GOING TO CRASH INTO THE ISLE!
TAKE CARE NOT TO BITE YOUR TONGUE, FRAN!
HWOOOOOOO
ACK!

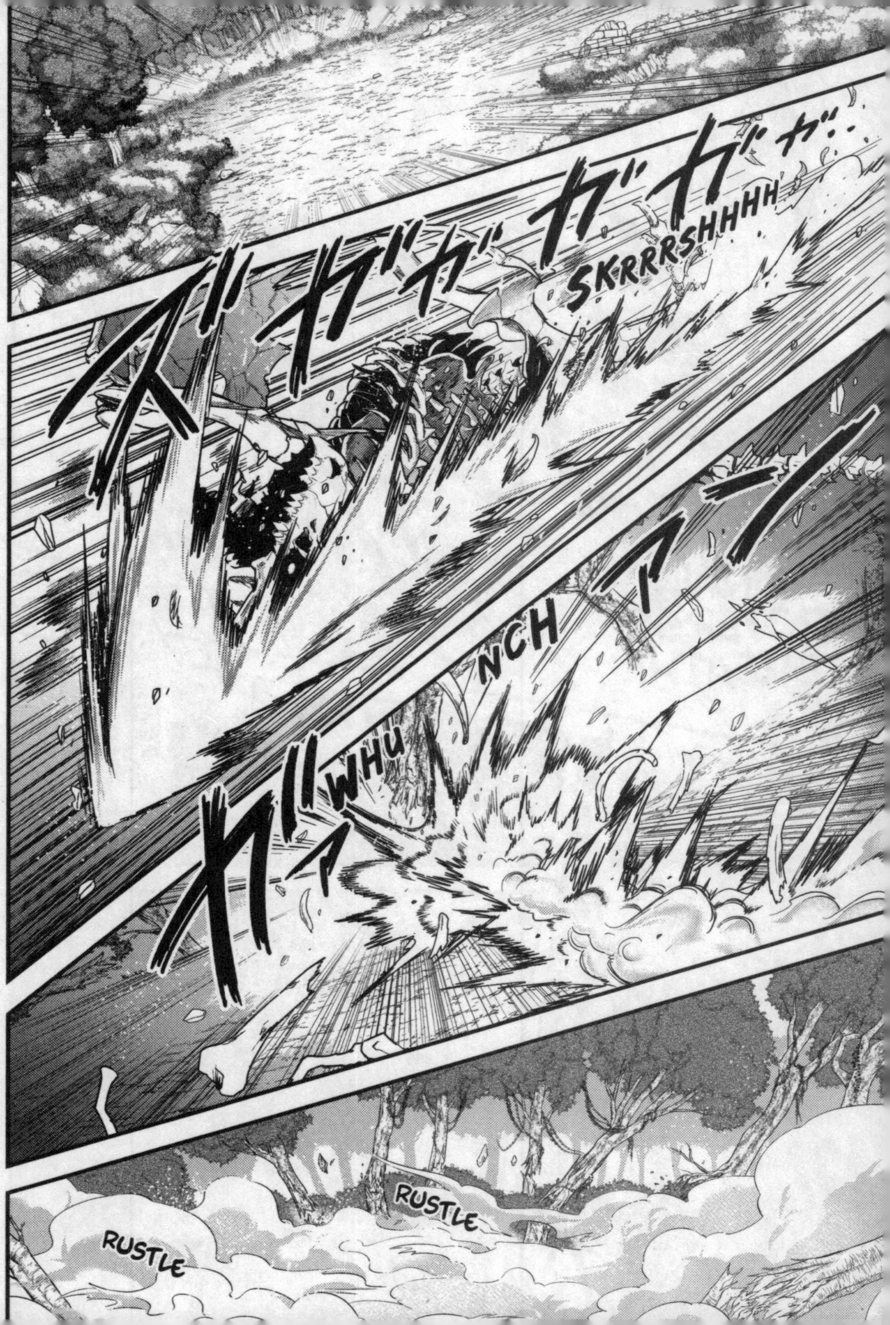
SKRRRSHHHH
WHUNCH
RUSTLE
RUSTLE

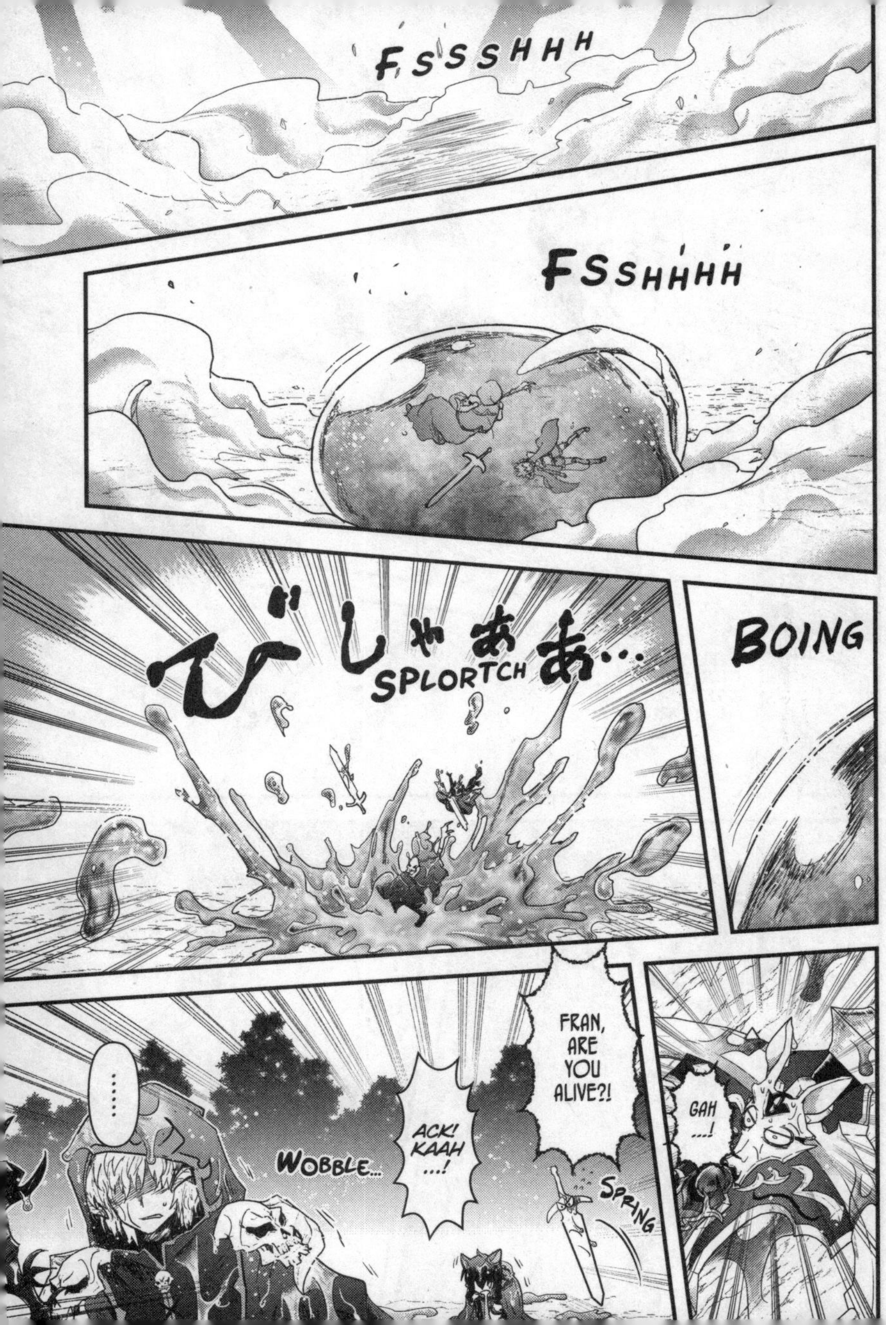

FSSSHHH
FSSHHHH
BOING
びしゃぁあ…
SPLORTCH
GAH...!
FRAN, ARE YOU ALIVE?!
ACK! KAAH...!
SPRING
WOBBLE...
......

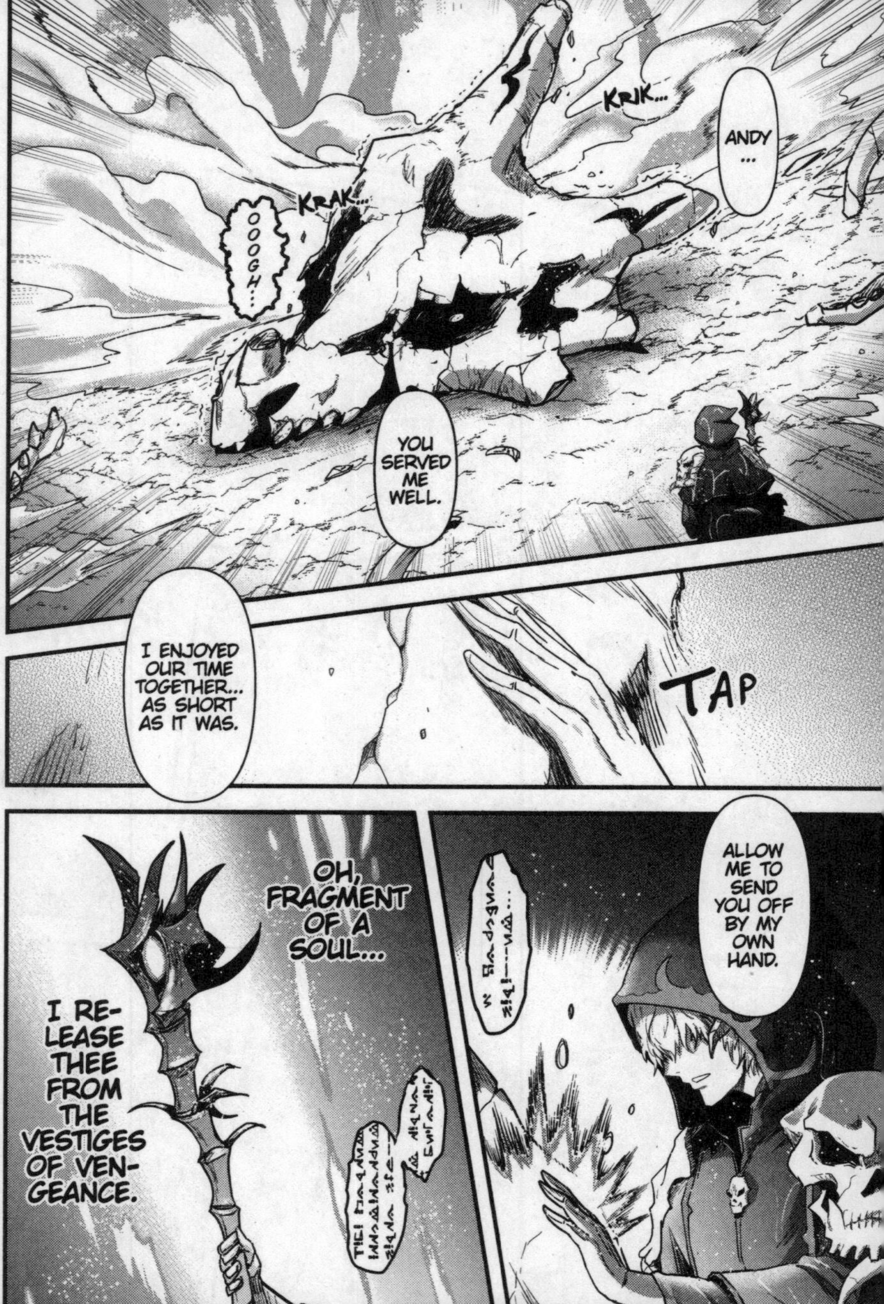
KRIK...
ANDY...
KRAK...
OOOGH...
YOU SERVED ME WELL.
TAP
I ENJOYED OUR TIME TOGETHER... AS SHORT AS IT WAS.
ALLOW ME TO SEND YOU OFF BY MY OWN HAND.
OH, FRAGMENT OF A SOUL...
I RE-LEASE THEE FROM THE VESTIGES OF VEN-GEANCE.

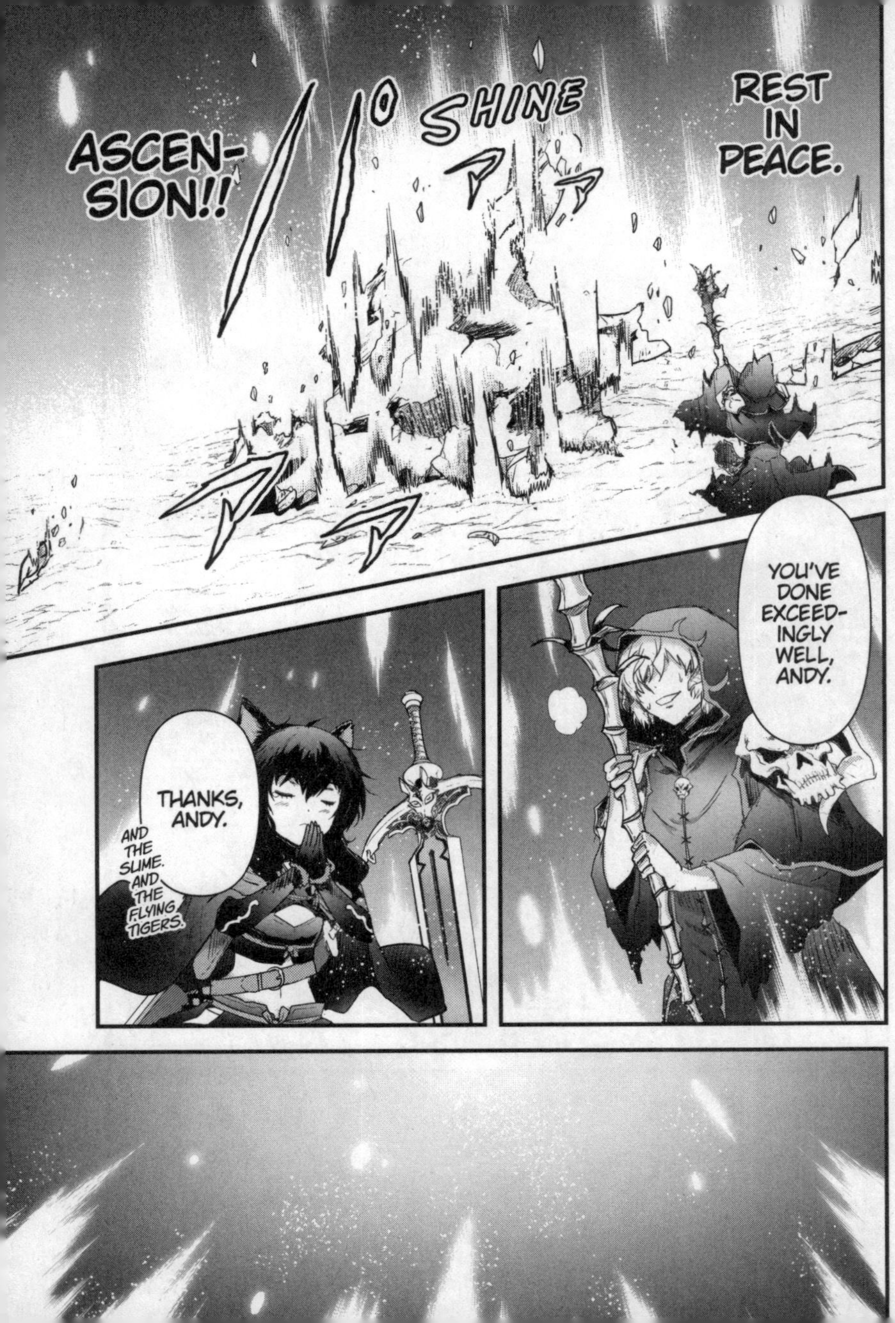
REST IN PEACE.
O SHINE
ASCEN-SION!!
YOU'VE DONE EXCEEDINGLY WELL, ANDY.
THANKS, ANDY.
AND THE SLIME. AND THE FLYING TIGERS.

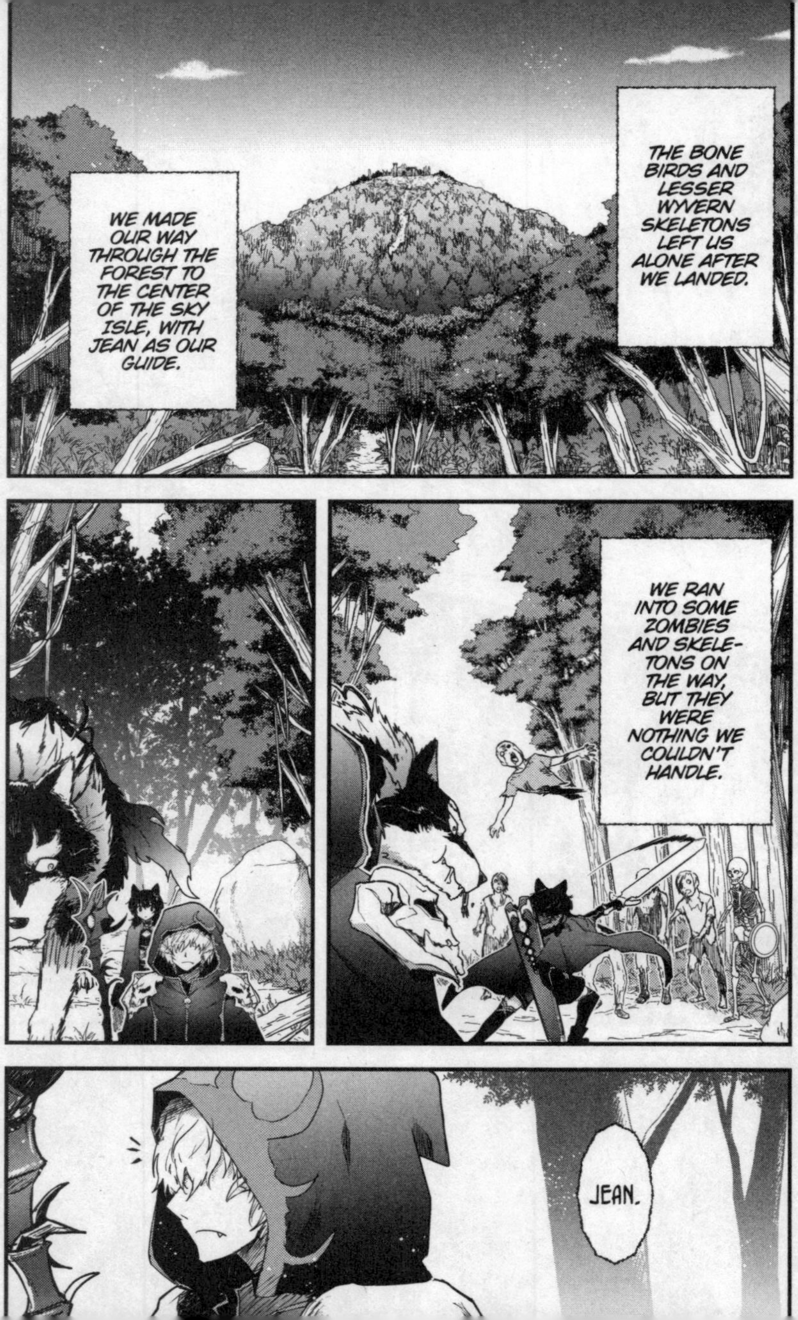
THE BONE BIRDS AND LESSER WYVERN SKELETONS LEFT US ALONE AFTER WE LANDED.
WE MADE OUR WAY THROUGH THE FOREST TO THE CENTER OF THE SKY ISLE, WITH JEAN AS OUR GUIDE.
WE RAN INTO SOME ZOMBIES AND SKELE-TONS ON THE WAY, BUT THEY WERE NOTHING WE COULDN'T HANDLE.
JEAN.

I HAVE A REQUEST ABOUT THE DUNGEON SPOILS.

I'D LIKE IT IF WE COULD KEEP ANY MAGICITE WE FIND. YOU CAN TAKE IT OUT OF OUR PAY, IF YOU WANT.

CERTAIN-LY. BUT WHAT WILL YOU USE IT FOR?

I'D LIKE TO KEEP SOME CARDS UP MY SLEEVE.

UHHH...

WHAT SHOULD I TELL HIM?

......

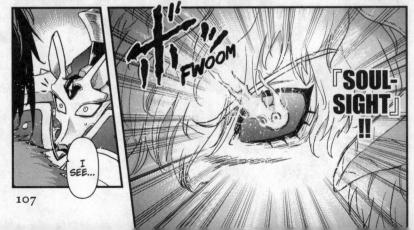

I SEE...

FWOOM

『SOUL-SIGHT』!!

107

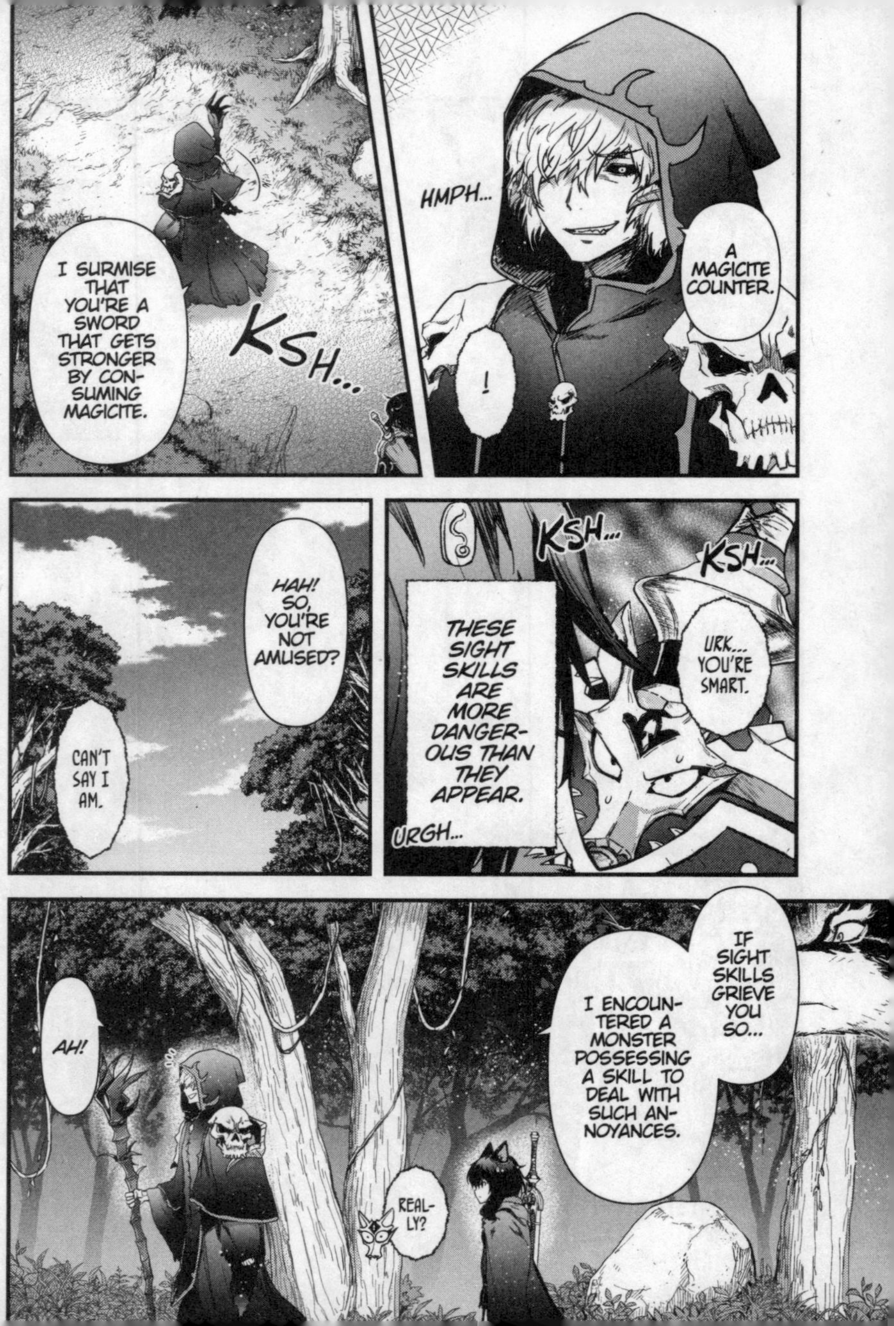
HMPH...
A MAGICITE COUNTER.
!
I SURMISE THAT YOU'RE A SWORD THAT GETS STRONGER BY CONSUMING MAGICITE.
KSH...
KSH...
KSH...
URK... YOU'RE SMART.
THESE SIGHT SKILLS ARE MORE DANGEROUS THAN THEY APPEAR.
URGH...
HAH! SO, YOU'RE NOT AMUSED?
CAN'T SAY I AM.
IF SIGHT SKILLS GRIEVE YOU SO...
I ENCOUNTERED A MONSTER POSSESSING A SKILL TO DEAL WITH SUCH ANNOYANCES.
AH!
REALLY?

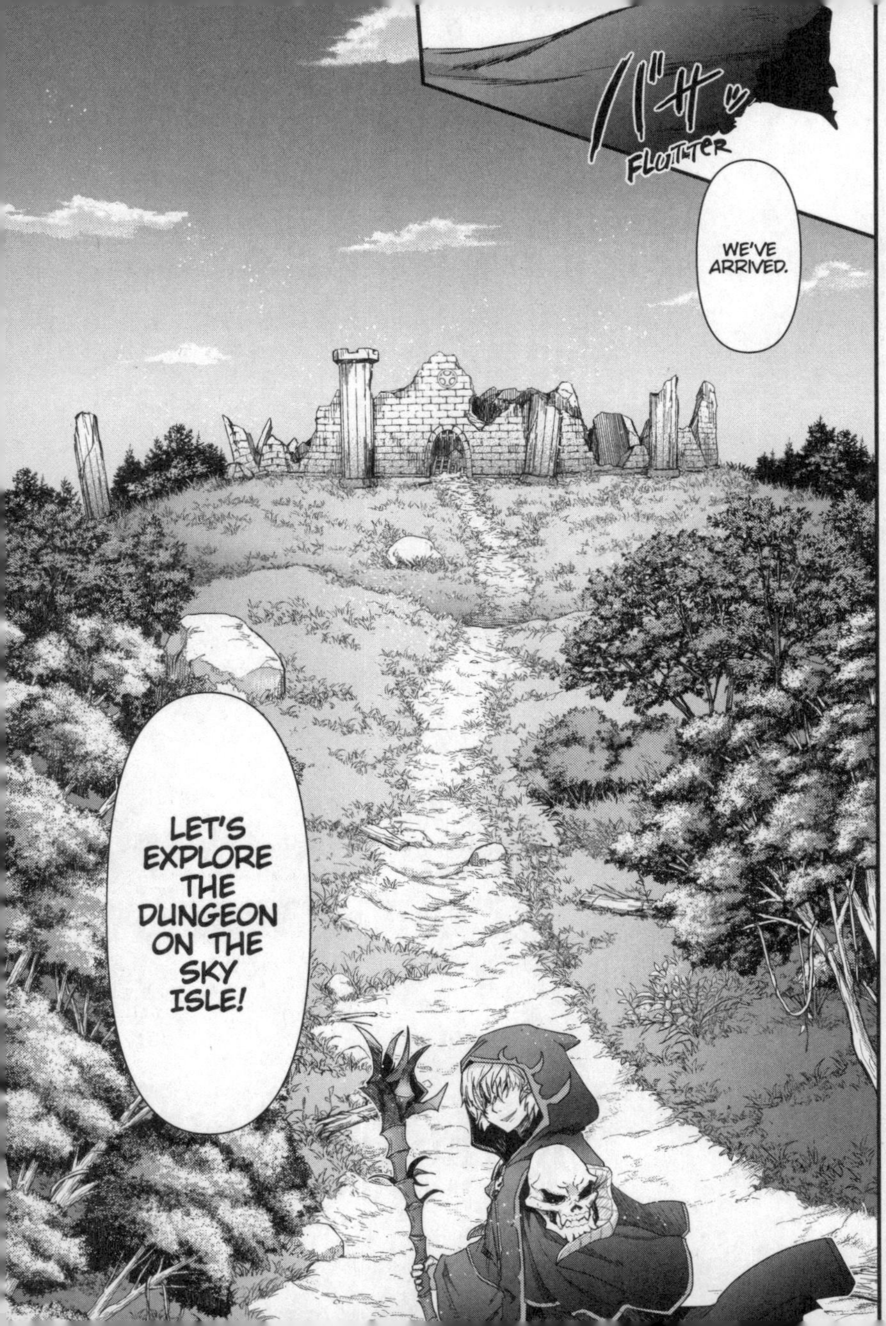
バサッ
FLUTTER
WE'VE ARRIVED.
LET'S EXPLORE THE DUNGEON ON THE SKY ISLE!

Reincarnated
as a sword

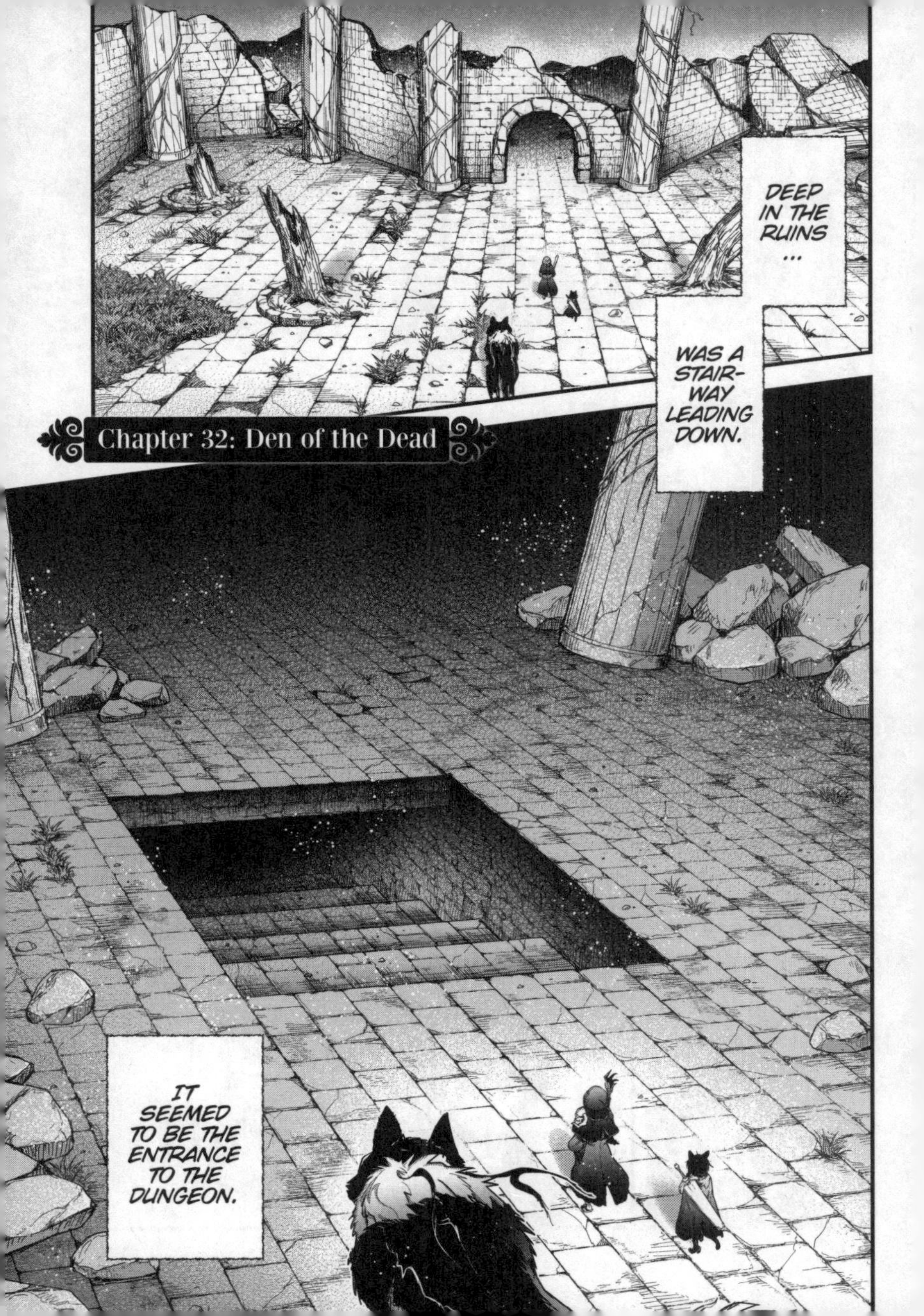
DEEP IN THE RUINS ...
WAS A STAIRWAY LEADING DOWN.
Chapter 32: Den of the Dead
IT SEEMED TO BE THE ENTRANCE TO THE DUNGEON.

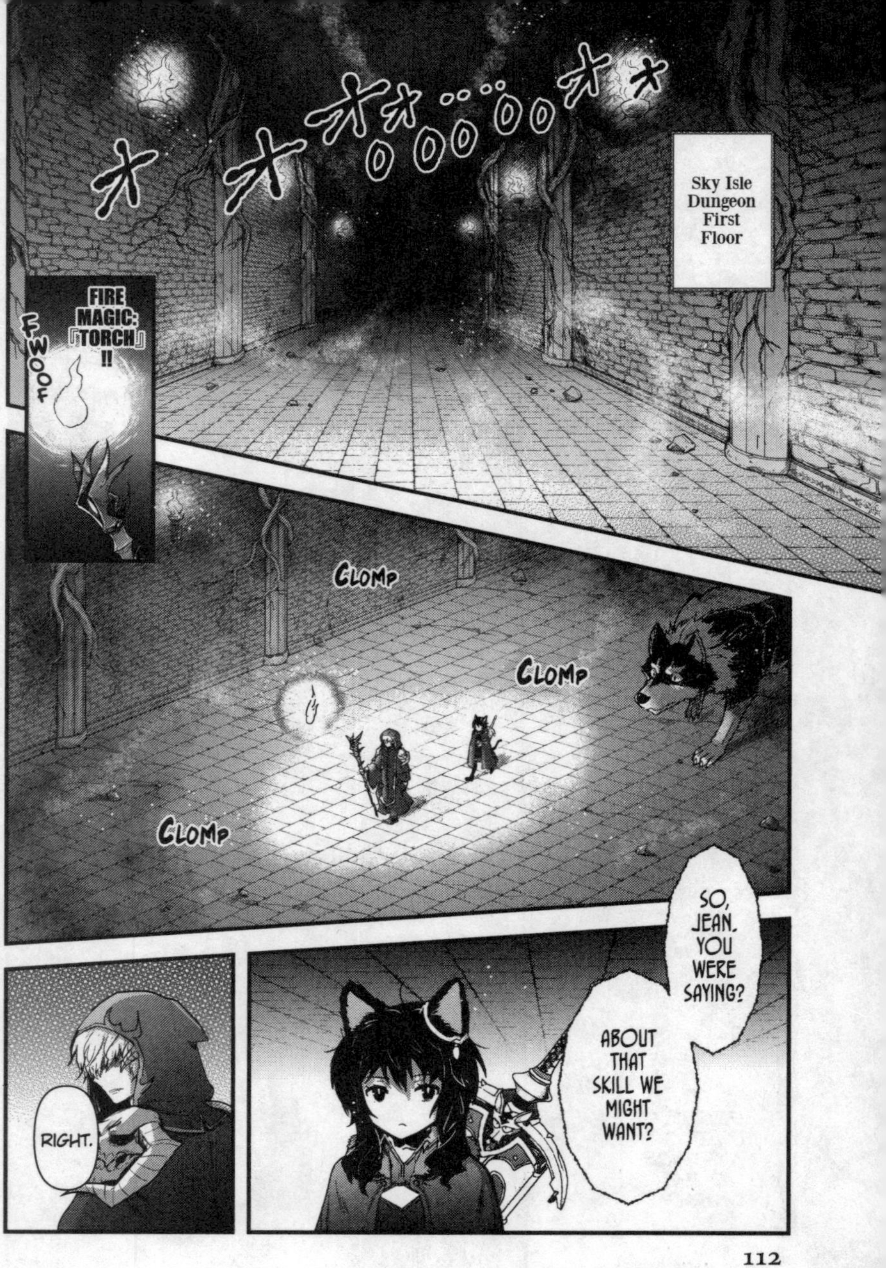
オオオォ OOOOO オオ
Sky Isle Dungeon First Floor
FIRE MAGIC: 『TORCH』!!
FWOOF
CLOMP
CLOMP
CLOMP
SO, JEAN, YOU WERE SAYING?
ABOUT THAT SKILL WE MIGHT WANT?
RIGHT.

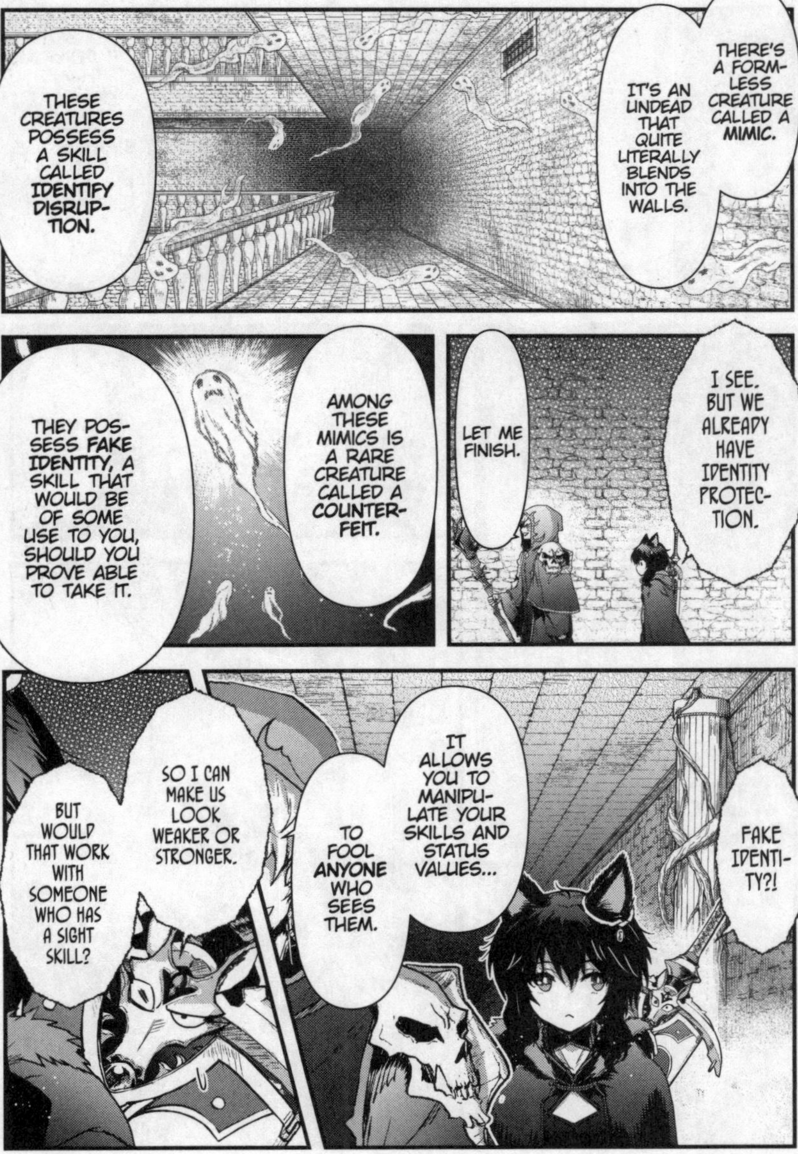
THERE'S A FORMLESS CREATURE CALLED A MIMIC.
IT'S AN UNDEAD THAT QUITE LITERALLY BLENDS INTO THE WALLS.
THESE CREATURES POSSESS A SKILL CALLED **IDENTIFY DISRUPTION.**
I SEE. BUT WE ALREADY HAVE IDENTITY PROTECTION.
LET ME FINISH.
AMONG THESE MIMICS IS A RARE CREATURE CALLED A **COUNTERFEIT.**
THEY POSSESS **FAKE IDENTITY,** A SKILL THAT WOULD BE OF SOME USE TO YOU, SHOULD YOU PROVE ABLE TO TAKE IT.
FAKE IDENTITY?!
IT ALLOWS YOU TO MANIPULATE YOUR SKILLS AND STATUS VALUES...
TO FOOL **ANYONE** WHO SEES THEM.
SO I CAN MAKE US LOOK WEAKER OR STRONGER.
BUT WOULD THAT WORK WITH SOMEONE WHO HAS A SIGHT SKILL?

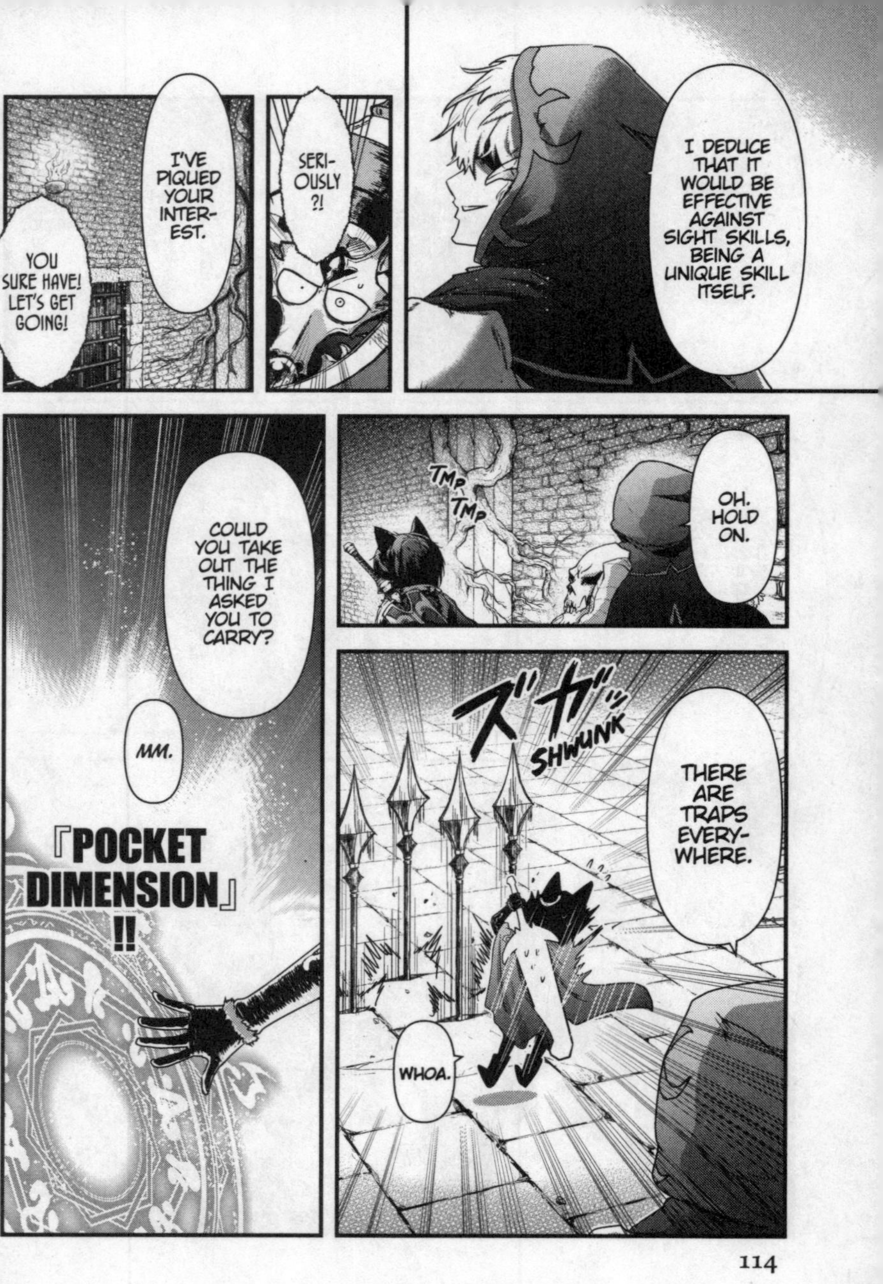
I DEDUCE THAT IT WOULD BE EFFECTIVE AGAINST SIGHT SKILLS, BEING A UNIQUE SKILL ITSELF.
SERI-OUSLY?!
I'VE PIQUED YOUR INTER-EST.
YOU SURE HAVE! LET'S GET GOING!
TMP TMP
OH. HOLD ON.
ズガッ
SHWUNK
THERE ARE TRAPS EVERY-WHERE.
WHOA.
COULD YOU TAKE OUT THE THING I ASKED YOU TO CARRY?
MM.
『POCKET DIMENSION』!!

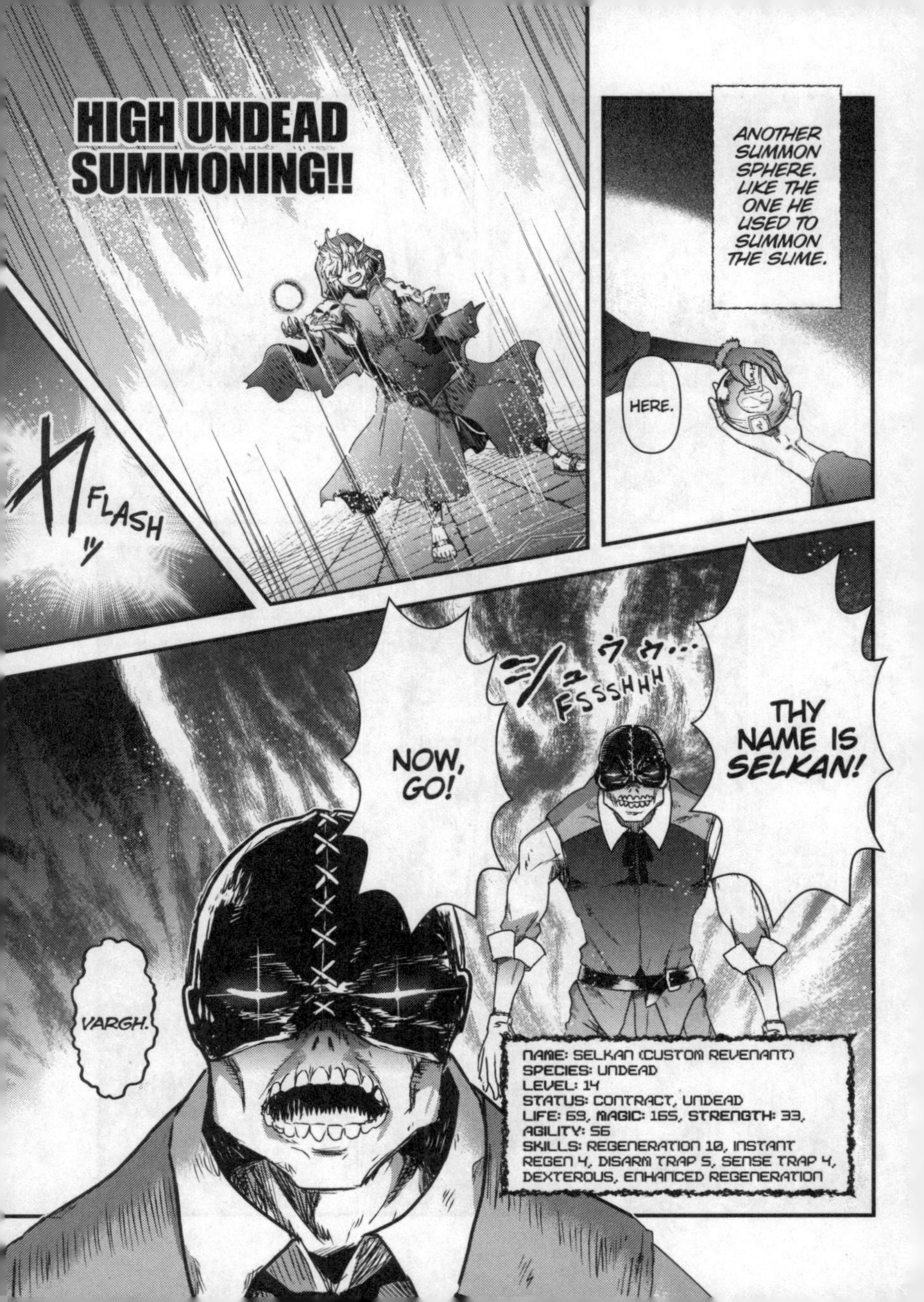
ANOTHER SUMMON SPHERE. LIKE THE ONE HE USED TO SUMMON THE SLIME.
HERE.
HIGH UNDEAD SUMMONING!!
FLASH
THY NAME IS SELKAN!
FSSSHHH
NOW, GO!
NAME: SELKAN (CUSTOM REVENANT)
SPECIES: UNDEAD
LEVEL: 14
STATUS: CONTRACT, UNDEAD
LIFE: 69, MAGIC: 165, STRENGTH: 33, AGILITY: 56
SKILLS: REGENERATION 10, INSTANT REGEN 4, DISARM TRAP 5, SENSE TRAP 4, DEXTEROUS, ENHANCED REGENERATION
VARGH.

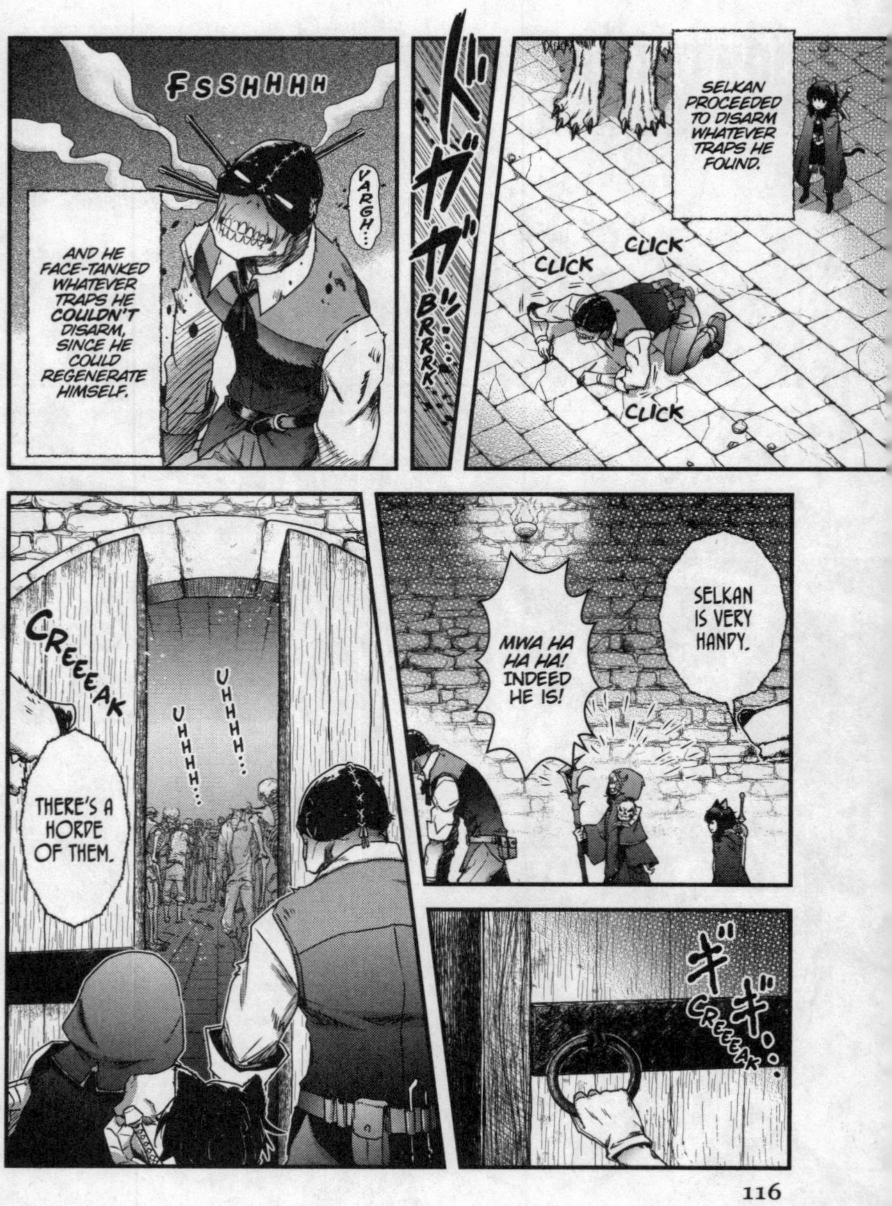
SELKAN PROCEEDED TO DISARM WHATEVER TRAPS HE FOUND.
CLICK
CLICK
CLICK
ドガガッ
BRRRRK...
FSSHHHH
VARGH...
AND HE FACE-TANKED WHATEVER TRAPS HE COULDN'T DISARM, SINCE HE COULD REGENERATE HIMSELF.
SELKAN IS VERY HANDY.
MWA HA HA HA! INDEED HE IS!
ギギ
CREEEAK...
CREEEAK
UHHHH...
UHHHHH...
THERE'S A HORDE OF THEM.

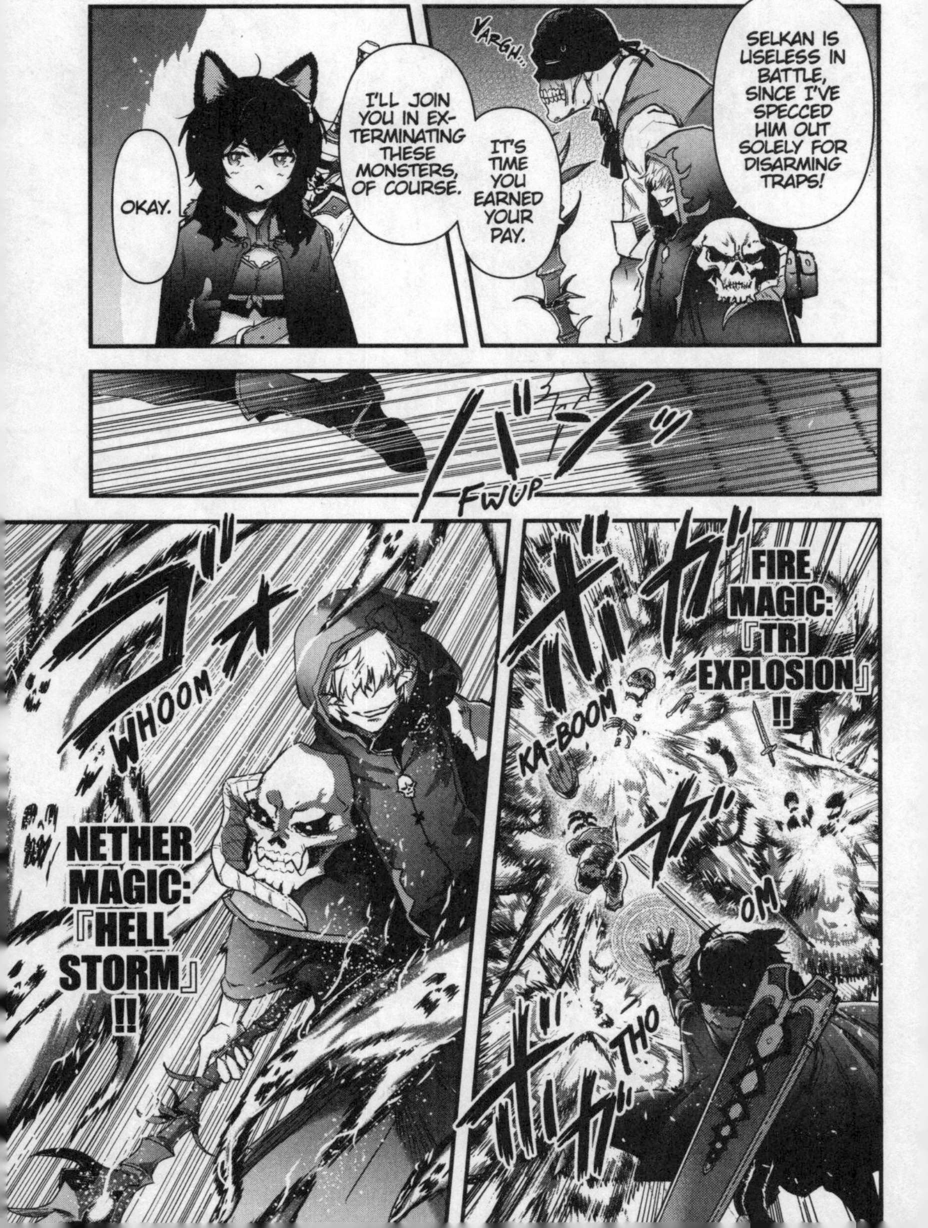

SELKAN IS USELESS IN BATTLE, SINCE I'VE SPECCED HIM OUT SOLELY FOR DISARMING TRAPS!
VARGH...
I'LL JOIN YOU IN EXTERMINATING THESE MONSTERS, OF COURSE.
IT'S TIME YOU EARNED YOUR PAY.
OKAY.
FWUP
FIRE MAGIC: 『TRI EXPLOSION』!!
KA-BOOM
OM
THO
WHOOM
NETHER MAGIC: 『HELL STORM』!!

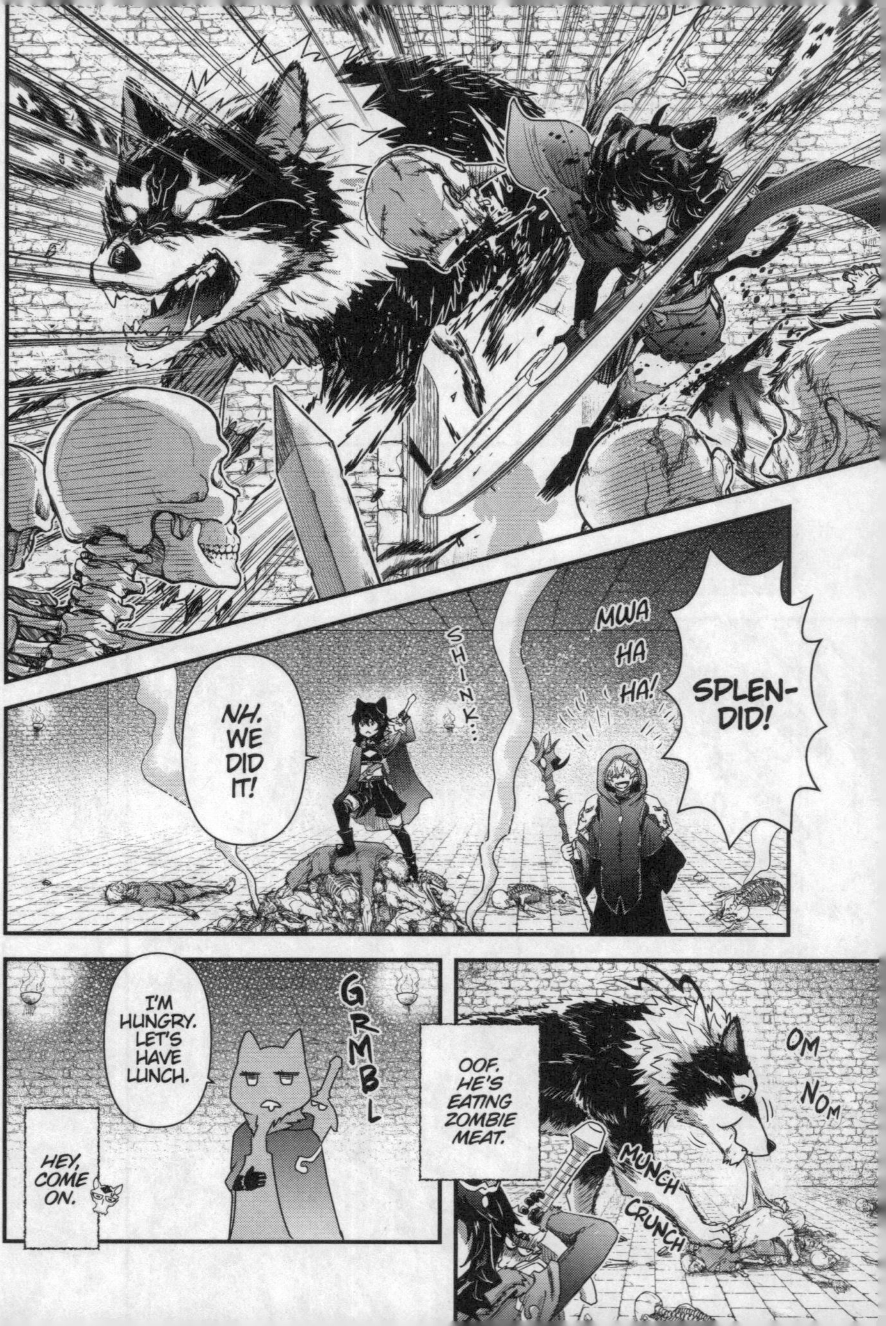
SPLEN-DID!
MWA HA HA HA!
SHINK...
NH. WE DID IT!
OM NOM
OOF. HE'S EATING ZOMBIE MEAT.
MUNCH
CRUNCH
GRMBL
I'M HUNGRY. LET'S HAVE LUNCH.
HEY, COME ON.

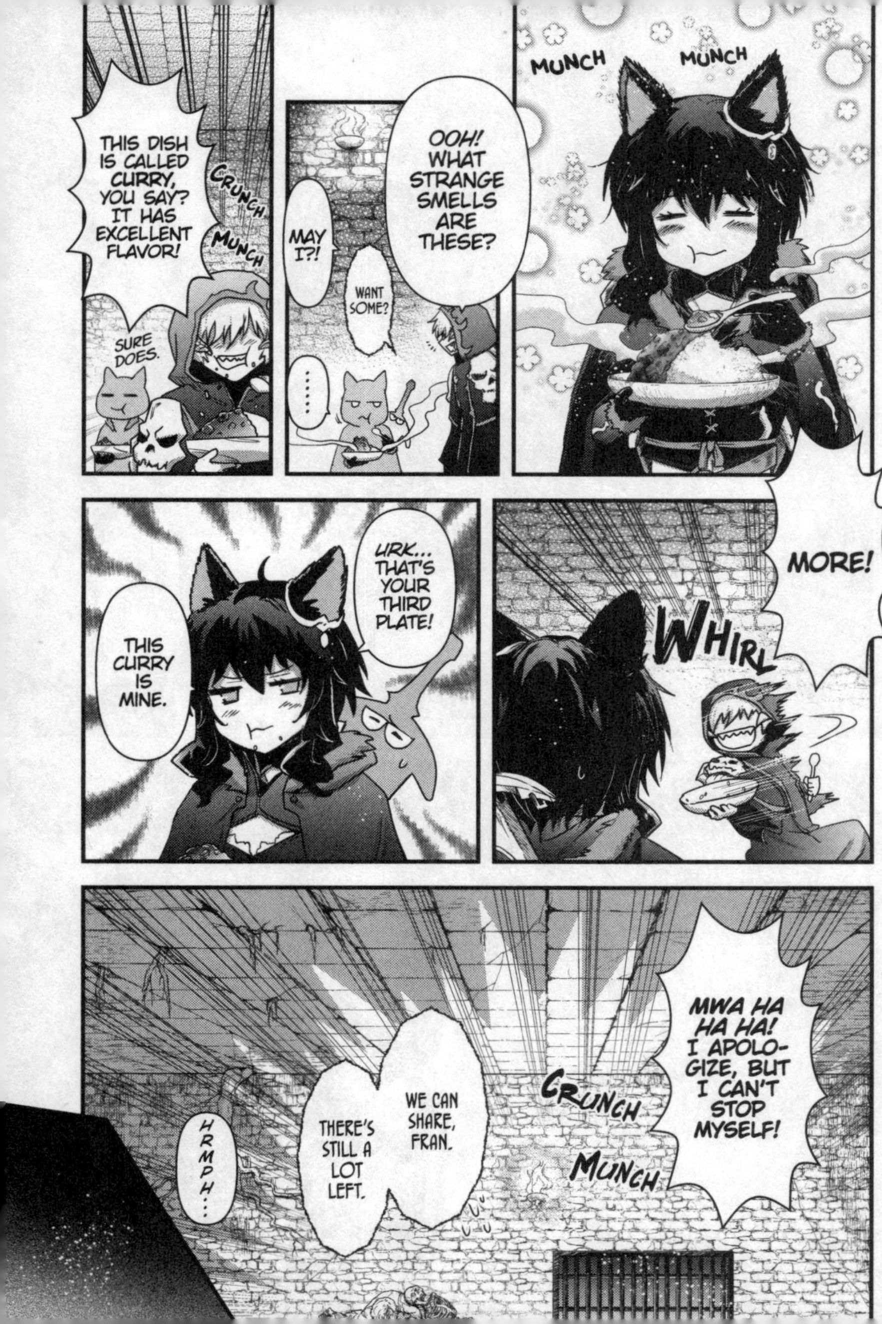
MUNCH
MUNCH
OOH! WHAT STRANGE SMELLS ARE THESE?
MAY I?!
WANT SOME?
......
THIS DISH IS CALLED CURRY, YOU SAY? IT HAS EXCELLENT FLAVOR!
CRUNCH
MUNCH
SURE DOES.
MORE!
WHIRL
URK... THAT'S YOUR THIRD PLATE!
THIS CURRY IS MINE.
MWA HA HA HA! I APOLOGIZE, BUT I CAN'T STOP MYSELF!
CRUNCH
MUNCH
WE CAN SHARE, FRAN.
THERE'S STILL A LOT LEFT.
HRMPH...

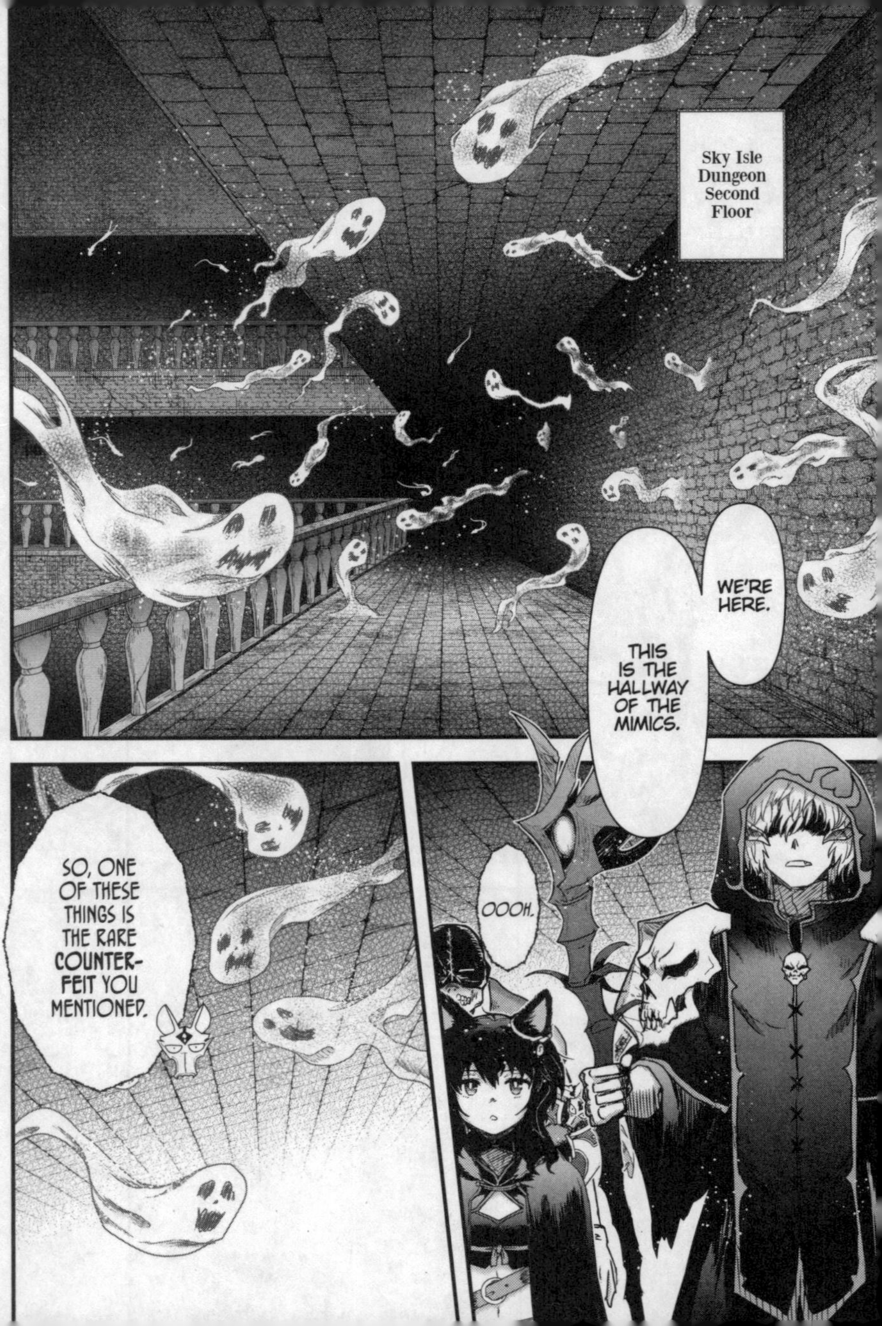
Sky Isle Dungeon Second Floor
WE'RE HERE.
THIS IS THE HALLWAY OF THE MIMICS.
OOOH.
SO, ONE OF THESE THINGS IS THE RARE COUNTERFEIT YOU MENTIONED.

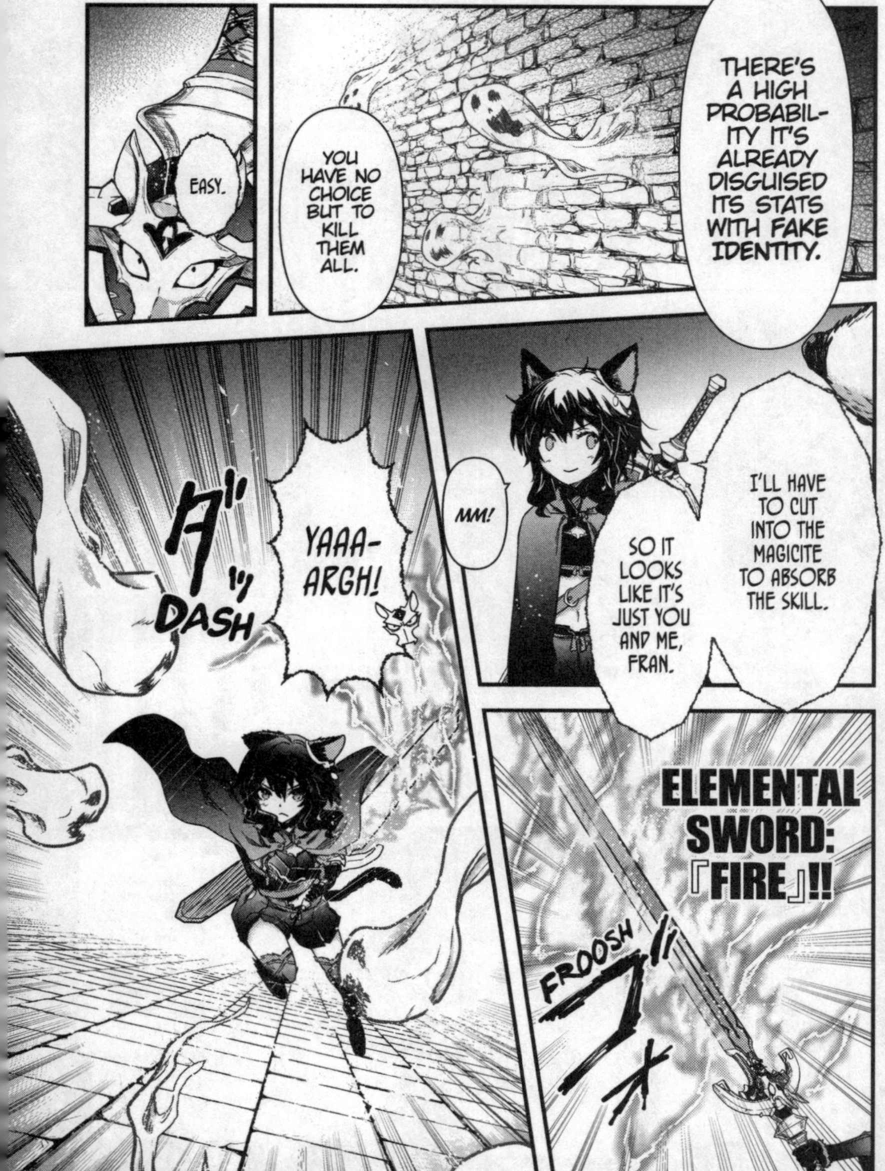
THERE'S A HIGH PROBABIL-ITY IT'S ALREADY DISGUISED ITS STATS WITH FAKE IDENTITY.
YOU HAVE NO CHOICE BUT TO KILL THEM ALL.
EASY.
I'LL HAVE TO CUT INTO THE MAGICITE TO ABSORB THE SKILL.
SO IT LOOKS LIKE IT'S JUST YOU AND ME, FRAN.
MM!
ELEMENTAL SWORD: 『FIRE』!!
FROOSH
YAAA-ARGH!
ダッ
DASH

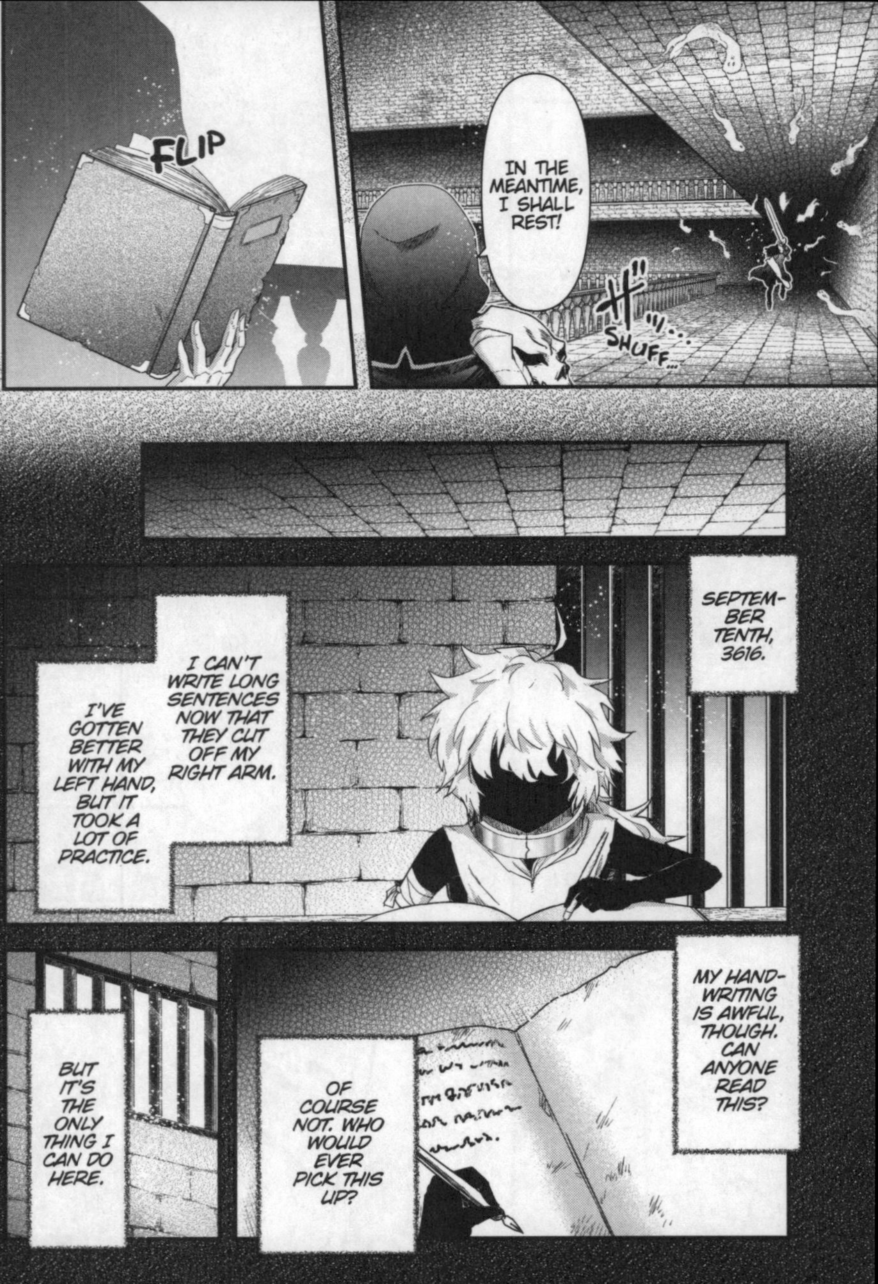
IN THE MEANTIME, I SHALL REST!
SHUFF...
FLIP
SEPTEMBER TENTH, 3616.
I CAN'T WRITE LONG SENTENCES NOW THAT THEY CUT OFF MY RIGHT ARM.
I'VE GOTTEN BETTER WITH MY LEFT HAND, BUT IT TOOK A LOT OF PRACTICE.
MY HANDWRITING IS AWFUL, THOUGH. CAN ANYONE READ THIS?
OF COURSE NOT. WHO WOULD EVER PICK THIS UP?
BUT IT'S THE ONLY THING I CAN DO HERE.

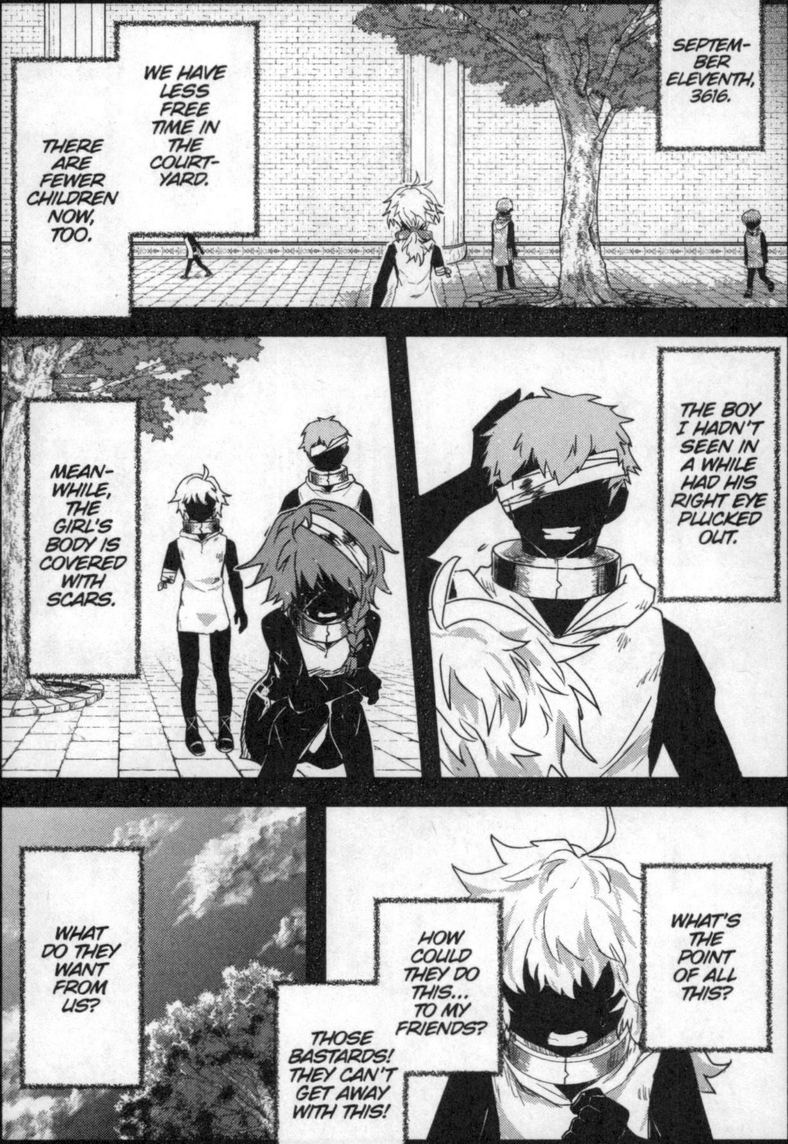

SEPTEMBER ELEVENTH, 3616.
WE HAVE LESS FREE TIME IN THE COURTYARD.
THERE ARE FEWER CHILDREN NOW, TOO.
THE BOY I HADN'T SEEN IN A WHILE HAD HIS RIGHT EYE PLUCKED OUT.
MEANWHILE, THE GIRL'S BODY IS COVERED WITH SCARS.
WHAT'S THE POINT OF ALL THIS?
HOW COULD THEY DO THIS... TO MY FRIENDS?
THOSE BASTARDS! THEY CAN'T GET AWAY WITH THIS!
WHAT DO THEY WANT FROM US?

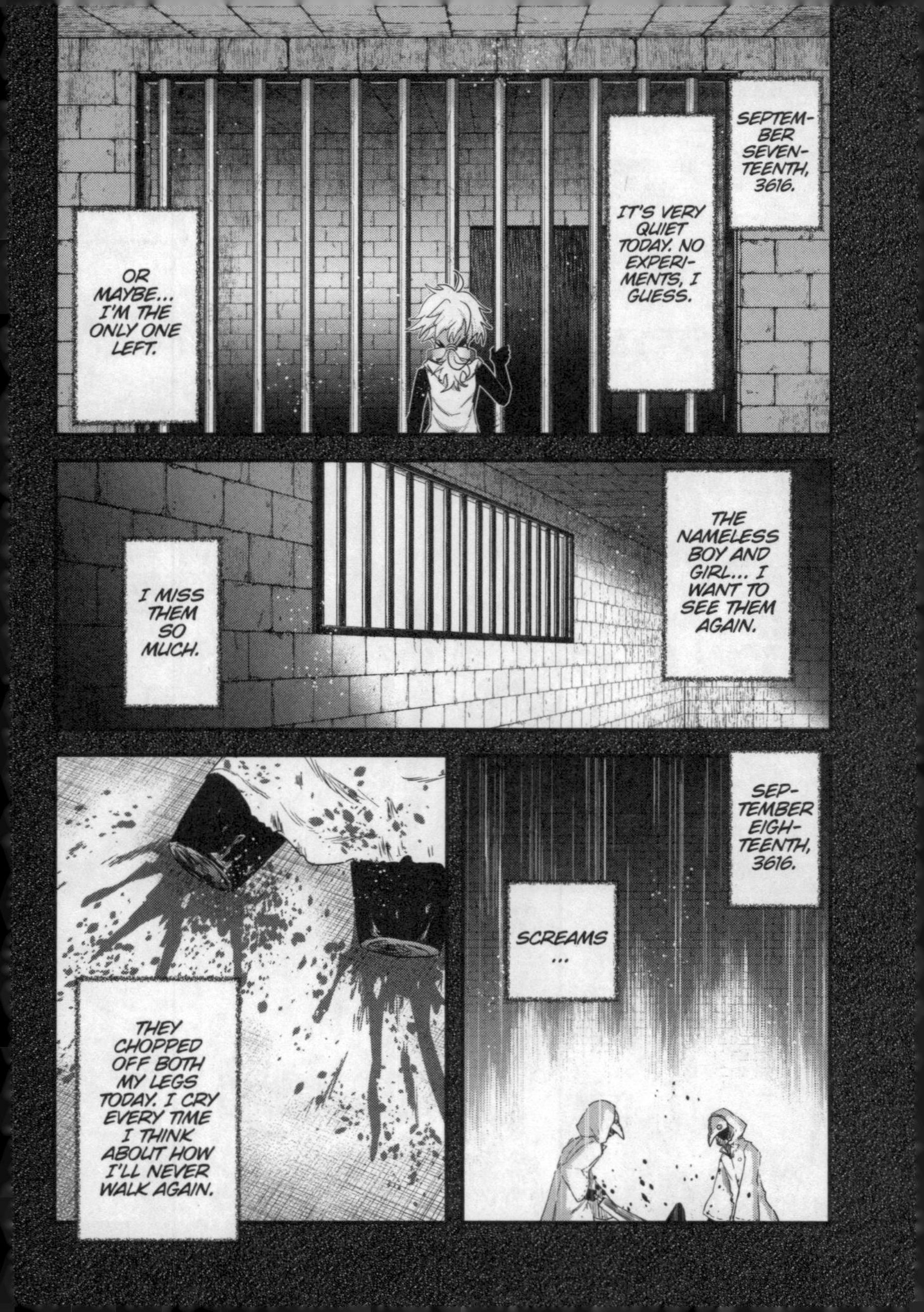
SEPTEMBER SEVENTEENTH, 3616.
IT'S VERY QUIET TODAY. NO EXPERIMENTS, I GUESS.
OR MAYBE... I'M THE ONLY ONE LEFT.
THE NAMELESS BOY AND GIRL... I WANT TO SEE THEM AGAIN.
I MISS THEM SO MUCH.
SEPTEMBER EIGHTEENTH, 3616.
SCREAMS...
THEY CHOPPED OFF BOTH MY LEGS TODAY. I CRY EVERY TIME I THINK ABOUT HOW I'LL NEVER WALK AGAIN.

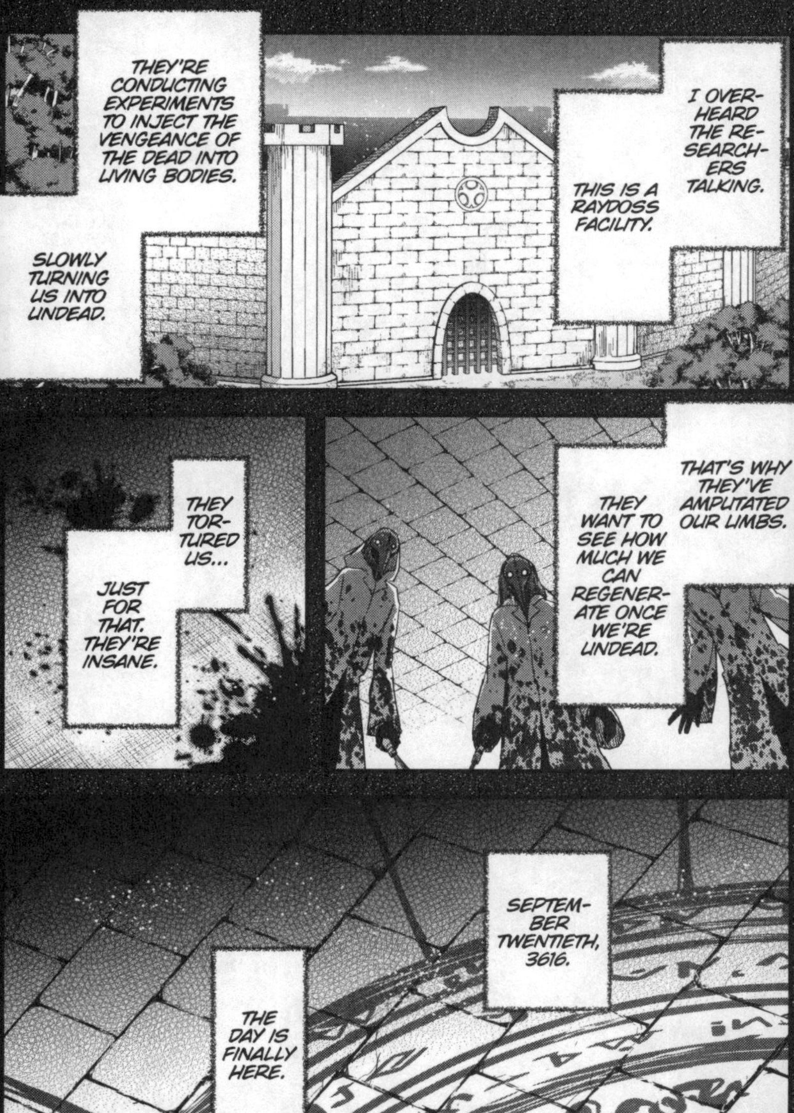
I OVERHEARD THE RESEARCHERS TALKING.
THIS IS A RAYDOSS FACILITY.
THEY'RE CONDUCTING EXPERIMENTS TO INJECT THE VENGEANCE OF THE DEAD INTO LIVING BODIES.
SLOWLY TURNING US INTO UNDEAD.
THAT'S WHY THEY'VE AMPUTATED OUR LIMBS.
THEY WANT TO SEE HOW MUCH WE CAN REGENERATE ONCE WE'RE UNDEAD.
THEY TORTURED US...
JUST FOR THAT. THEY'RE INSANE.
SEPTEMBER TWENTIETH, 3616.
THE DAY IS FINALLY HERE.

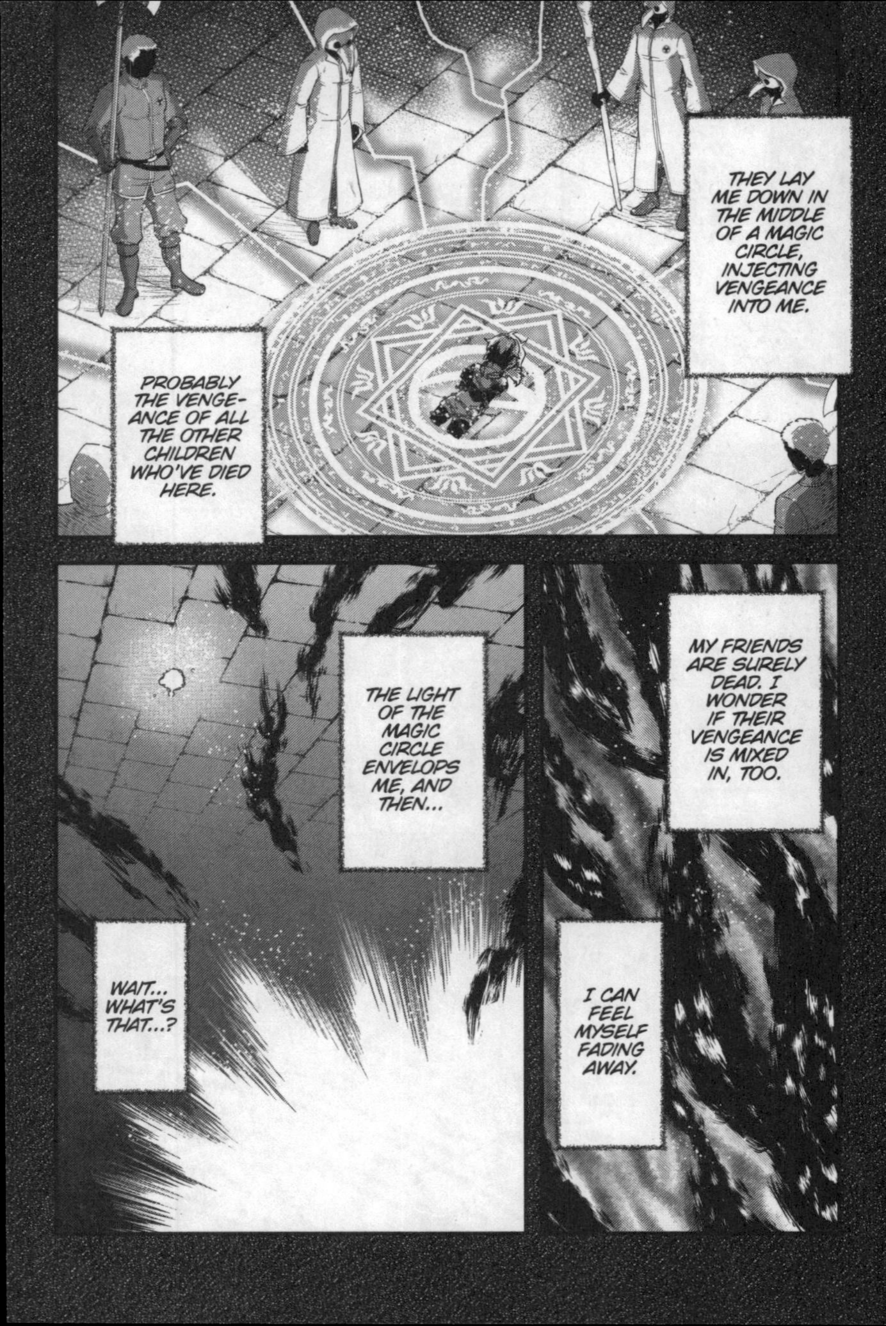
THEY LAY ME DOWN IN THE MIDDLE OF A MAGIC CIRCLE, INJECTING VENGEANCE INTO ME.
PROBABLY THE VENGE-ANCE OF ALL THE OTHER CHILDREN WHO'VE DIED HERE.
MY FRIENDS ARE SURELY DEAD. I WONDER IF THEIR VENGEANCE IS MIXED IN, TOO.
I CAN FEEL MYSELF FADING AWAY.
THE LIGHT OF THE MAGIC CIRCLE ENVELOPS ME, AND THEN...
WAIT... WHAT'S THAT...?

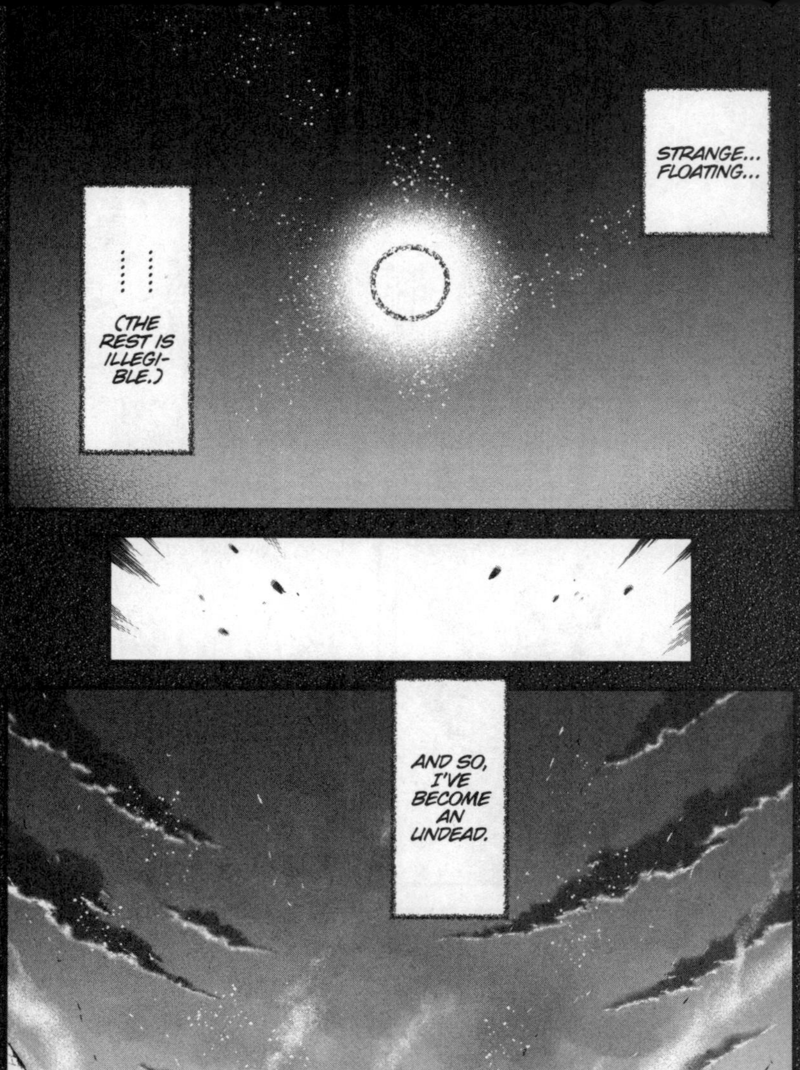
STRANGE... FLOATING...
......
(THE REST IS ILLEGIBLE.)
AND SO, I'VE BECOME AN UNDEAD.

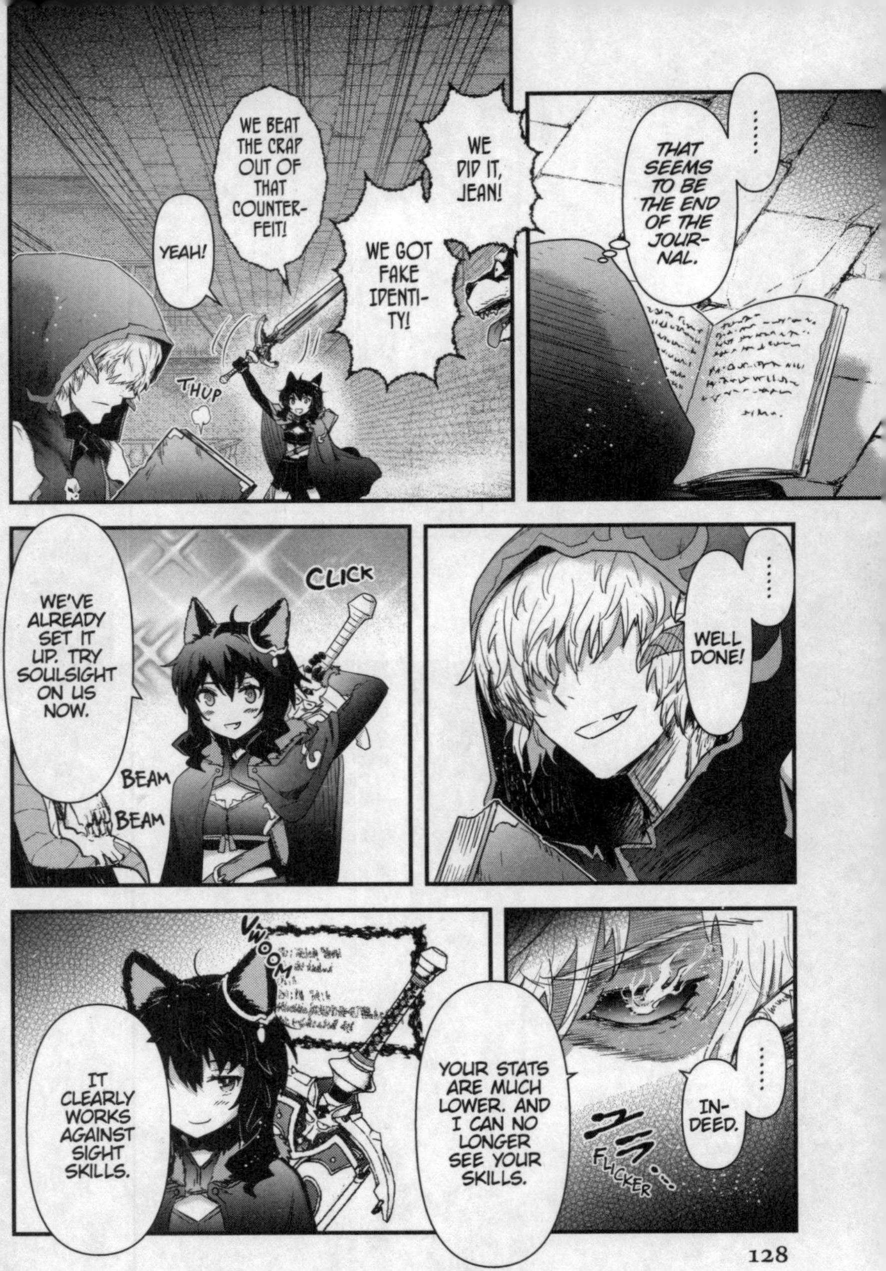
......
THAT SEEMS TO BE THE END OF THE JOURNAL.
WE DID IT, JEAN!
WE BEAT THE CRAP OUT OF THAT COUNTERFEIT!
WE GOT FAKE IDENTITY!
YEAH!
THUP
......
WELL DONE!
CLICK
WE'VE ALREADY SET IT UP. TRY SOULSIGHT ON US NOW.
BEAM
BEAM
......
INDEED.
FLICKER
VWOOM
YOUR STATS ARE MUCH LOWER. AND I CAN NO LONGER SEE YOUR SKILLS.
IT CLEARLY WORKS AGAINST SIGHT SKILLS.

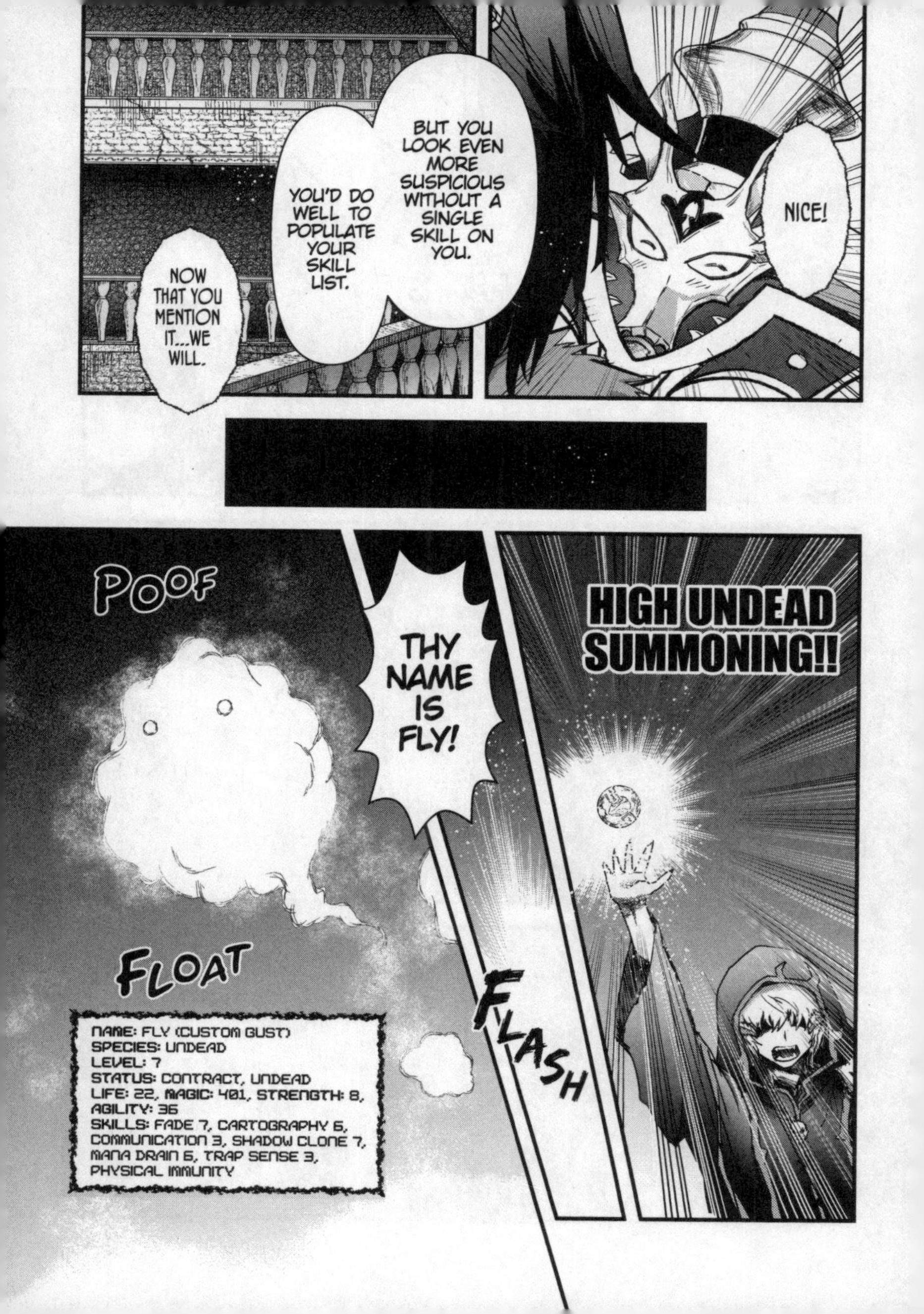
NICE!
BUT YOU LOOK EVEN MORE SUSPICIOUS WITHOUT A SINGLE SKILL ON YOU.
YOU'D DO WELL TO POPULATE YOUR SKILL LIST.
NOW THAT YOU MENTION IT...WE WILL.
HIGH UNDEAD SUMMONING!!
FLASH
THY NAME IS FLY!
POOF
FLOAT
NAME: FLY (CUSTOM GUST)
SPECIES: UNDEAD
LEVEL: 7
STATUS: CONTRACT, UNDEAD
LIFE: 22, MAGIC: 401, STRENGTH: 8, ABILITY: 36
SKILLS: FADE 7, CARTOGRAPHY 6, COMMUNICATION 3, SHADOW CLONE 7, MANA DRAIN 6, TRAP SENSE 3, PHYSICAL IMMUNITY

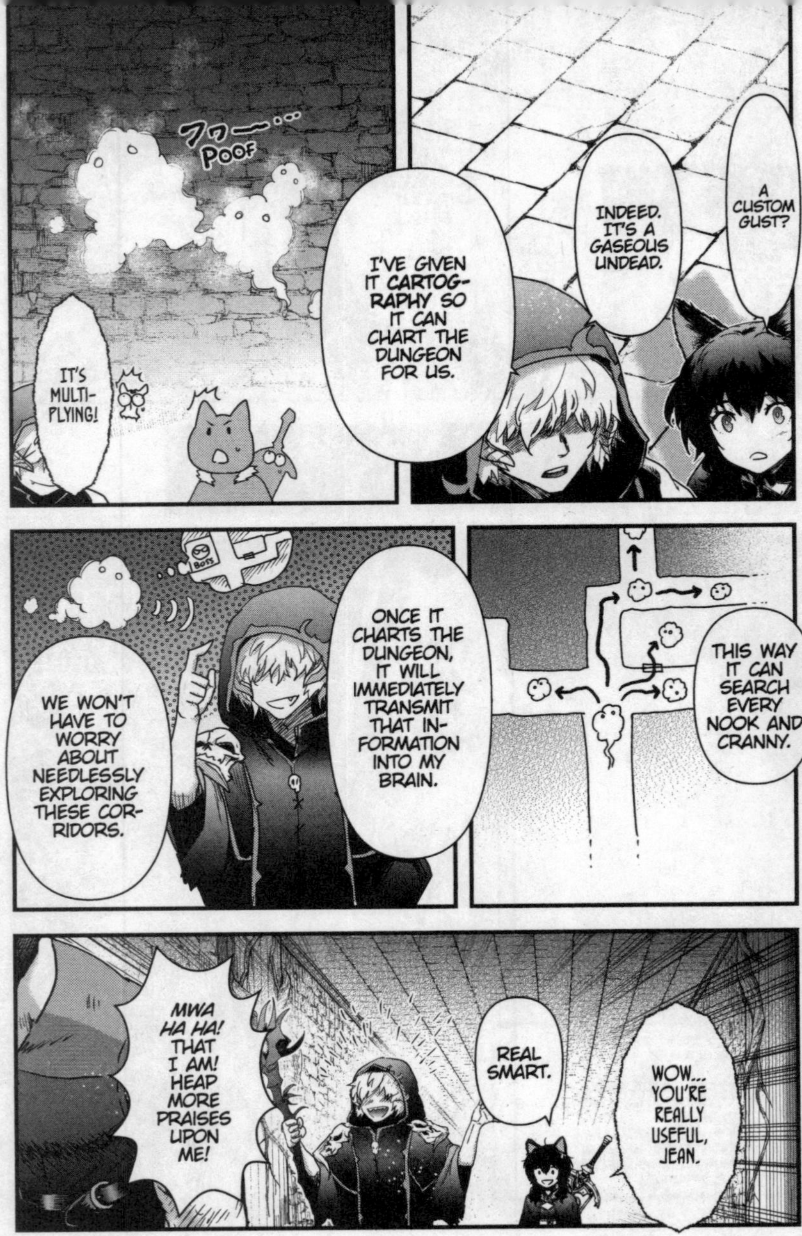
A CUSTOM GUST?
INDEED. IT'S A GASEOUS UNDEAD.
I'VE GIVEN IT CARTOGRAPHY SO IT CAN CHART THE DUNGEON FOR US.
フワ~...
POOF
IT'S MULTI-PLYING!
THIS WAY IT CAN SEARCH EVERY NOOK AND CRANNY.
ONCE IT CHARTS THE DUNGEON, IT WILL IMMEDIATELY TRANSMIT THAT IN-FORMATION INTO MY BRAIN.
BOSS
WE WON'T HAVE TO WORRY ABOUT NEEDLESSLY EXPLORING THESE COR-RIDORS.
WOW... YOU'RE REALLY USEFUL, JEAN.
REAL SMART.
MWA HA HA! THAT I AM! HEAP MORE PRAISES UPON ME!

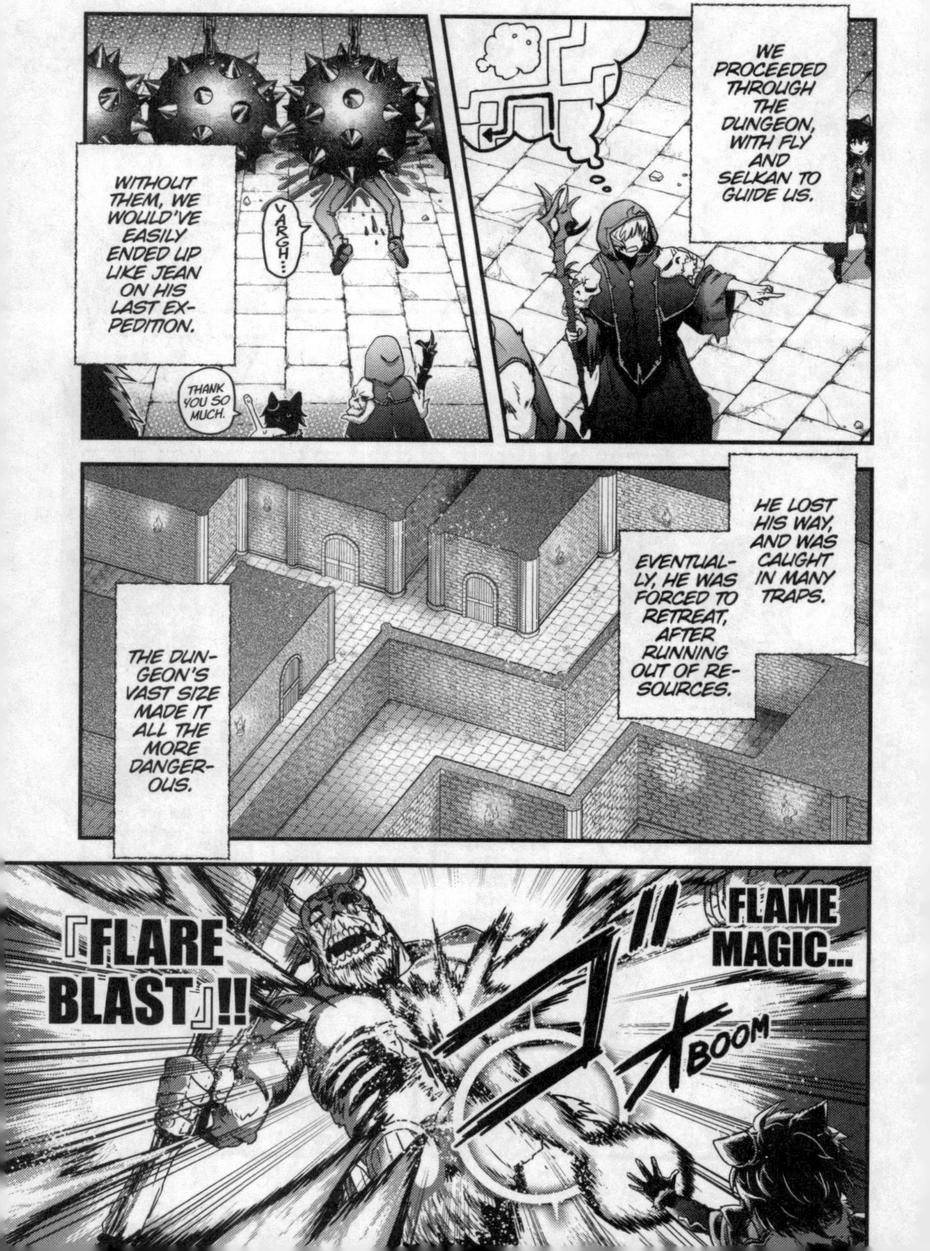
WE PROCEEDED THROUGH THE DUNGEON, WITH FLY AND SELKAN TO GUIDE US.
WITHOUT THEM, WE WOULD'VE EASILY ENDED UP LIKE JEAN ON HIS LAST EXPEDITION.
VARGH...
THANK YOU SO MUCH.
HE LOST HIS WAY, AND WAS CAUGHT IN MANY TRAPS.
EVENTUALLY, HE WAS FORCED TO RETREAT, AFTER RUNNING OUT OF RESOURCES.
THE DUNGEON'S VAST SIZE MADE IT ALL THE MORE DANGEROUS.
FLAME MAGIC...
『FLARE BLAST』!!
BOOM

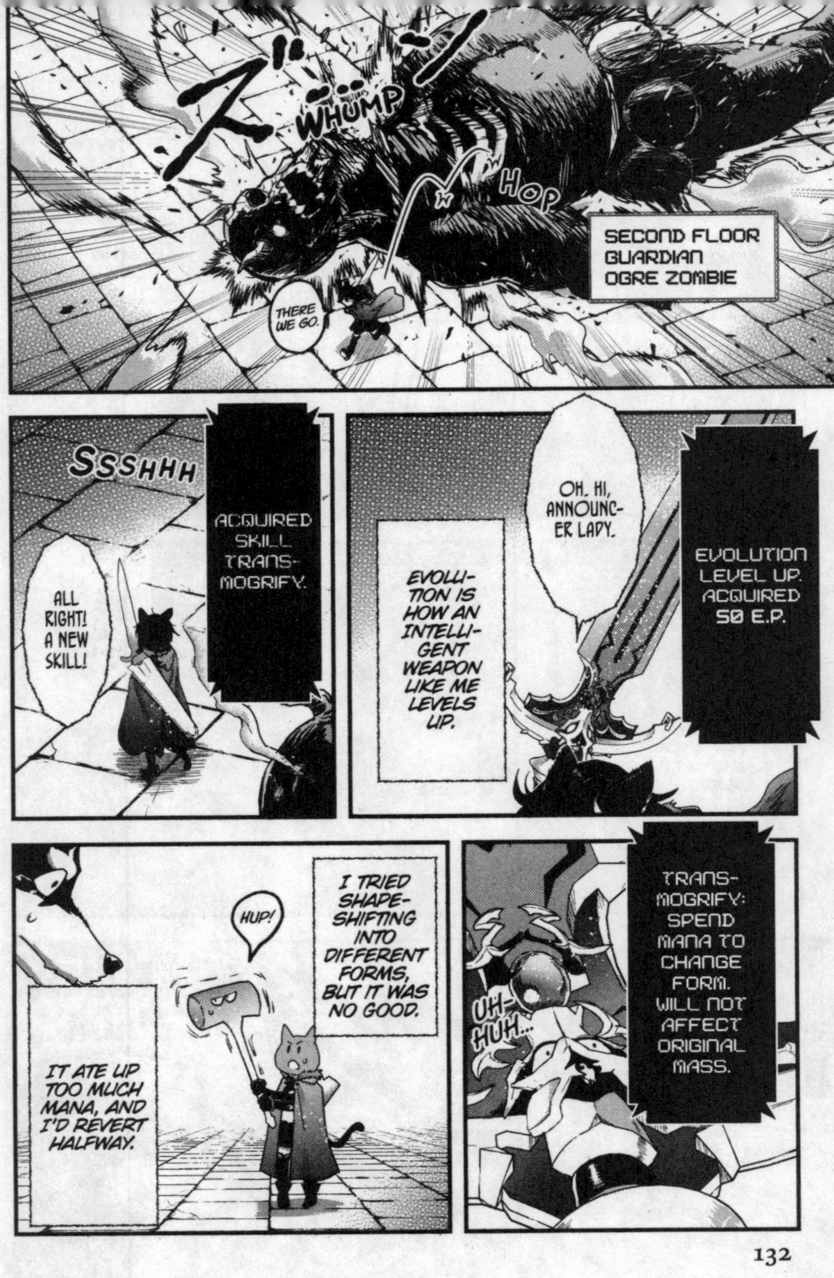
WHUMP
HOP
SECOND FLOOR GUARDIAN OGRE ZOMBIE
THERE WE GO.
EVOLUTION LEVEL UP. ACQUIRED 50 E.P.
OH. HI, ANNOUNCER LADY.
EVOLUTION IS HOW AN INTELLIGENT WEAPON LIKE ME LEVELS UP.
SSSHHH
ACQUIRED SKILL TRANSMOGRIFY.
ALL RIGHT! A NEW SKILL!
TRANSMOGRIFY: SPEND MANA TO CHANGE FORM. WILL NOT AFFECT ORIGINAL MASS.
UH-HUH...
I TRIED SHAPESHIFTING INTO DIFFERENT FORMS, BUT IT WAS NO GOOD.
HUP!
IT ATE UP TOO MUCH MANA, AND I'D REVERT HALFWAY.

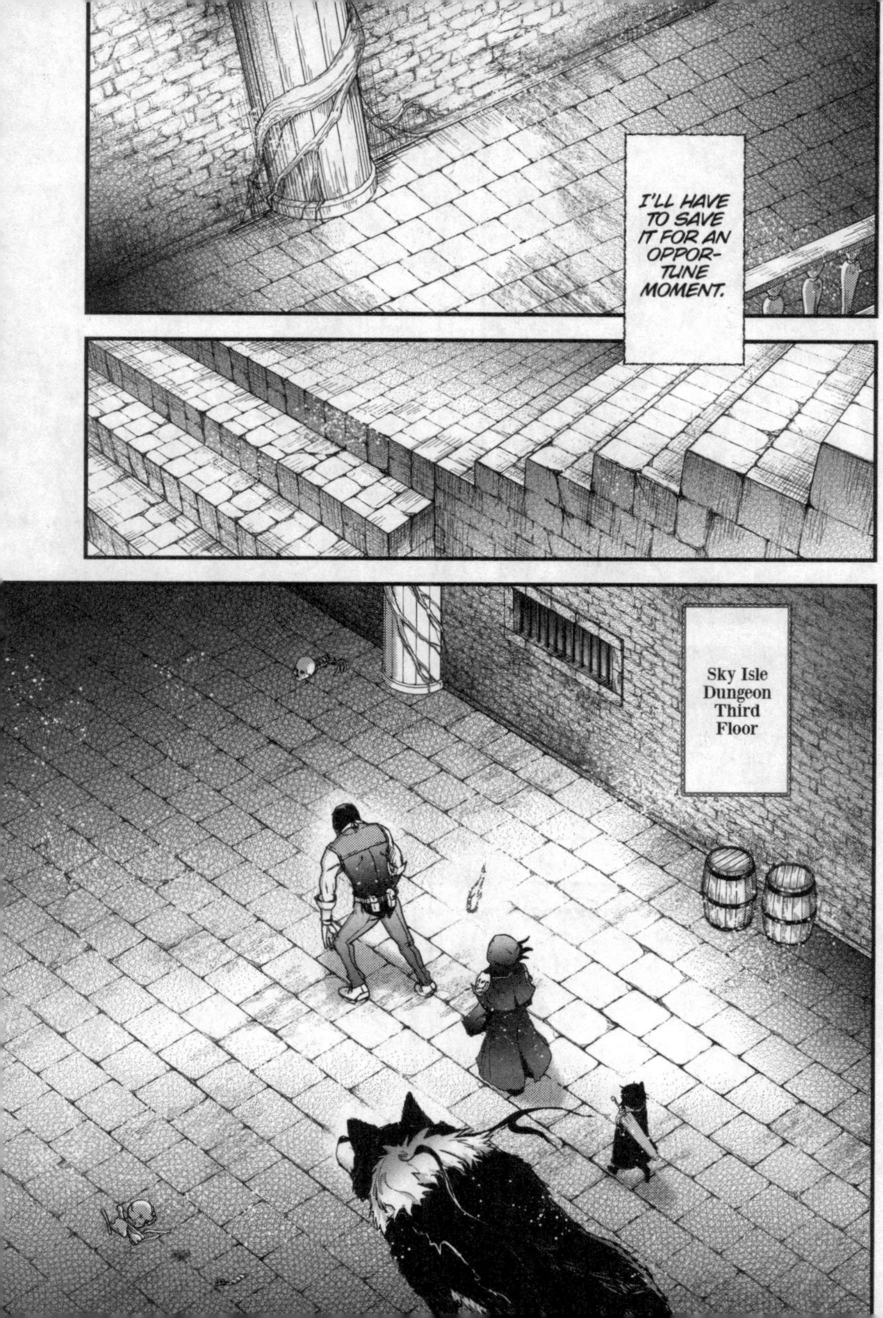
I'LL HAVE TO SAVE IT FOR AN OPPOR-TUNE MOMENT.
Sky Isle Dungeon Third Floor

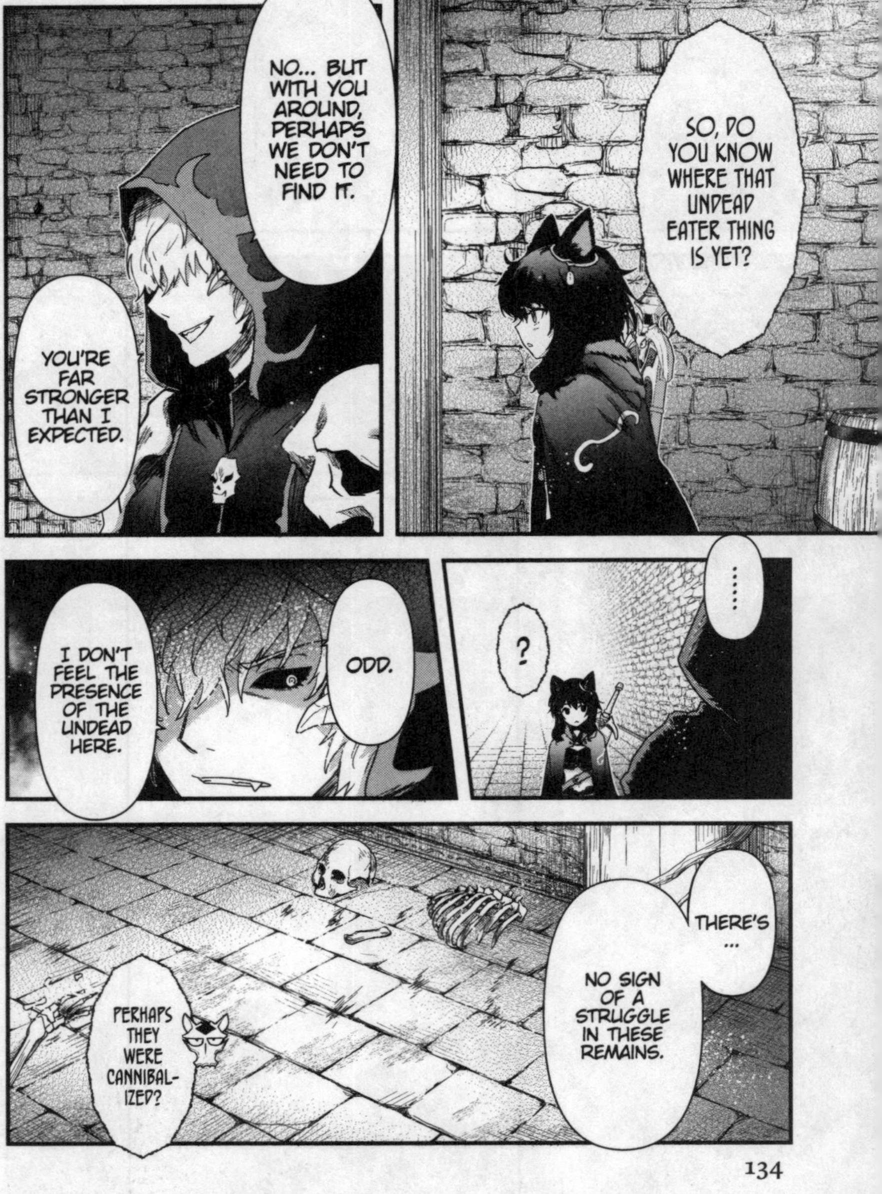
SO, DO YOU KNOW WHERE THAT UNDEAD EATER THING IS YET?
NO... BUT WITH YOU AROUND, PERHAPS WE DON'T NEED TO FIND IT.
YOU'RE FAR STRONGER THAN I EXPECTED.
......
?
ODD.
I DON'T FEEL THE PRESENCE OF THE UNDEAD HERE.
THERE'S...
NO SIGN OF A STRUGGLE IN THESE REMAINS.
PERHAPS THEY WERE CANNIBAL-IZED?

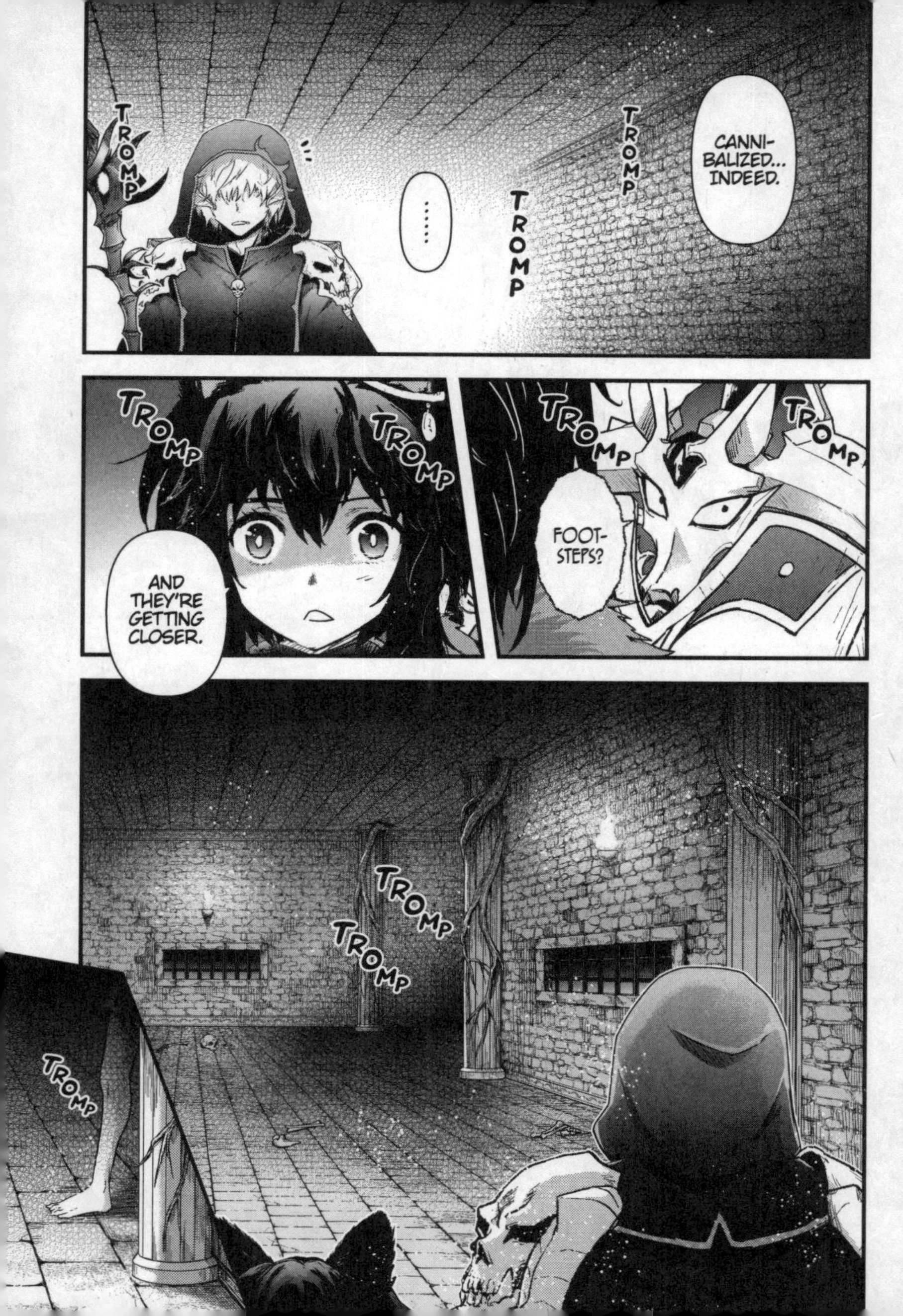
CANNI-BALIZED... INDEED.
TROMP
TROMP
......
TROMP
TROMP
TROMP
FOOT-STEPS?
TROMP
TROMP
AND THEY'RE GETTING CLOSER.
TROMP
TROMP
TROMP

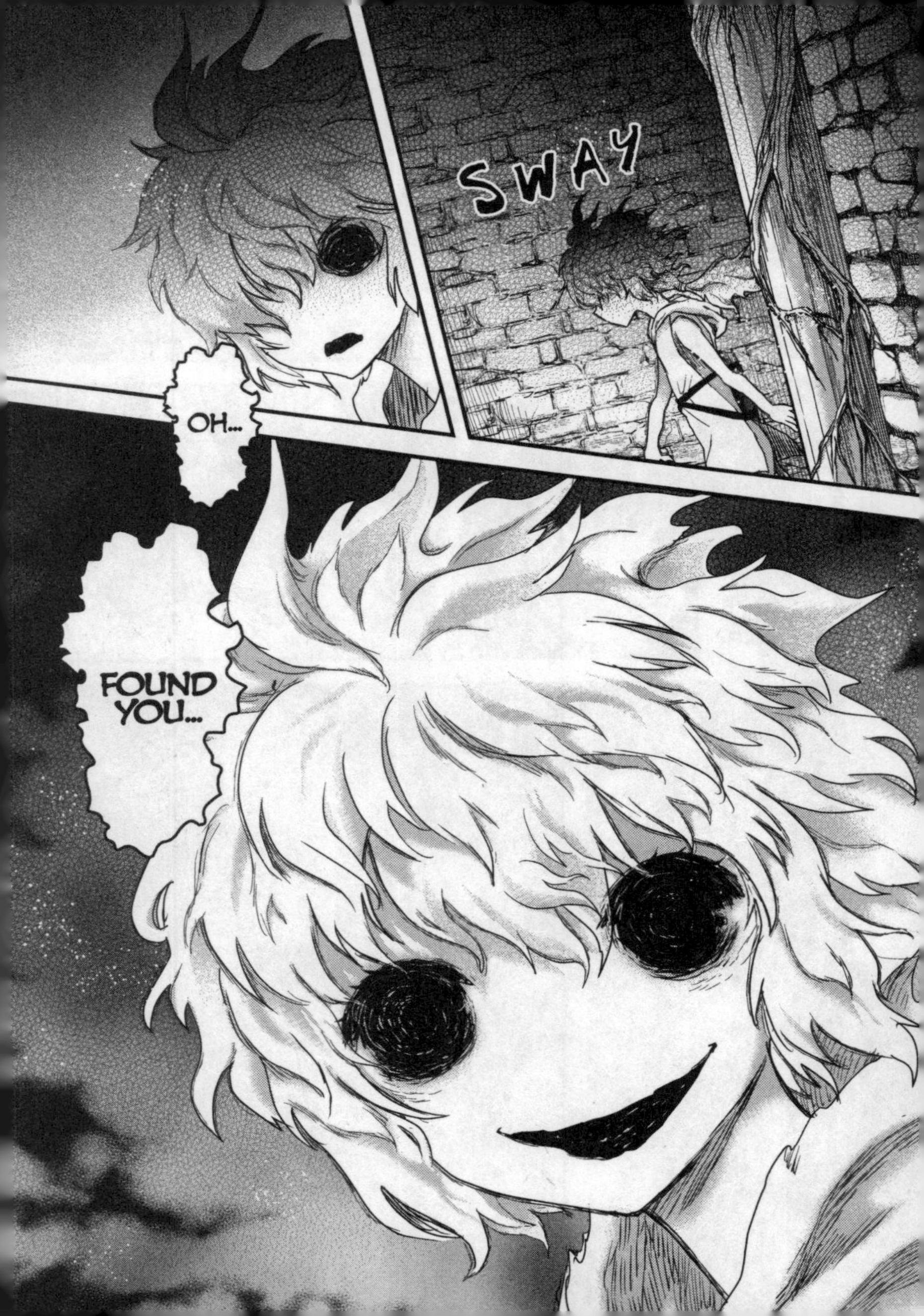
SWAY
OH...
FOUND YOU...

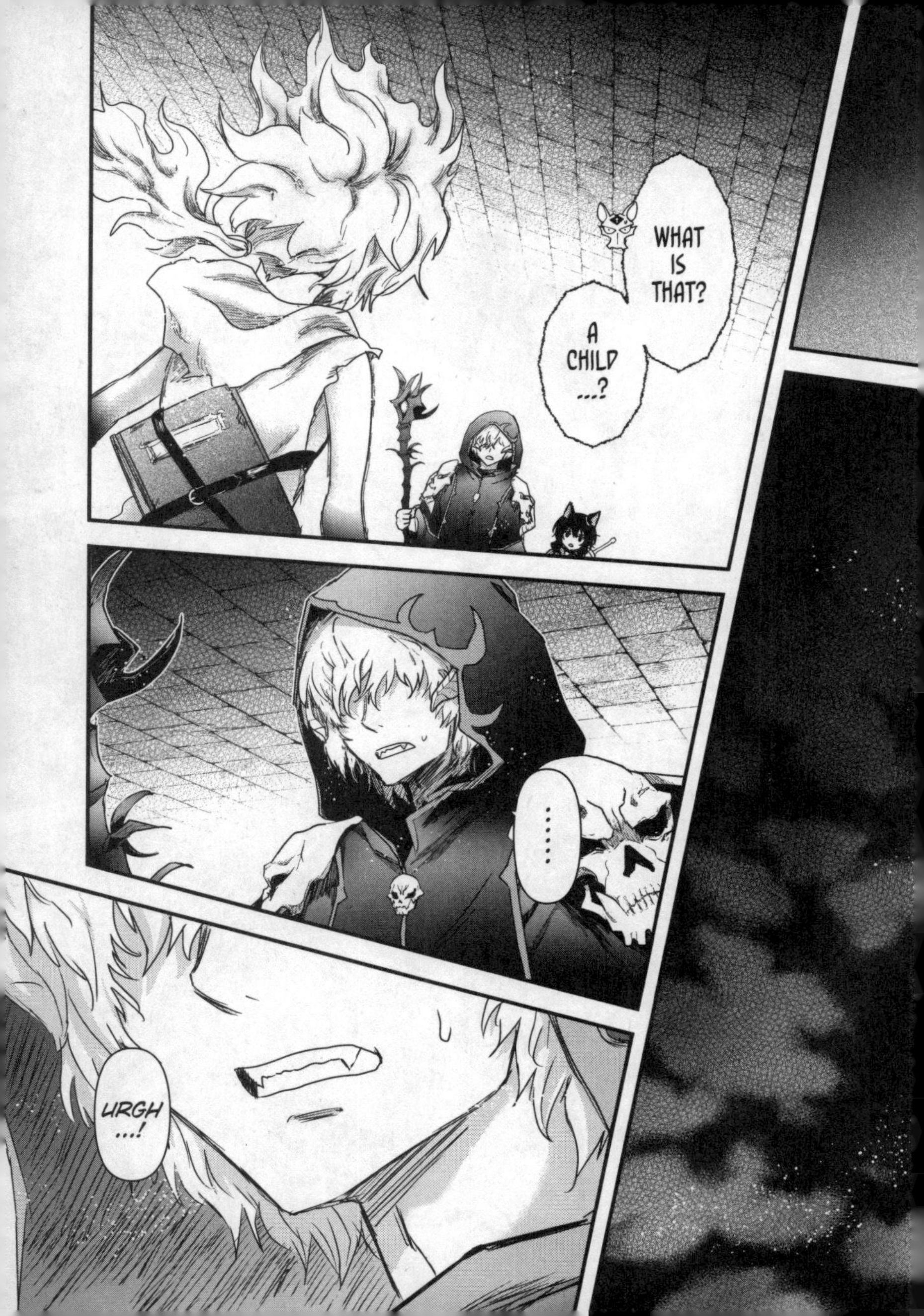
WHAT IS THAT?
A CHILD ...?
......
URGH ...!

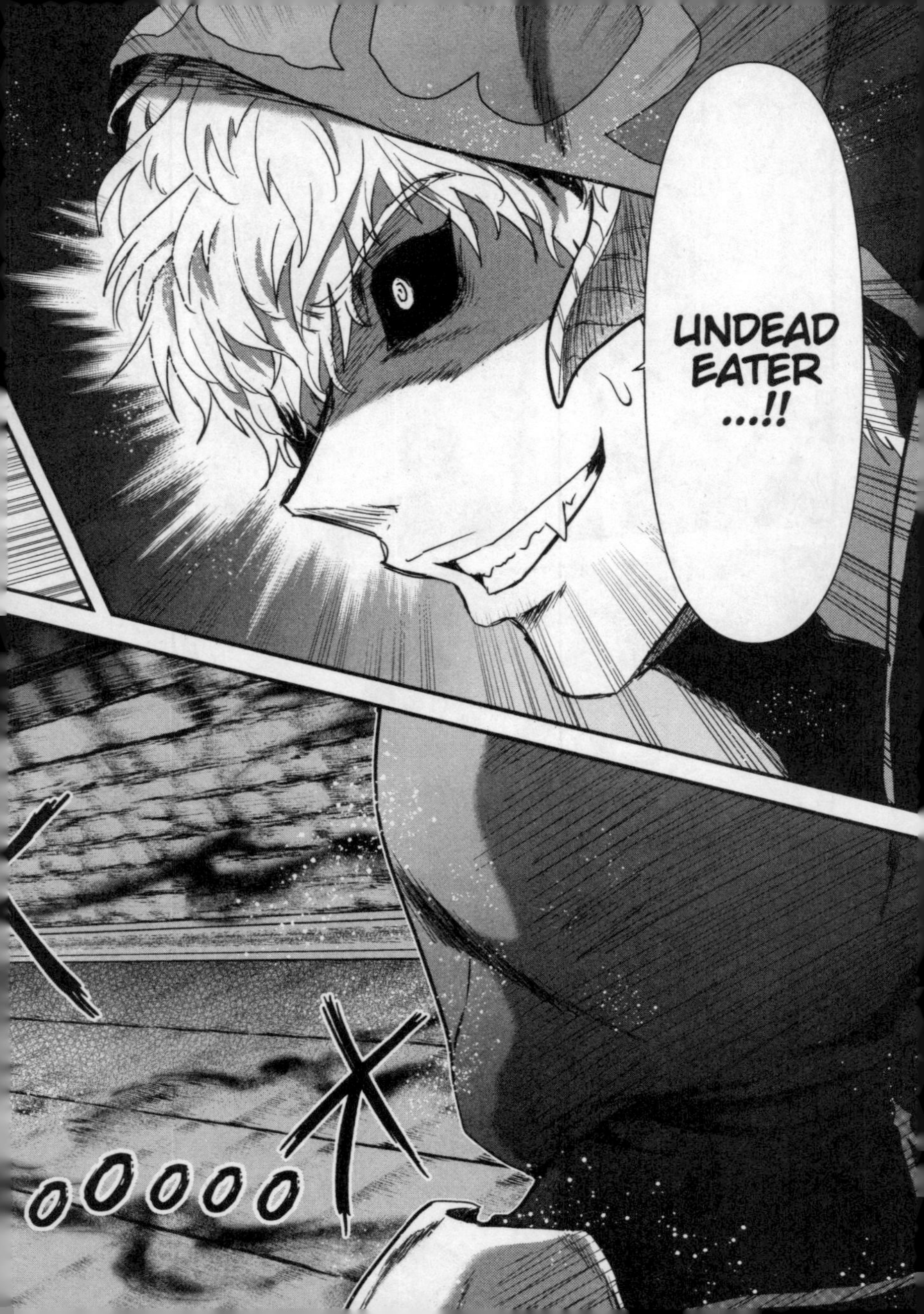
UNDEAD EATER ...!!

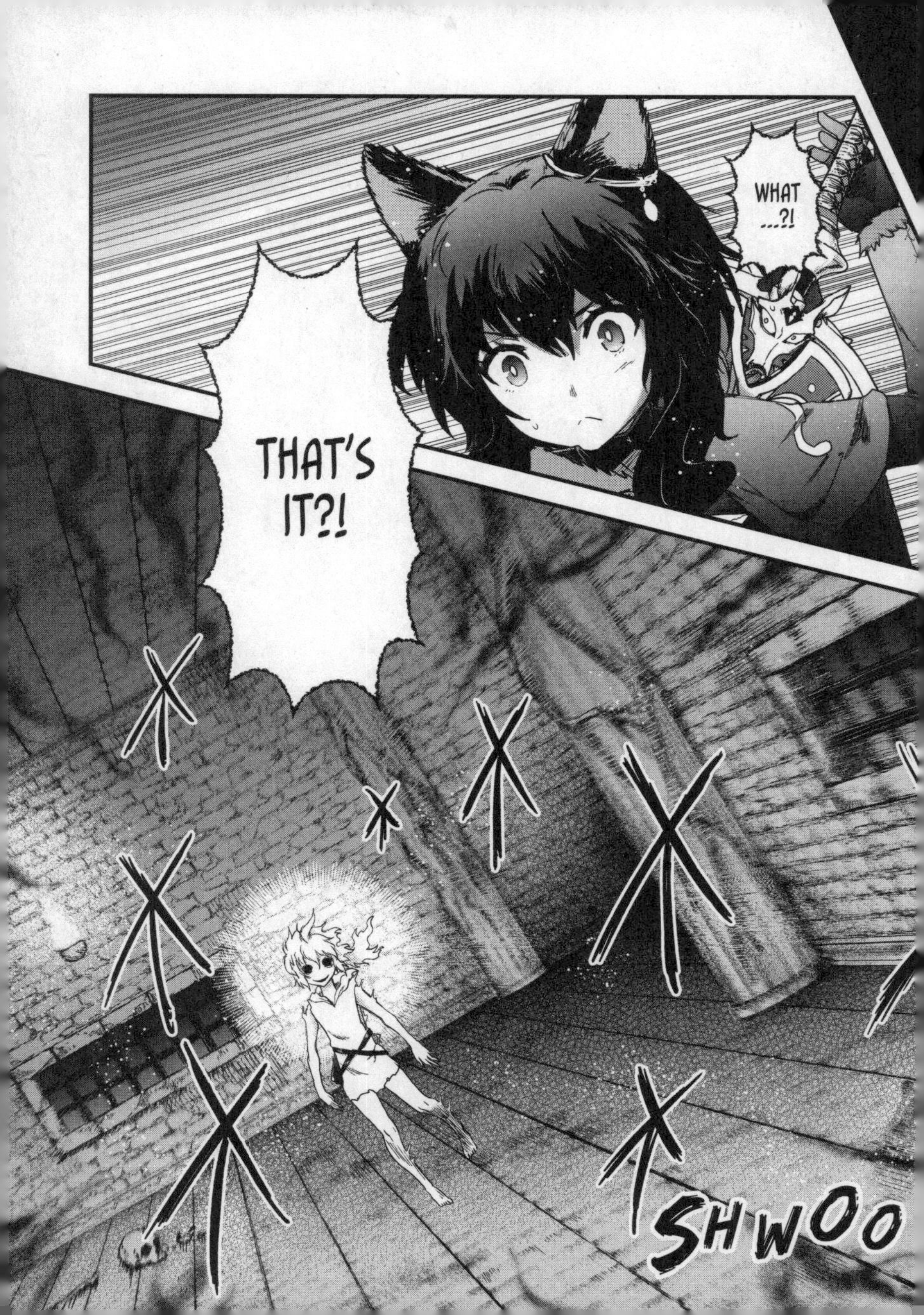
WHAT ...?!
THAT'S IT?!
SHWOO

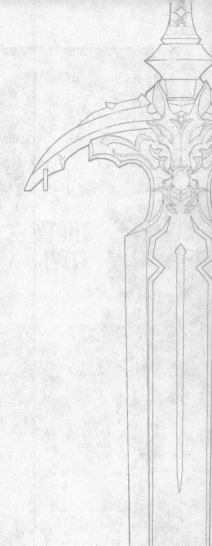

Reincarnated
as a sword

Reincarnated as a Sword
Bonus Story
Fran and Stealing
the Dragon's Whiskers

*And that's how I played Daruma is Falling Down as
a child and earned the fear of all my friends.*

"What's a Daruma?"

Oh, right. You wouldn't know what that is.

It was a lovely day for a talk, and so I'd decided to
tell Fran how I used to play Daruma is Falling Down.

*A Daruma is this red, round doll with the face of a
man.*

But it was a difficult concept to explain to someone
who wasn't from my world.

"The face of a man?" Fran tilted her head, unable to
picture it.

It always gets back up, even if you knock it down.

"This thing with the face of a man."

Y-yeah.

"So, he doesn't fall down even when he does?"

What?

"You said he's supposed to fall down."

Right. We were talking about the children's game.

"So, *why* did the Daruma fall down?"

Why? Uhhh...

141

Now that she mentioned it, why *was* the game called that?

I mean, it's a nice name.

"Is it...?"

A-anyway, how you play the game is more important, all right?

"Mm."

I gave Fran a lecture on how to play Daruma is Falling Down, also known as Red Light, Green Light in the West. She tapped her fist on her open palm.

Any questions?

"I know that game. We call it Stealing the Dragon's Whiskers."

Stealing the Dragon's Whiskers? That's a strange name for it.

"Better than 'Daruma is Falling Down.'"

Fair. Ours was a strange name as well. So, how do you play it?

"Easy. First, you get a dragon..."

Fran proceeded to explain the rules of Stealing the Dragon's Whiskers. The game was indeed quite similar to Daruma is Falling Down. It even had a backstory.

"These veteran adventurers are sneaking into a dragon's den."

And they're out to steal the dragon's whiskers. But why the whiskers?

"A dragon's whiskers can be used to make medicine."

And they'll fetch a pretty penny?

"No. The leader of the adventurers has a sick daughter who'll die in a few days without this medicine."

That's quite an intense story!

"But they know they can't beat the dragon in a fight.

So they decide to cut its whiskers off while it's asleep. All to save the little girl's life."

You go, adventurers!

"But whiskers are quite important for a dragon. It can't walk without them."

I guess they're like feelers on an ant. Cats and catfish can't function without them, either.

"The dragon can't let its whiskers be cut off. Only death awaits a whiskerless dragon in the wild."

Who came up with this story?! At least let the adventurers kill an *evil* dragon!

Contrary to the weight of the backstory, its rules were fairly simple. The dragon would turn away and say, "stealing the dragon's whiskers," while the adventurers approached. If any adventurer was moving when the dragon turned to face them, they were out. The difference was the turn limit. If the adventurers couldn't touch the dragon in ten turns, they lost. I wondered if this reflected the amount of time the child had left because of her illness. The game truly was dark!

B-but that's beside the point. The point of a game is to have fun with it! So, you wanna give it a go?

"Mm. I'd love to."

Oh? You sound confident.

"I'm good at it."

I'll be the dragon and you be the adventurer, then. All right?

"Sure." Fran nodded, smiling confidently. She must have been really good at this game.

Ready?

"Mm."

I started by measuring her abilities.

Stealing the dragon's whiskers.

I turned around after saying the words at a normal speed. Fran had completely stopped.

"…"

Pretty good. Let's see how you handle this! Steeealing theeeee dragon's whiskers!

"…"

V-very good!

She didn't even sway. How about this?!

Stealing the dragooooooon's whiskers!

"Heh heh."

Urgh… You've earned that smug face!

I couldn't knock Fran out, no matter how much I changed the tempo. Her sense of balance was impeccable. She'd been good at the game before, and now she was even better, thanks to all the balance Skills she'd equipped. It was enough to give an acrobat vertigo.

There was one turn left. I couldn't let her lose her respect for me as her teacher. I had to do something.

Hey! What's that?! Stealing the dragon's whiskers!

"Hrmph."

Mwa ha ha! You moved!

"No fair. That was cheap."

People do this all the time back on Earth. Cut me some slack. I was feeling very childish.

"Hrngh. Again!"

Sure, sure! I'll play with you as many times as you want.

"Mm!"

The rounds only grew worse as we went on. Fran was particularly cute when I tricked her with the smell of curry. But what could I do? She'd practically sicced a horned rabbit on me! Surely I was allowed to use

144

illusions to throw off her sense of balance.

We carried on for hours. Fran's stamina and competitive spirit amazed me. In the end, I admitted defeat.

I just hope you had fun.

"Mm!"

We wouldn't be stealing any dragon's whiskers for a while after this.

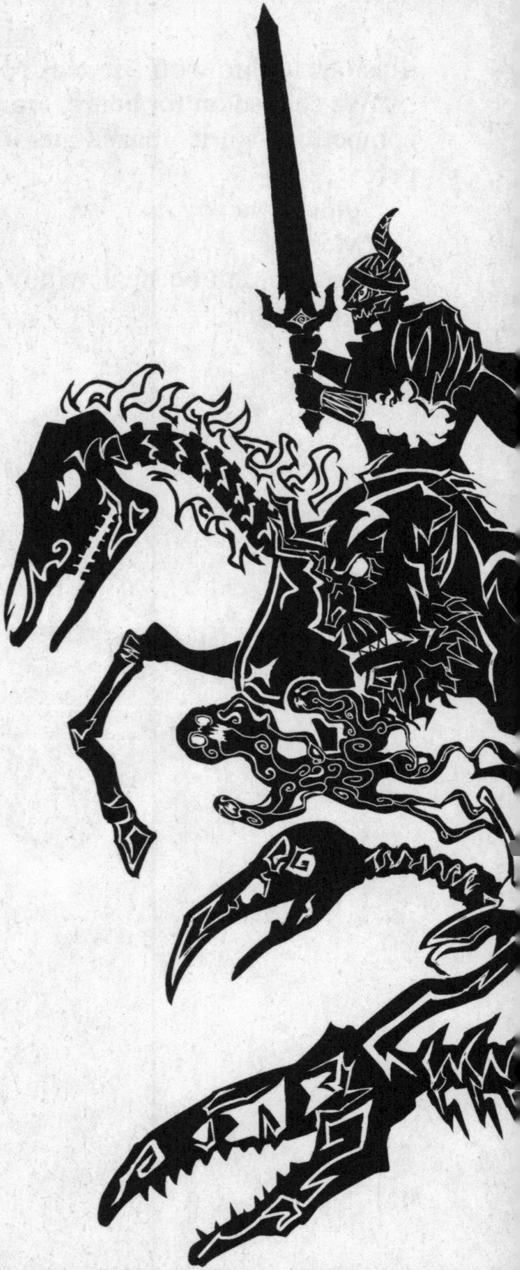

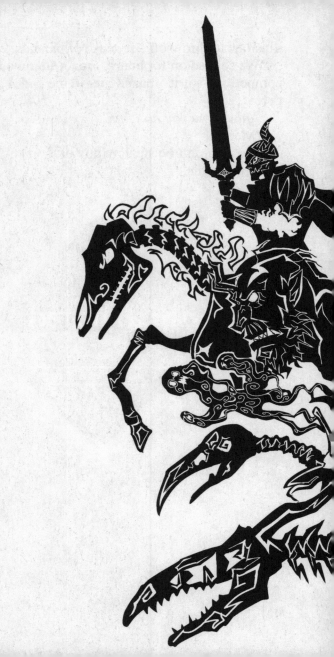

Reincarnated
as a sword

to be continued

CONCEPT ART

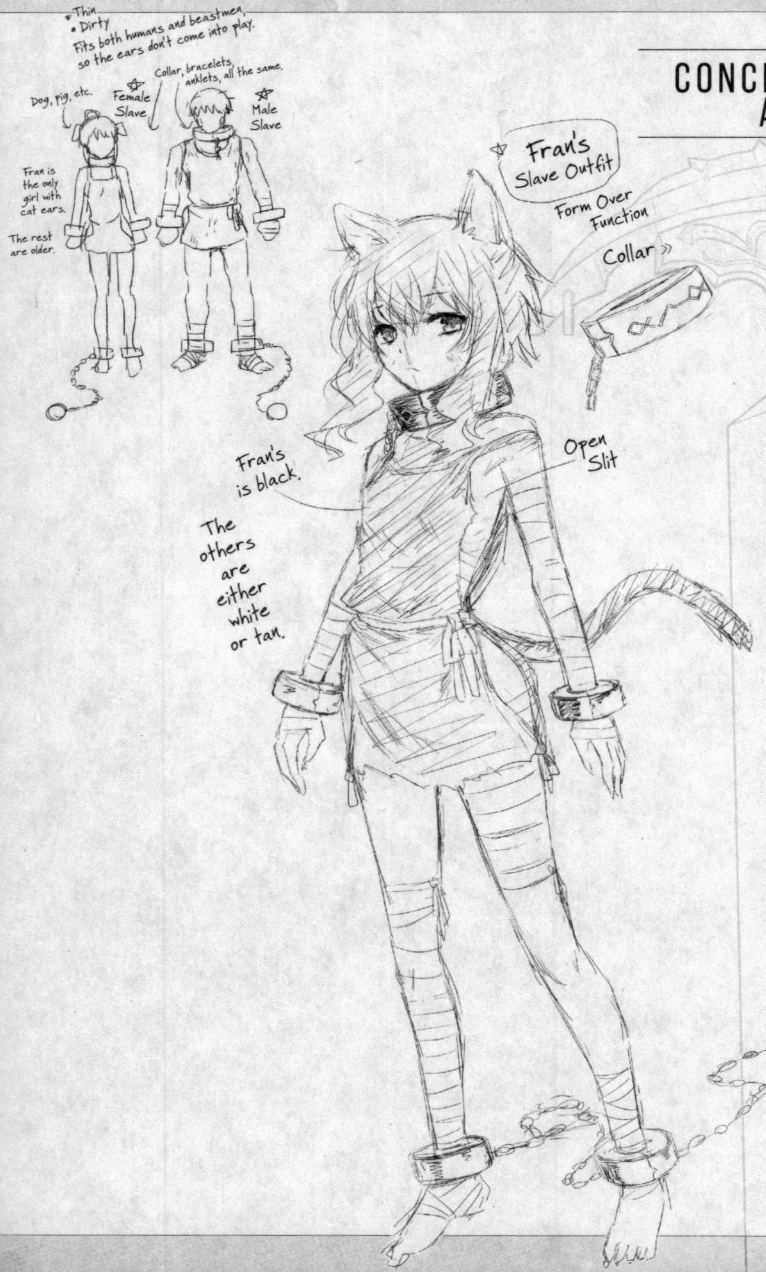

• Thin
• Dirty
Fits both humans and beastmen, so the ears don't come into play.
Collar, bracelets, anklets, all the same.
Dog, pig, etc.
Female Slave
Male Slave
Fran is the only girl with cat ears.
The rest are older.
Fran's Slave Outfit
Form Over Function
Collar
Open Slit
Fran's is black.
The others are either white or tan.

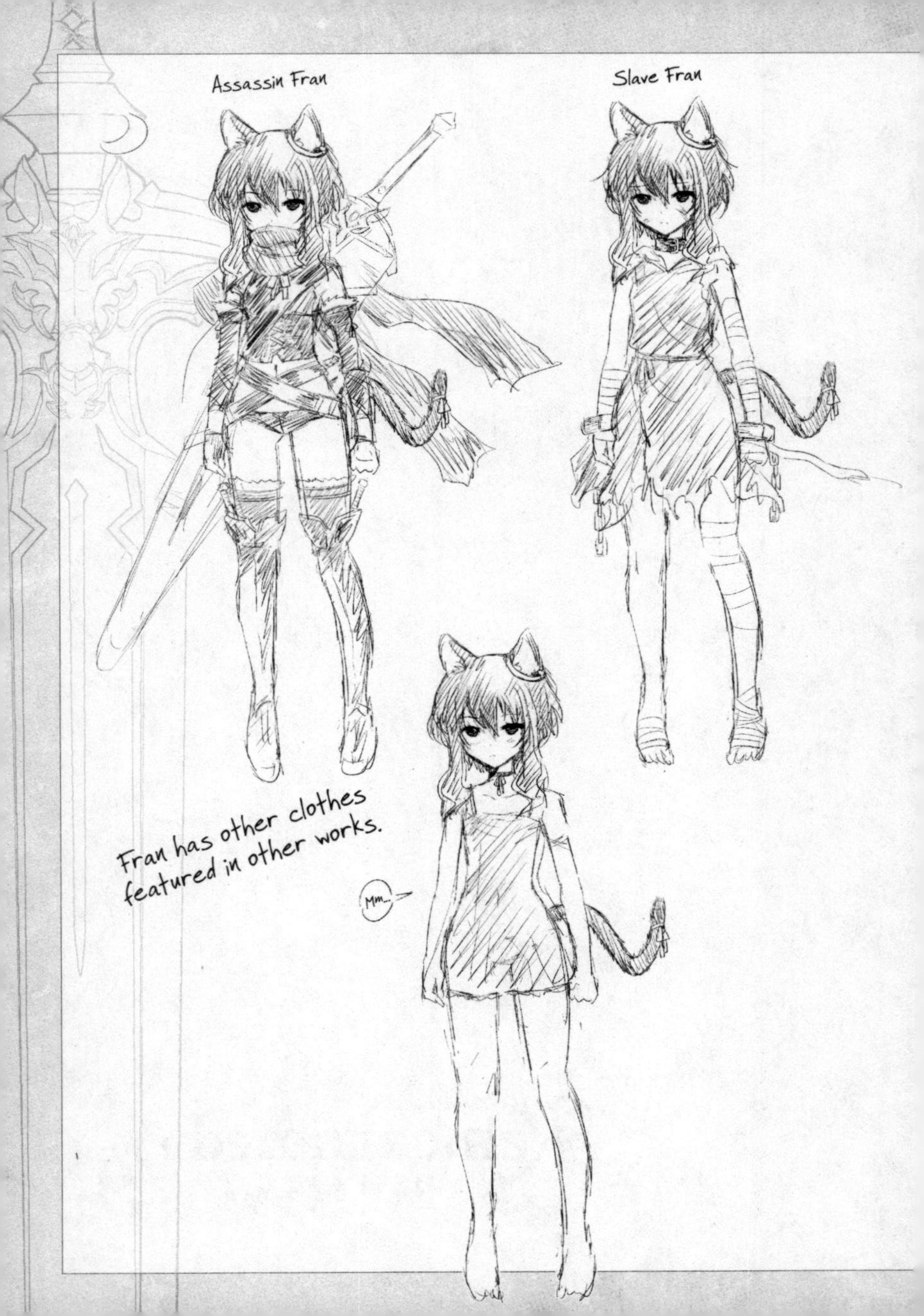
Assassin Fran
Slave Fran
Fran has other clothes featured in other works.
Mm...

Reincarnated
as a sword

SEVEN SEAS ENTERTAINMENT PRESENTS

Reincarnated as a Sword

story by **YUU TANAKA** art by **TOMOWO MARUYAMA** character designs by **Llo** **VOL. 6**

TRANSLATION
Michael Rachmat

LETTERING AND RETOUCH
Rai Enril

COVER DESIGN
Nicky Lim

PROOFREADER
Danielle King
Dawn Davis

EDITOR
Peter Adrian Behravesh
J.P. Sullivan

PREPRESS TECHNICIAN
Rhiannon Rasmussen-Silverstein

PRODUCTION MANAGER
Lissa Pattillo

MANAGING EDITOR
Julie Davis

ASSOCIATE PUBLISHER
Adam Arnold

PUBLISHER
Jason DeAngelis

TENSEI SHITARA KEN DESHITA Vol. 6
by TANAKA YUU / MARUYAMA TOMOWO / Llo
© 2019 TANAKA YUU, MARUYAMA TOMOWO / MICRO MAGAZINE,
GENTOSHA COMICS INC.
All rights reserved.

Original Japanese edition published in 2019 by GENTOSHA COMICS Inc.
English translation rights arranged worldwide with GENTOSHA COMICS Inc.
through Digital Catapult Inc., Tokyo.

Seven Seas press and purchase enquiries can be sent to Marketing Manager
Lianne Sentar at press@gomanga.com. Information regarding the distribution
and purchase of digital editions is available from Digital Manager CK Russell
at digital@gomanga.com.

Seven Seas and the Seven Seas logo are trademarks of
Seven Seas Entertainment. All rights reserved.

ISBN: 978-1-64827-236-3
Printed in Canada
First Printing: June 2021
10 9 8 7 6 5 4 3 2 1

FOLLOW US ONLINE: *www.sevenseasentertainment.com*

READING DIRECTIONS

This book reads from **_right to left_**, Japanese style.
If this is your first time reading manga, you start
reading from the top right panel on each page and
take it from there. If you get lost, just follow the
numbered diagram here. It may seem backwards at
first, but you'll get the hang of it! Have fun!!

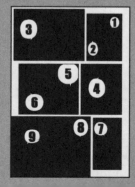